LETTERS TO LIMBO

ROBERT LAIRD BORDEN

ROBERT LAIRD BORDEN, Prime Minister of Canada from 1911 to 1920, was born in the village of Grand Pré, Nova Scotia, in 1854. He practised law in the province before entering politics. In 1896 he was elected to the House of Commons, and in 1901 was chosen leader of the Liberal-Conservative party.

After his retirement in 1920, Sir Robert kept on the sidelines of political debate, although he was often consulted by those in power and was frequently tempted to express his views on current issues. During the last four years of his life, 1933 to 1937, he recorded some of his thoughts and experiences in the form of 'Letters to Limbo.' Some of these he read over and revised, others he left as dictated. The wide range of his interests is revealed in the topics: union government for Canada? / reminiscences of household pets / inaccuracy of the press / bestowal of honours in Canada / business conditions in the United States / Dean of Canterbury and Social Credit / appraisal of Sir Arthur Currie / King Edward VIII and Mrs. Simpson.

All the letters but four are presented in this volume. They reveal some of the inner thoughts and strongest beliefs of Sir Robert, giving an insight into the man and his times. Whimsical and humorous, or serious and wellargued, these letters paint a portrait in words of one of the great figures in Canadian history.

HENRY BORDEN is a nephew of Sir Robert Borden and the editor of his memoirs. He has had a distinguished career in law and business, and is a former member and chairman of the Board of Governors of the University of Toronto.

The Right Honourable Sir Robert Laird Borden, PC, GCMG, KC

Letters to Limbo

BY THE RIGHT HONOURABLE
SIR ROBERT LAIRD BORDEN, PC, GCMG, KC
PRIME MINISTER OF CANADA 1911–1920
EDITED BY HENRY BORDEN, SM, CMG, QC

UNIVERSITY OF TORONTO PRESS

Toronto and Buffalo
Reprinted in paperback 2014

ISBN 978-0-8020-1839-7 (cloth)
ISBN 978-1-4426-5211-8 (paper)
Microfiche ISBN 0-8020-0164-5

Foreword

One hundred and seventeen years ago – on June 26, 1854 – Robert Laird Borden, Prime Minister of Canada from 1911 to 1920, was born in the village of Grand Pré, Nova Scotia. He left school at the age of 14. Subsequently, after a period of teaching and study, he entered into 'articles' with a firm of lawyers in Halifax and in due course was admitted to the practice of law in his native province. In 1896 he was elected to the House of Commons as one of the representatives from Halifax and in 1901 was selected as leader of the Liberal-Conservative party. From 1905 until his death on June 10, 1937, he made Ottawa his home.

After Sir Robert's retirement in 1920 from active participation in public affairs he followed a policy of keeping on the side lines in so far as political issues were concerned, although as time went on he was consulted frequently by those in charge of our country's government. He was often strongly tempted to express his views on current issues. During the last four years of his life he developed the habit of occasionally dictating his thoughts to his secretary or by these means recording some incident or experience. This he did in the form of a 'Letter to Limbo.' Some of these he read over and revised, others he left as dictated. These 'Letters to Limbo' have been reproduced in this volume with the exception of one which is in rough draft form only and of three which are of no particular significance and which I am sure Sir Robert himself would have omitted. I have merely attempted to assist the reader by notes designed to make the references to individuals and circumstances more readily understandable after the passing of so many years. The footnotes and words in square brackets are mine.

My uncle was a serious and thoughtful man, yet he had a deep, but quiet, sense of humour. He was an indefatigable worker and expected his associates and colleagues to accomplish as much work in a day as he himself did. In this he told me more than once that he was disappointed. This was understandable because he had tremendous powers of application and concentration and great physical stamina. Possessed of much patience, he was, however, no person to argue with when aroused. He was humble and kindly, and in his later years enjoyed the company of younger people with whom he would talk, discuss, and laugh as if they were his equal in learning and experience. While he was a great believer in the British Empire and in the Commonwealth, he was first and foremost a Canadian. I recall very vividly an incident that took place at the week-end residence of Mr Lloyd George, then the Prime Minister of Great Britain, one Sunday afternoon in July, 1918. Mr Lloyd George had called an emergency meeting of the Imperial War Cabinet to deal with a grave military situation in France with which the Allies were faced. During the afternoon, at the tea hour, I found myself in the room with those members of the Cabinet who had arrived. The discussion naturally revolved around the war, disposition of troops and matters of that kind. I do not remember the statement of Mr Lloyd George which provoked my uncle's remarks but I have never forgotten his words, the pointed finger, his voice shaking with emotion: 'Mr Prime Minister, I want to tell you that, if ever there is a repetition of the battle of Passchendaele, not a Canadian soldier will leave the shores of Canada so long as the Canadian people entrust the government of their country to my hands.' Within seconds I was asked by my uncle to leave the room and I, therefore, do not know what transpired as the result of that statement.

There was no 'side' to Sir Robert. He disliked pomp and ceremony. He never felt wholly comfortable with his knighthood, although he did not in any way minimize the honour which he felt had been given to the Canadian people when it was conferred on him, as their Prime Minister, in 1913. A few hours before his death, when he knew he could not long survive, he said to me: 'Remember, Henry, none of this Sir "stuff" at the cemetery, just plain "Robert Laird Borden, born Grand Pré, N.S. – 1854; died Ottawa, Ont. – 1937." ' His wish was respected and that is the wording on the headstone marking his grave in Beechwood Cemetery, Ottawa.

I am deeply grateful for the privilege of having known so intimately such a forceful, kindly, and inspiring character. These 'Limbo Letters' have been edited and put together by me as a labour of love and token of respect and admiration for a great Canadian.

Toronto, Canada
May, 1971

HENRY BORDEN

Acknowledgments

The Editor gratefully acknowledges permission to publish the following:

An extract from Sir Robert's *Canada in the Commonwealth* from the Clarendon Press, Oxford; quotations from the Marquess of Crewe's *Life of Lord Rosebery* from John Murray (Publishers) Limited; extracts from *Lord Minto – A Memoir* by John Buchan from Thomas Nelson & Sons Limited and the estate of the late Lord Tweedsmuir; the poem by Sir Henry Newbolt, *Vitae Lampada* from *Poems New and Old* from Mr Peter Newbolt.

Permission was obtained from the Macmillan Company of Canada Limited to include the quotations from *A Dryad in Nanaimo* by Audrey Alexandra Brown included in the article by Hon. Martin Burrell published in the *Ottawa Journal* of December 15 1934, and in the article by Thomas B. Robertson published in the *Winnipeg Free Press* in January, 1935.

The Editor is likewise grateful to the *Ottawa Journal*, the *Winnipeg Free Press*, the *Globe and Mail*, the Southam Press, and the *Montreal Star* for permission to include various articles and due acknowledgement is made to other Canadian newspapers for articles as noted.

The Editor also acknowledges with gratitude the much appreciated assistance and advice received by him from members of the University of Toronto Press and particularly those of the Editorial Department.

Contents

LETTERS TO LIMBO

ROBERT LAIRD BORDEN

Preface

Ottawa, March 6, 1933

TO: *THE LIMBO RECORDER AND GUARDIAN*

Limbo, Erewh

Sir,

One who has filled a certain place in public affairs, so-called, and who has retired from active participation but not from active interest therein, feels impelled, from time to time, to lift up his voice in the press or otherwise but frequently with no great satisfaction to himself. In your vast museum there is a marvellous collection of systems, beliefs, thoughts, theories, creeds, hopes, fears, methods and many other things that have been abandoned or cast away and which doubtless you have classified as 'interesting souvenirs of humanity's attempts toward higher endeavour.' What an amazing collection you must possess! What yearnings! What unwisdom! What pathos! And there is much still to come, including the greater part of present-day literature and perhaps all of present-day journalism. It seems to me desirable that I should refrain from encumbering the press but that I might be permitted to confide to your keeping such worthless thoughts and suggestions as may occur to me from time to time. So make timely preparation, for I shall add to the deluge that is presently descending upon you.

Yours in sympathy,

Introduction

Sir Robert's 'Letters to Limbo' were started by him in 1933 and in that calendar year he wrote twenty. In the period 1934 to May of 1937 he added fifty-five, making a total of seventy-five of such letters covering a wide variety of subjects.

Four of these letters have been omitted from this volume – one because it was written not long before his death in 1937 and was only in rough draft form and three because the editor feels it would have been Sir Robert's wish not to include them as they contain nothing of historical or public interest.

The first Limbo letter was no doubt occasioned by the death, early in 1933, of Mr John S. Ewart KC. It is dated March 6, 1933, and is an appraisal of his late friend, who was born in Toronto in 1849, called to the bar of Ontario in 1871 and to that of Manitoba in 1882. He practised his profession in Winnipeg until 1904 when he removed to Ottawa and was one of the leaders of the Canadian bar. He was a forceful public speaker and a prolific author and essayist, – the best known of his works being *The Kingdom of Canada, Imperial Federation, The Colonial Conferences, The Alaska Boundary, and other Essays*, published in 1908.

March 6, 1933

THE LATE JOHN S. EWART

Sir,

During the past ten years I have been in very close association with the late John S. Ewart; and on many occasions he has lavished upon me praise which probably was not wholly deserved but which, nevertheless, I greatly appreciated, as is the custom with men of advanced years. Oliver Wendell Holmes said that while he was a young man he was content to have his praise in tea-spoonfuls, in middle life in table-spoonfuls but in old age he was content with nothing less than ladle-fuls.

However, for several years my relations with Ewart were by no means cordial. During the election of 1917, he made a most unjust and unprovoked attack upon me which I did not fail to resent, although I treated it with the silent contempt which it deserved. But that episode passed into forgetfulness and I did not permit it to interfere with the extremely intimate association which grew up after my retirement from public life.

Of Ewart's intellectual brilliancy there could be no doubt. His mind was extraordinarily acute. He was endowed with fine courage and marvellous persistence. His systematic arrangement of material was of great assistance to him and he did not fail to explore all sources that were helpful to the main purpose of his activities during the past thirty years. And his industry, which was concentrated upon practically one topic during that period, was wonderful.

He carried on for many years in the *Kingdom Papers* and in public addresses a propaganda which was not without effect but which probably reached a much smaller circle of readers and auditors than might be imagined. So far as that propaganda advocated the recognition of Canada's nationhood, I was in full sympathy. Indeed, my own efforts from the first were devoted to the fulfillment of that ideal. The constitutional resolution which, with full approval of the British government, was unanimously adopted upon my motion by the Imperial War Conference in 1917 established a principle to which I had devoted myself from the beginning of my public career. But my ideal also included the unity of the British Commonwealth which I regarded as a supreme duty of its constituent nations, not only to themselves but to the world, to humanity. However, if I have a correct appreciation of Ewart's ideal, he aimed at nothing less than the dissolution of the British Commonwealth.

With many of Ewart's views I was in whole or partial agreement, while others I regarded as both unfortunate and undesirable. In these I include his intense antagonism to Great Britain and to British statesmen. He seemed always to start from the premise that Great Britain must be wrong. This feeling, I fear, was not entirely absent from his mind during the War period; and it was exemplified on the last occasion when I had an opportunity of hearing him speak. It was at the University Club and *inter alia* he took into consideration the attitude of United States towards Great Britain and other nations in respect of war debts. He argued that United States was perfectly justified in exacting the last farthing. Indeed he did not seem to get beyond the Coolidge formula, 'Well, they hired the money didn't they?'

How this intense antagonism arose, I do not attempt even to conjecture. There were rumours that he was disappointed at lack of adequate appreciation of his labours when he represented Canada as counsel in the arbitration with United States over the fisheries of North America at The Hague in 1910. Whatever may have been the cause, the feeling undoubtedly existed; and it seemed even to carry with it a desire for the complete separation of Canada from the British Commonwealth. This is evidenced by his eventual admission when charged by the *Ottawa Journal* that such was his purpose. However, although I vehemently disagree in this respect I do not condemn him, for I believe that sincere conviction in that regard should be respected and not treated with contempt.

In his treatment of constitutional relations he failed, in my judgment, to give adequate weight to the force and elasticity of convention upon which government in Great Britain has by gradual steps attained its present development. In some aspects convention is more useful than statutory enactment, as it is easily and indeed automatically molded by the needs arising from new conditions. Witness the recent reversion in Great Britain when the principle of cabinet solidarity was *ex necessitate* disregarded for the time being.

His methods in controversial argument and discussion were not always of the highest type. In many instances, which I cannot at the moment recall but of which a firm impression remains in my mind, he tore a sentence or two from the context and attributed to the author or speaker a meaning which certainly was never intended. More than one young man who worked with him and under his guidance spoke to me of this tendency which seemed to disregard the limits of legitimate argument.

During his later years certain of his views did not seem to me reasonable or logical. I was quite astonished at his concept of what is involved in responsible government. Occasionally he used to submit to me pamphlets which he was about to publish in order to invite my criticism or suggestions. A copy of my correspondence with him, in which my disagreement was expressed, is attached and sufficiently explains itself.

He was never in public life for which indeed his temperament was quite unsuited. I have been told that in his earlier years on political platforms in Manitoba he was quite ineffective, as he was easily diverted by any interrupter with whom he would immediately engage in argument. His intellectual trend was theoretical rather than practical, a weakness which I think he sometimes realized.

But although not in active political life he filled no inconsiderable place in our public life in its wider significance. And even when one did not agree with his views, one was constrained to acknowledge and respect his unfailing courage and his perfect sincerity.

In one respect he was to me an enigma. That a man of his intellectual force and brilliancy should have no interest whatever in the glories of our English literature was inexplicable. The great names in the world of letters appealed to him in vain. I once asked his opinion of some great work of fiction and he replied with mild scorn that he never 'wasted' his time in such useless reading. On another occasion he told me that he had vainly endeavoured to read a novel of great renown (I cannot recall the name) but that he never succeeded in getting beyond the first few pages. So far as I am aware, even Shakespeare was to him a sealed book. In truth, he was the very reverse of a many-sided man.

On the other hand, he was an active athlete in his younger days, a fine lacrosse player, for example; and indeed he was an adept at nearly every game that he attempted.

Some rather foolish things have been said and written as to the influence of his propaganda in the development of constitutional relations through which Canada and other Dominions have entered the portal of full nationhood. That development was due to the valour, the endurance and the achievement of the Canadian Army in France and Belgium which inspired our people with an impelling sense of nationhood never before experienced. When the Dominions, with Canada in the lead, insisted upon recognition at the Peace Conference, at the beginning of 1919, and when Clemenceau learned that these Dominions had put a million men in the field or in training, he said that this record was enough for him; and so Canada and the other Dominions at that Conference entered into the Society of Nations to take their place in the concert of the League.

7 MARCH 6, 1933

Ewart told me once that in his early years he had been much concerned with things spiritual and that at one time he was strongly inclined to put aside other activities and to devote his energies to the Christian ministry. Thus he set himself with great earnestness to consider problems of existence and to determine the path to which his convictions would lead him. But, evidently he became discouraged by the confusion of many discordant voices and so the idea was abandoned. What he confided to me might be illustrated by quotation:

'Myself when young did eagerly frequent
Doctor and Saint and heard great argument
About it and about; but evermore
Came out by the same door wherein I went.'

During the past ten years I have greatly enjoyed my intimate association with him. His conversation was stimulating and often entertaining as he had a keen sense of humour and was a good raconteur. I shall miss him greatly; and, although I differed intensely from him in certain respects, I shall preserve a happy memory of our association.

Yours in sympathy,

October 30, 1931

400 Wilbrod Street, Ottawa

Rt. Hon. Sir R.L. Borden, GCMG

Dear Borden,

I have expanded the clause in my Paper on Sir Charles Metcalfe to which you took some exception. It will now read as follows:

13. The question of responsible government was not involved. For that was a system of relationship between the Counsellors and the Assembly. It made no prescription as to the relations between the Counsellors and the sovereign, although it undoubtedly was well calculated to exercise great influence upon these relations. Distinction between the thing and the effects which it produced has lost some of its importance as the King has lost some of his prerogative of dissent, but in earlier days it was well marked. Joseph Howe, for example, while arguing powerfully in support of the system admitted that, quite consistently with

> its operation, many questions as to the relations of the governors and the counsellors demanded definition. 'These bounds', he said, 'must be clearly defined in the Act of Parliament which establishes the new system, or in the instructions sent to the Governors, to be communicated to the Legislatures'.

Perhaps what I now say may be worthy of your further consideration.

Sincerely yours,
(Sgd) John S. Ewart

November 2, 1931

J.S. Ewart, Esq, KC

My dear Ewart,

Thanks for your letter of the thirtieth ultimo which I have perused with interest. My view of the question which we discussed seems not altogether in accord with your own. An understanding or convention that the Governor shall in the ordinary course act upon the advice of his ministers respecting domestic affairs (subject to any established constitutional exception) seems to me an essential of responsible government. The selection of advisers who command the confidence of the peoples' representatives but whose advice in such matters he is entitled to over-ride or disregard, by the direction of the Colonial office or upon his own arbitrary judgment, does not fill the measure of responsible government as I understand it.

The scope of 'domestic affairs' has gradually advanced and developed during three-quarters of a century and perhaps has not yet reached its full limit.

It seems to me that Lafontaine and Baldwin based themselves on the position which I have above indicated.

Right or wrong, this is the view I firmly entertain; and I hope you will not wish me to argue the question. Even where I fail to agree, I have every respect for your opinion.

Yours faithfully,

In 1931 the Marquess of Crewe published his biography of Lord Rosebery, who had been Prime Minister of the United Kingdom (1894–5) and had died in 1929. Sir Robert's Limbo letter was written after his reading of these two volumes and a significant point of the letter is his reference to the origin of the expression 'British Commonwealth of Nations.' See, on this point, W.K. Hancock, *Survey of British Commonwealth Affairs, I, Problems of Nationality, 1918–1936* (London, 1937), pp. 52–62.

March 6, 1933

LORD ROSEBERY BY THE MARQUESS OF CREWE

Sir,

Recently I have read with very great interest Lord Crewe's *Life of Lord Rosebery* [John Murray (Publishers) Limited]; and I have laid aside the book with the deepest admiration for the remarkable intellectual brilliancy, both in oratory and letters, which distinguished that remarkable man. My wonder is that thus equipped, and possessing also the immense advantages of great wealth and high position and inspired, for the most part, with high ideals, he bequeathed to his country and to the world so little of great achievement or of inspiring tradition. Elsewhere I have spoken of him as a man of brilliant wit but without a real sense of humour. This I must modify by admitting a sense of humour that is allied to wit; but I think he was devoid of the humour which impels one occasionally to laugh at oneself. At page 659 (Volume II) there is the following quotation:

> I saw in some book the other day that I was described as a failure, and this led me into a train of thought which whirled me from myself. But let me at once say that according to the usual apprehension of the word the description is sufficiently accurate.

On the same page it is recorded that Rosebery in his last days declared that his main fault had been pride. His biographer considers, however, that self-consciousness was his bane. Lord Crewe says 'He found it hardly possible to get outside his own personality, to look at himself as one of the outside crowd might; or to look at contemporary movements without wondering whether he ought, or ought not, to take a part in them.' In my judgment his biographer in these words has solved the riddle. Rosebery found it impossible to forget himself. He lacked a certain grim earnestness which places far in the background one's purely personal considerations and presses on to the achievement of purpose or ideal with no thought of the sacrifice entailed.

Gladstone's estimate of Rosebery's character (p. 661) is in the following words: 'I can say three things of him: (1) He is one of the very ablest men I have known. (2) He is of the highest honour and probity. (3) I do not know whether he really has common sense.'

A critic has declared that Rosebery always coveted *palmam sine pulvere*, to which his biographer gives the significance of 'mud.'

His oratory has sometimes been characterized as theatrical; he was a Cicero rather than a Demosthenes. But his speeches on the hustings are said to have been most moving; an electric thrill passed through those who listened. Thus, he was perhaps a greater success on the platform than in the senate. In his literary efforts a certain theatrical tendency is also noticeable. Thus in his *Life of Pitt* he pictured Addington as possessing 'the indescribable air of a village apothecary inspecting the tongue of the State.' In this he descends to what would be termed in United States 'smartness.'

The expression 'British Commonwealth of Nations' was first employed, as I thought, either by Smuts or by myself shortly after the constitutional resolution of 1917 had been adopted. Mr Ewart criticized it as indefensible and, perhaps, from his standpoint he was right. But the phrase was subsequently embalmed in an Act of Parliament and it served its purpose. However, I find (p. 186) that on January 18, 1884 (nearly fifty years ago) Rosebery invented this phrase in his speech at Adelaide, Australia.

> Does this fact of your being a nation, and I think you feel yourselves to be a nation, imply separation from the Empire? God forbid! There is no need for any nation, however great, leaving the Empire, because the Empire is a commonwealth of nations.

It is to be regretted that his wonderful gifts did not lead him to higher achievement; but we have the legacy of his ideals at least. I regret never having heard him speak in Parliament or on the platform. Sir Charles Hibbert Tupper told me of his eloquent address at the unveiling of Sir John Macdonald's monument in St Paul's Cathedral. In 1909 (if I remember correctly) at a dinner in London I sat by a bishop who paid Rosebery this tribute 'He should be recognized and hailed "Orator in Ordinary for the British Empire." '

Yours in sympathy,

In 1933 Canada was in the depths of the great depression. Rt. Hon.

R.B. Bennett, the leader of the Conservative party, was Prime Minister, his party having been elected to power in the general election of 1930. Unemployment, on an unprecedented scale, with all its related problems, was causing untold misery and hardship throughout the country. It was, therefore, quite natural that many responsible citizens wondered whether a Union or National government would not be better able to cope with the many difficulties facing the nation.

Sir Robert, who had formed the Union government in 1917, made these thoughts the theme of the following short Limbo letter.

March 7, 1933

UNION GOVERNMENT FOR CANADA?

Sir,

Doubtless you are receiving considerable consignments of nonsense respecting the practicability and advantages of Union government in Canada.

The Conservatives, who can retain power for more than two years, are not disposed to deprive themselves of that advantage, although in some respects it is not particularly pleasurable.

The Liberals who eagerly anticipate a general election, which they imagine would advance them to power with a fine majority, are equally indisposed to welcome the proposal. But, in truth, a general election might result in no majority for either party, with the CCF holding the balance of power. In that case, conditions might drive Liberals and Conservatives into each others' arms.

Conservative leaders claim that the present government can accomplish everything that a Union government could achieve. Any one who recalls the experience of 1917 to 1920, will not readily accept that view.

Three essential conditions are required for the constitution of an efficient Union government.

1 It must have a leader under whom the principal elements of both parties would be prepared to unite.

2 It must have a definite programme for submission to the electorate.

3 It must submit that programme to the electorate and receive its mandate therefor.

Such a government could render important service to Canada at this juncture. It is doubtful, to say the least, whether it could be constituted.

Yours in sympathy,

Echo Beach Fishing Club (commonly known as 'Echo Beach') is a trout fishing club located at Echo Lake, the head waters of the Blanche river some twenty miles north of Buckingham in the province of Quebec. It was founded in the early 1860s. Sir Robert, who was a great lover of nature, as well as a keen fisherman, was a member of the Club from 1908 until his death in 1937. Although during the period when he was Prime Minister he found little opportunity to use the facilities of the Club, he made good use of them after his retirement and during the five or six years before his death he took in a party practically each summer for 10 days or two weeks. These invariably included two or three younger couples, including my wife and myself, as Sir Robert much enjoyed the company (and antics!) of younger people.

By 1919 his health had been undermined, resulting in his retirement as Prime Minister in early July, 1920. In an effort to recover his health he accepted the invitation of Lord Jellicoe to accompany him on a tour of the *Caribbean* in the battle cruiser *New Zealand* in early 1920. However, the object of the excursion was not attained.

March 18, 1933

SUNSETS – IN OTTAWA AND ELSEWHERE – DAWN

Sir,

February and March exchanged roles this year. Today was a typical winter scene with radiant landscape, brilliant sunshine and glorious countryside.

Ottawa sunsets are frequently of exceptional beauty; and one of them, noted in my diary last winter, is still vivid in my memory. The western horizon was a great glowing furnace of molten gold from which radiated multi-coloured streamers of a hundred different hues; but always the central golden radiance dominated the scene.

Another sunset of some years ago I can still see as its picturesque beauty arrested my attention when I emerged one winter evening from my office in the Eastern Block. There was a great mountain of deepest azure cloud in the western heavens; in its centre was a wide, clear-cut portal through which streamed the sunset's glory. It seemed that one looked through the barriers of time to the glory of eternity. For many minutes I stood motionless, my soul entranced by the mystery of that never-to-be-forgotten scene, invested as it was with a meaning that I dimly realized but could not wholly comprehend.

Another memorable scene was on the voyage from Trinidad to Southampton when I was the guest of Lord Jellicoe on the battle cruiser *New Zealand*. He had placed at my disposal the rooms which had been fitted up for the accommodation of Lady Jellicoe who did not accompany him on his cruise to the West Indies. Waking early one morning I saw the morning star more beautiful than ever before. Strange to say it had a distinct pathway across the water. Charles Dickens speaks somewhere of the moon's pathway on the waters as the 'path to Heaven,' according to his childish imagination. The radiance of this new and most beautiful path of the morning star upon the silence of the waters seemed a good omen and a promise of hope in my endeavour to rally my jaded energies for renewed effort.

To one impressed by the varying moods of nature, the daily concerns of life seem very trivial in the presence of such beauty.

Lord Morley in his *Recollections*[1] quotes a translation from one of the minor Greek poets which still dwells in my memory:

> I hold him happiest
> Who, before going quickly whence he came,
> Hath looked ungrieving on these majesties,
> The world-wide Sun, the stars, water and clouds
> And fire. Live, Parmeno, a hundred years,
> Or a few weeks, these thou wilt always see,
> And never, never any greater things.

Last summer while I was at Echo Beach, I made notes in my diary which one of my friends copied and which I here reproduce:

> August 23 A sun-bath of forty-five minutes. Yesterday and today bathed in Home Lake where the forest and hill protect one from any breeze drawing from the north or north west. This

1 Lord Morley, d. 1923. *Recollections* published 1917.

morning there was a wonderful chorus of birds. The hills to the south were hidden by a mountain of mist bathed in sunshine. Gradually a great portal opened in this mountain disclosing the beautiful hills beyond and leaving on each side a great pinnacle of mist which slowly melted away.

August 25 Bright sunshine with light clouds drifting from south west. While having sun-bath at Home Lake and while B... was busily identifying rare species of birds, a gull, high in the shining clouds, floating with motionless wings, cried to us joyously.

For several years I have slept out of doors during the summer months. In the silence of the night, broken occasionally by distant sounds, to watch, when I was wakeful, the majestic march of the stars across the heavens was a new revelation. It is no exaggeration to say that sometimes the earth seemed far away. Then in the early morning came first the promise of dawn, when one could just distinguish the lacery of the tree-tops against the eastern sky. Then the cry of the darting night-hawk with its curious appeal; this soon followed by a bird symphony, led and dominated by the throbbing and rapturous contralto of the robin. Sometimes, but not always, there was the little breeze that precedes the dawn so beautifully described by Tennyson in the following lines:

And drawn from out the distant gloom
A breeze began to tremble o'er
The large leaves of the sycamore,
And fluctuate all the still perfume,

And gathering freshlier overhead,
Rock'd the full-foliaged elms, and swung
The heavy folded rose, and flung
The lilies to and fro, and said

'The dawn, the dawn', and died away;
And East and West, without a breath,
Mixt their dim lights, like life and death,
To broaden into boundless day.

I have taken the liberty to substitute the word 'drawn' for 'suck'd' in the first line of this quotation; and I marvel at my daring!

I remain, dear Sir, Yours in sympathy,

March 28, 1933

A GRIEVANCE (DISAPPOINTMENT IF IT SHOULD BE REMEDIED) – TABLE OF PRECEDENCE

Sir,

So far as I am aware I am the only subscriber to your valuable and interesting journal. Thus, I feel at liberty to ask the hospitality of your columns even in respect of so trivial a matter as that which I now bring to your attention.

A few years after my retirement from public life I established for myself a self-denying ordinance which debarred me from taking part in further partisan activities.

For nearly three years I was chief of a Union government in which strong Liberals and Conservatives united their efforts for the service of their country in a time of supreme stress. This intimate association with former political opponents, who were loyal to me throughout the period of the Union government, removed the emotion of partisanship which had been strong during my leadership of the Liberal-Conservative party.

However, Mr Meighen, during his premiership, occasionally asked my advice and cooperation; and I could not well refuse so devoted a friend.

In October, 1927, I was strongly urged to attend the Liberal-Conservative convention in Winnipeg; and with considerable reluctance I finally consented. Speaking at that convention, I absolutely refrained from any partisan utterance.

During the general election of 1930, Mr Bennett, in his appeal to the country, went altogether too far in his promises to relieve unemployment and to 'blast' the way to more extended markets. In the course of his campaign his language, on occasion, seemed to imply that he regarded Great Britain as a foreign country and had little concern for the essential unity of the British Commonwealth of Nations. This commenced to attract attention among the Loyalists and the Orangemen; and Liberal speakers, as well as the Liberal press, began to declare openly that I was not in sympathy with the views which he thus expressed.

I had set forth in somewhat different phraseology my conception of Canada's relation to Great Britain and other nations of the Commonwealth in contradistinction to her relation to foreign nations. To me Mr Bennett's phraseology seemed rather clumsy and maladroit; and I thought the situation might be improved if I should repeat what I had said many years before and suggest that this was Mr Bennett's real meaning. Accordingly, I made public the following statement:

> Since retiring from public life about eight years ago, I have deliberately refrained from taking an active part in political discussion, nor did I intend to do so on this occasion. But, as my name has been dragged into the controversy by prominent supporters of the government, and even by the Prime Minister himself, it becomes my right, as well as my duty, to make my position clear.
>
> I am whole-heartedly in accord with the fiscal policy which Mr Bennett has eloquently proclaimed in every part of Canada. Twenty-five years ago I took substantially the same ground. The British Empire first and within the British Empire, Canada first; the preservation of our home market for our own producers; the maintenance of our industries to give employment to our people; Canada's unimpaired control over her tariff; subject to these considerations, a system of reciprocal trade preference within the Empire. Briefly stated, such was the policy that I advocated and to which I still adhere.
>
> On March 18, 1902, I declared in the House of Commons (1. *Hans.* 1902, pp. 1334 *et seq*) that the manufactures of Canada were of as much value to the Empire as the manufactures of Great Britain, and on the public platform I declared that a mill or a factory in Canada was worth as much to the Empire as a mill or a factory in Great Britain. It is charged that Mr Bennett's policy is lacking in loyalty to the Empire. If so, I must be classed in the same category. But I am content to leave the record of my devotion to the Empire to the judgment of my fellow countrymen.
>
> When the British Preference was first established it was argued that a sentimental preference to Canada would result. The Liberal government discovered that no such sentimental preference had resulted; and in 1902, in a memorandum presented by Sir Wilfrid Laurier and Mr Fielding to the British government, they practically threatened to abolish the preference unless Great Britain would exempt the products of the colonies from customs

duties. The record can be seen in Mr Fielding's speech of April 16, 1903 (1. *Hans.* 1903, pp. 1406–7) and in my reply of April 17, 1903 (1. *Hans.* 1903, p. 1488).

Reference has been made in a Liberal journal to a speech delivered by me in London on July 31, 1918. The position I then took is perfectly consistent with what I have already said. The people of Great Britain alone must determine the fiscal policy of the United Kingdom; on the other hand the people of Canada have the same right to control the fiscal policy of our country. No Canadian would desire a British government to adopt a policy regarded as unfair or oppressive by the British people; on the other hand a Canadian government is derelict to its duty unless it safeguards the interests of the Canadian people.

Any policy that sends abroad raw materials which can be economically utilized in our own industries; any policy that drives our labouring population to seek employment in a foreign country; any policy which sends abroad good Canadian money to pay for articles that can be economically and usefully produced by the labour of our own people and the employment of our own raw materials is economically unsound and destructive of our country's welfare. Any policy that has the effect of driving people out of our country is a most disastrous remedy for unemployment.

The clamor which had arisen, especially throughout Ontario, ceased.

I was then urged most strongly to preside at Mr Bennett's meeting on July 21, 1930; and with a good deal of reluctance I finally consented. At that meeting he urged me to repeat from the platform the views which I had expressed in my public statement and I did so.

After Mr Bennett had been in power a few months I sent to him a letter and memorandum, copies of which are appended. A few weeks thereafter he sent me a letter saying that with the appointment of a new Governor General the table of precedence would be revised and he would bear in mind my communication.

On February 2, 1931, I sent to Mr Bennett the following memorandum:

1 A memorandum is, perhaps, the least tiresome form of raid upon your time.

2 On Saturday last at the Lemieux luncheon, Mr Mackenzie King

came to me and expressed the opinion that the table of precedence should be amended by giving to ex-Prime Ministers, in the order of their accession to office, precedence immediately after the members of the Cabinet.

3 Pray do not acknowledge.

Throughout Mr Bennett's regime, I furnished him, from time to time, with memoranda recalling the attitude of the Liberal party under Sir Wilfrid Laurier in connection with many matters which were the subject of controversy between Mr Bennett and Mr Mackenzie King; and he frequently made use of the information thus furnished.

Further, I was of very useful and confidential service to Perley in 1930 and at a previous election – a service which I would be most unwilling to repeat.

Mr Bennett has been in power for three years; but he has quite forgotten to implement his promise of January 15, 1931. Similarly my friend Perley, who has never forgotten his own position, has been wholly indifferent to the situation set forth in my memorandum of December 26, 1930. On the other hand, Bennett and Perley have been extremely considerate to me in many respects. Copies of the December memorandum were sent to the Prime Minister for transmission to Perley and to Rhodes; and to both of these gentlemen I made oral mention of the circumstances.

At first I felt somewhat hurt and resentful at this treatment; but later I virtually dismissed the matter from my mind; and I should now feel greatly disappointed if Mr Bennett should remember his promise.

My friend T.E. Kenny, in 1896, told me that while he was working hard in that election campaign he went late at night, after a very exhausting day, into the Halifax Club and saw a number of strong Conservatives enjoying themselves in a game of whist. He looked at them for a moment and then said: 'To see you gentlemen thus enjoying yourselves and failing to take the slightest interest in this election makes me realize more fully than ever what a d——— old fool I am.'

So, when I look back at my renunciation of my self-denial ordinance, my efforts on behalf of the Liberal-Conservative party during the past twelve years, various subscriptions of no inconsiderable amounts to the funds of that party, I realize that Mr Kenny's observation on that occasion is strictly applicable to myself.

I remain, Sir, Yours in sympathy,

19 MARCH 28, 1933

LETTER OF DECEMBER 26, 1930 REFERRED TO IN THE FOREGOING LIMBO LETTER

Private and Personal

My dear Prime Minister,

In sending the enclosed memorandum respecting a matter of most trifling importance, I do not in the least desire or intend to suggest that there should be an early revision of the table of precedence; but if at any time such a revision should be undertaken you may perhaps think it worth while to take into account the considerations expressed in this memorandum.

At private dinners in his own house Mr King was most courteous and considerate in placing my wife and myself. From time to time at a public dinner he had the habit (which I did not particularly appreciate) of asking my wife or myself (as the case might be) to advance to a higher place rendered vacant by the unexpected absence of a Minister or a Minister's wife.

I remain, Yours faithfully,

MEMORANDUM OF DECEMBER 26, 1930

1 Shortly after Sir Robert Borden's retirement from the Premiership, the then Governor-General (the Duke of Devonshire) assigned to him a place immediately after that of the Chief Justice of Canada in the table of precedence.

2 After Mr Mackenzie King came into power in 1922, he revised the table of precedence, giving to the Prime Minister (as I think was quite appropriate) a much higher place than before. At the same time he assigned to Sir Robert Borden a much lower place than that accorded to him by the Duke of Devonshire. For example, Sir Robert was postponed to Mr Lemieux and to Senator Belcourt.

3 Mr King had become an eloquent exponent of Canada's service to the Empire and the world in the Great War. Considering that Sir Robert Borden (who is an Imperial Privy Councillor) had served as Prime Minister of his country during the entire war period and for two and a half years of reconstruction and that this service had never received any formal recognition, Mr King's action in this regard seemed petty and unworthy.

4 About two or three years ago, Mr King called on Sir Robert Borden and this subject was introduced. Sir Robert asked bluntly why Mr King had thought it appropriate to lower his place in the table,

to postpone him to persons who had never served as Ministers of the Crown, and whose appointment to the Privy Council was simply by courtesy, why no consideration was given to Sir Robert's service as Prime Minister, nor to his position as an Imperial Privy Councillor, etc, etc. To all this, Mr King returned more or less evasive answers, suggesting that the changes had been made without his knowledge. Sir Robert Borden then inquired whether, in Mr King's opinion, the office of Prime Minister was of less distinction and importance than the office of Chief Justice. Mr King agreed that it was not. Thereupon Sir Robert demanded Mr King's reason for a then recent change by which a retired Chief Justice of Canada should have precedence next after the Chief Justice, while no consideration was given to a retired Prime Minister. Mr King practically denied that any such change had been made, asserting positively that he had never heard of it. Sir Robert Borden assured him that it had been made and, of course, by his authority. Finally Mr King declared his intention of appointing a Committee to revise the table; and he expressed the hope that Sir Robert Borden would act as a member of that committee. Since then Mr King, apparently, has given the matter no attention.

In 1906 Sir Robert purchased a home in Ottawa, known as 'Glensmere'. It was located on the east side of Wurtemburg Street and the property extended to the west shore of the Rideau river. Between the house and the river the land fell sharply and the Bordens, over the years, made rock gardens, set out trees and paved many walkways down and along the slope. Each of these was named, such as 'Pleasance Walk' to which he refers in the following letter.

The house was occupied by Sir Robert and his wife until the latter's death in 1940. It was subsequently sold to the government of Nationalist China and occupied by the Ambassador of that country until resold to developers in 1969. It was then demolished and the property is now the site of a high-rise apartment development.

April 11, 1933

BIRDS AT GLENSMERE AND AT ECHO BEACH

Sir,

About four years ago we erected a bird-house with twenty-four apartments designed as an abode for purple martens which, however, have never seen fit to occupy it. But tree swallows have occasionally made their home therein. We very seldom saw them, as the male seems to bring food to the sitting female only twice a day – about ten or eleven in the morning and about five in the afternoon. We never saw the young birds, as by some mysterious method they always succeeded in departing without coming under our observation. In this respect their practice is in exact antithesis to that of the robins whose young are very much in evidence after leaving the nest and whose insistent demands for food continue several days thereafter.

Until the occasion I am about to mention I never saw a tree swallow alight on the ground. The incidents which are recorded in my letter of June 23, 1932 (copy attached) were most surprising. These incidents were the subject of some correspondence with Mr J. Philip Bill, Mr R.W. Tufts and Mr P.A. Taverner. This correspondence is annexed and I hope it will interest you.

Another curious incident was the discovery that a large bird, which for several days I could not observe, was nesting in our wild-garden. One Sunday afternoon I was conducting some friends along Pleasance Walk when one of them observed the bird which proved to be a black-crowned night heron.

The same evening as I went to shut the south gates of the avenue, the same bird, or its mate, flew out of the shrubbery within three yards of where I was standing.

I have identified at least twenty-five different species of birds, most of which nest on our property. A person with more knowledge than I possess probably might identify at least forty species.

During my visit to Echo Beach in August 1932, to which I have already alluded in a previous letter, I was accompanied by my nephew Henry Borden and his wife and by J. Philip Bill who has a great knowledge of birds. During our sojourn there Bill identified some thirty species, a list of which is attached. I had an excellent view of the oven bird and the winter wren which I had never seen before.

On a previous occasion at Echo Beach, Bill and I went far into the woods for the purpose of sighting a pileated woodpecker. We heard his notes and could almost locate his habitat but we failed to see him. A year or two afterwards, while fishing on Pickwick lake, I heard a sound as of someone using an axe or a hatchet in the bush. Upon inquiry of the guide I was told it was a woodchuck. I asked what a woodchuck was like and I was told 'just a woodchuck.' As the guide spoke, out flashed a pileated woodpecker which I recognized.

Our bird colony at Glensmere has been much disrupted and sometimes decimated by the presence and attacks of crows and bronze grackles who devour the eggs and sometimes the young of other birds, while the grackles themselves suffer from the crows. It is interesting to see a group of grackles pressing to attack a thieving and cowardly crow; in like manner the robins attack the grackles. I have never seen the flickers do this; but perhaps the grackles may dread their sharp and powerful bills.

This year the flickers have become wonderfully tame; and they approach as close to one as do the robins. They seem to have no fear but five or six years ago they were extremely shy.

But the most confiding of all is the hummingbird. We have an urn filled with flowers on our verandah; and very frequently, while sitting within a foot of this urn, I have seen a hummingbird, motionless in the air, supported by wings moving so rapidly that the eye cannot detect the motion, gathering honey within two feet of where I was sitting.

Sometimes birds are killed by flying against a window opposite another on the other side of the house. One day when I was sitting on the verandah some object struck the window within a yard of me and fell upon the tiles. I picked it up and discovered it was a robin apparently dead. However, after I had held it in my hand for about two minutes it suddenly revived and flew away.

Many years ago while I was arranging a pile of branches for burning, a wren, seated on the other side of the pile, discoursed to me for about half an hour, evidently dwelling upon his domestic affairs, upon the fine family that he had raised and his hope that another family would be in existence before the summer was over. It was most amusing and one would have said that he was really talking to me. This spring at Echo Beach while I was sitting at the boathouse near Home lake, no less than seven wrens alighted in the sand within two feet of where I was sitting, one of them not more than two inches away. After a little they flew away and then returned.

I remain, Sir, Yours faithfully,

LIST OF BIRDS IDENTIFIED DURING SIR ROBERT BORDEN'S VISIT TO ECHO BEACH AUGUST 19–28, 1932

1 Belted Kingfisher
2 Downy Woodpecker
3 Ruby-throated Hummingbird
4 Wood Pewee
5 Blue Jay
6 Northern Raven
7 Purple Finch

8 American Goldfinch
9 Song Sparrow
10 Cedar Waxwing
11 Black and White Warbler
12 Oven-Bird
13 Nuthatch
14 Black-Capped Chickadee
15 American Robin
16 Common Loon
17 Herring Gull
18 Red-Breasted Merganser
19 Great Blue Heron
20 Marsh Hawk – adult and juvenile
21 Sparrow Hawk
22 Blackburnian Warbler
23 Pine Siskin
24 Red-eyed Vireo
25 Parula Warbler
26 Black-throated Blue Warbler
27 Slate-colored Junco
28 Bald Eagle
29 Pileated Woodpecker
30 Crested Flycatcher
31 Spotted Sandpiper
32 Winter Wren

June 23, 1932

To J. Philip Bill, Esquire
Department of Justice
Ottawa

My dear Philip,

Tree swallows have not been in evidence for several weeks. This morning, while I was engaged in an interview, my wife observed about one hundred of them which suddenly made their appearance and engaged in unusual proceedings. They swooped close to the ground, sometimes alighted. Their great numbers and the immense swiftness of their flight close to the ground caused great alarm to the other birds. The robins and even the grackles crouched down in evident apprehension.

The majority of the tree swallows disappeared after ten or fifteen minutes. But after my interview I went out on the lawn and saw about a dozen of them still going through the same evolutions. They would fly so close to the ground as to touch it with their wings, rising and falling gracefully.

The grace and swiftness of their flight are wholly admirable. At times one would say that they were weaving an invisible garment in the air. Flying at tremendous speed they wheel and reverse their direction without any apparent effort.

What may be the purpose of this unexpected visit is an enigma to me; and I shall watch their further proceedings with much interest.

As you doubtless know, the new infra-red method of photography enables the country to be photographed far beyond the horizon. Recent numbers of the *London Times* gave illustrations of these photographs. A writer in the *Times* has suggested that birds may possess infra red vision and that this may account for the ease with which they find their destination in annual migration.

I remain, Yours faithfully,

Department of Mines,
National Mines of Canada, Ottawa
June 28, 1932

To Mr J. Philip Bill

Dear Mr Bill,

The copy of Sir Robert Borden's letter re tree swallows hawking close to the ground received. Of course it is unsafe to be dogmatic about the cause of the peculiar actions of the birds, but this seems like a probable explanation.

If I remember correctly June 23rd was an unreasonably cold day, so cold indeed that we lit a fire in our furnace. I have noticed on other similar unusually cold days in early summer that many treetop birds haunt the ground and the lower shrubbery and I have concluded that it was for the chilled insects that drop from the trees or are unable to rise to their usual heights in the air. Probably these swallows found the upper air, where they usually feed, practically devoid of insects and they were particularly hungry. They discovered over this more or less sheltered spot an aggregation of insect food that they were quick to take advantage of. Probably one or more of the swallow population found the largess and their apparent successful hunting was noted and seen by others cruising in the neighborhood that joining the feeders soon built up the aggregated flock. That other birds should show some apprehension at these diving bullets that swung so unusually close to their heads as if in attack is not very surprising.

The problem of the range of colors to which the eyes of various non-humans are attuned to is an interesting one. Because our eyes are adapted to a certain range of the spectrum is not indicative that other animals' color perception is confined to the same band. The vision range in many species may be shifted far towards infra-red or towards ultra-violet or even expanded towards both. In any such case the world must have an entirely different appearance to them than it has to us. In fact it is not improbable that objects that are very inconspiciously colored to us may be highly conspicuous to them and vice versa. This is one point in which all our theories of coloration, color protection, mimicry &c. fail to take into consideration for they are usually based upon the assumption that all eyes are similar to ours. I am aware that there has been some study of this subject made but it must be scattered in many publications that the ornithologist does not often have access to. Dr Casey-Wood who has conducted considerable research on the eyes of birds has published some observations on the color sense of the Australian Bower-Bird in *The American Journal of Ophthalmology* between 1923 and 1925 but I have never seen it. Probably some of the local eye-specialists may have files. If birds have an infra-red vision sense it would not permit curved vision over the horizon but it would cut through various hazes and render distant vision clearer. In such way it certainly would assist in migration though that it would confer any very extraordinary migrational powers I am inclined to doubt. Just how far birds are dependent on sight and geographic memory in migration is questionable. Most modern explanations stress them heavily and even to the exclusion of any other factor. Doubtless they are of prime importance to many species but no sight or route memory conceivable explains the unerring way in which pelagic species find their ways over unmarked wastes of open sea. I have little doubt that birds have some direction-finding or orientation sense that is absent in man or so slightly developed that we can not recognize it.

Sir Robert's description of the low-flying swallows reminds me of a pleasant little experience I had once in the Okanagan Valley. The Violet-grass Swallows were building and industriously hunting for feathers and cottony down to line their nests. We scattered bits of cotton-batting about and they immediately carried them off. Finally I shredded out some long wisps of cotton and held them out at arms length and the birds dove down and plucked them from my hand again and again. Some of these wisps were long trailers and it was amusing to see a bird with a long streamer of white cotton after it pursued by half a dozen others snatching at the ends and stealing it piece-meal.

Hoping these suggestions will be of interest, I remain,

Yours sincerely,
(Sgd) P.A. Taverner

June 29, 1932

My dear Sir Robert,

I am sure you will be greatly pleased and interested in Mr Taverner's endeavour to solve your enigma concerning the unusual assemblage and actions recently of the tree swallow. As I told you, I sent him a copy of your very interesting letter of the 23rd instant. He is the Government Ornithologist. His remarks concerning your reference to the infra-red method of photography reflect, I am sure you will agree, that he is practically and ably at home on the subject.

My brother Gordon has written as follows:

> I was very much interested in Sir Robert Borden's letter of June 23.
>
> I have never seen tree swallows doing anything like what he noticed. As a matter of fact I rarely have seen them in large bodies except possibly in the fall. This, incidentally, in spite of the fact that Hanover is a favorite haunt of tree swallows. It seems to me that there must have been some food supply where they were congregating – perhaps a hatching of some sort of almost invisible insects.

Yours very sincerely,
(Sgd) J. Philip Bill

Department of the Interior
National Parks of Canada

July 4, 1932
Wolfville, NS

Dear Philip,

I am just in receipt of the copy of the letter you sent me which was received by you from the Right Honourable Sir Robert Borden and which I have read with profound interest.

His recital of the actions of the tree swallows is certainly unusual and I cannot say that I have ever seen, or heard, of such a performance by them before. You may, or may not, know that the tree swallow is the first, or one of the first, of our summer birds to leave us in the autumn and strangely enough it is one of the first to arrive in the spring. After the middle of August they are rarely seen here and the tendency is for them to become gregarious immediately after their nesting responsibilities for the year are ended, anticipating the southward migration. Doubtless they are ended in Ottawa earlier than here, though those which nested on my premises have been on the wing for some time. It occurs to me that Sir Robert's swallow visitation and the unusual behaviour which he describes might be accounted for as follows: A band of birds which are through nesting and which were feeding close to the ground on a swarm of insects of microscopic proportions for his description of their acrobatic powers of flight (which are well-known in the swallow tribe) would suggest that the birds were in pursuit of food.

In his final paragraph he speaks of the infra-red method of photography which enables one to photograph the country far beyond the horizon. I have never heard of such a thing and am tremendously interested. The suggestion which he quotes from the *London Times* that birds may possess infra-red vision is of interest and represents a possible solution to some of the migration problems which have confronted bird students for many years. With your permission, I would like to write a short note for the press concerning this phase of Sir Robert's letter.

I spent a few days on the Island of Grand Manan, which is off the coast of the mainland of New Brunswick, recently and witnessed a very unusual spectacle while there, namely, a thousand or more herring-gulls sailing in wide circles high overhead, all feeding on a swarm of large winged insects, presumably flying ants. The concourse was slowly moving in our direction and when it was directly overhead we were able to note the minute specks as they reached for them with their long necks. The fisherman who was with me stated that he had frequently seen this performance but always at a considerable altitude and on hot windless days when the insects would be flying high. That gulls were ever entitled to be classified as fly-catchers was a new one to me.

I am, Yours faithfully,
(Sgd) R.W. Tufts,
per J.C.
Chief Federal Migratory
Bird Officer, Maritime Provinces

July 12, 1932

To J. Philip Bill, Esquire

My dear Philip,

Please say to Mr Tufts that I would not care to have my name mentioned in any communications to the press respecting my recent letter.

I think I must have been quite mistaken in supposing that the new infra-red photography enables objects beyond the horizon to be photographed. Kindly correct this in writing to Mr Taverner.

I am much interested in Mr Tufts' comments. However, his explanation of the extraordinary gyrations of the birds on the occasion when I noticed them does not accord with my observation. They really did not seem to be feeding although, occasionally, they alighted on the ground. Further, his explanation would not account for their close approach to us and apparent disregard of our presence, although on other occasions they maintained a very considerable distance in their flights.

My suggestion is – the unusual chilliness of the day, (noted by Mr Taverner in his letter of June 28), the gathering of a great number of young birds (four of them perched on the branches of the sprinkler) and, perhaps, some strong unexplainable stimulus.

Yours faithfully,

April 25, 1933

ACQUISITION OF GLENSMERE – OTTAWA

Sir,

On two occasions I have purchased land, employed an architect and completed all the preparations for building a house.

On the first occasion, during the autumn of 1892 or the beginning of 1893, we had purchased a lot and employed an American architect who came to Halifax to prepare the necessary plans. The arrangements were about completed when we were given an opportunity of purchasing a property called 'Pinehurst' near the head of the northwest Arm. There were four acres of land and a very pretty, one might say 'bijou', house upon which we expended a considerable amount of money before we sold it about fourteen years afterwards, upon our removal to Ottawa.

Our residence at Pinehurst was one of the most enjoyable periods of my life. There was a glorious view of the northwest Arm of which the aspect almost continually varied, in sunshine, shadow, cloud and mist. I made myself quite unpopular in the early morning by endeavouring to arouse my wife and my younger brother to enjoy with me the most beautiful view which the waters of the Arm presented immediately after sunrise.

After I found it necessary to remove to Ottawa during my political leadership, I purchased a lot on Marlborough Avenue. It was a most desirable location and again plans were prepared and everything was all ready to let the contract. My wife had attended the wedding of Corinne Fitzpatrick and when she returned therefrom she said that there was only one house in Ottawa which, above all others, she would like us to acquire and that was the house in which we have lived for twenty-seven years.

We discovered that the house, which was owned by Mrs Hayter Reid, was for sale. I called on Sir Charles Fitzpatrick who then occupied it and inquired whether he intended to purchase. He asked me to give him two months in which to decide and I assured him that in the meantime I would take no action. Before that period had elapsed he told me to proceed and accordingly I got into touch with the owner's representative; and eventually I purchased the house on April 25, 1906, on the understanding that the Fitzpatricks were to remain until about the end of June. They then moved out and we took over the house. In the meantime, Mrs Hayter Reid, who was engaged in the decoration of Canadian Pacific hotels in the west, requested that her furniture might remain until her return. This was rather inconvenient but we acquiesced. Upon her return, she arrived for luncheon with a friend from Quebec. Her chief interest appeared to be in a closet in the attic from which she emerged triumphant with a little child's cap which was a sort of heirloom in her family. She then proceeded to the basement where there was another clothes-closet and emerged with a small child's chair. Thereafter nothing interested her except the brass-knocker on the front door which she greatly prized and which she decided to remove. I demurred to this as it was my property; whereupon she said that if she did not have the knocker I must pay her ten dollars to which I cheerfully agreed. She then proceeded to make a demonstration about the fire-irons but her friend interposed and told her that this was really going too far.

But, I have omitted to mention an episode which she related with much unction. She had heard that we were willing to negotiate for the house which she was most anxious to sell. Arriving in Ottawa she endeavoured to get into touch with Sir Charles Fitzpatrick who was presiding in the Supreme Court of Canada. Nothing daunted by his official duties she telephoned the court demanding to speak to him. She was refused several times; and finally Sir Charles came to the telephone, evidently in a towering rage. The following conversation then took place:

> Mrs. Reid: Sir Charles Fitzpatrick, I want to know once and for all whether or not you intend to buy my house.
> Sir C.F. You go to H———.

There were many inscriptions in several parts of the house, some of which, unfortunately, have been obliterated. In the drawing-room above an alcove designed for music was a long scroll containing many poetic quotations in praise of music. The only one I can recall was from Milton:

> Lap me in soft Lydian airs,
> Married to immortal verse,
> Such as the meeting soul may pierce,
> In notes, with many a winding bout
> Of linked sweetness long drawn out.

Then in the middle of the scroll there were three or four bars of 'Home Sweet Home.' Over one of the doors in the hall was this inscription: 'The honour of the house is hospitality' and over the other 'The happiness of the house is contentment.' Over the fireplace in the hall, in old English lettering and spelling was this cheerful quotation:

> Now fayre betyde who here abyde and happie
> may ye be.
> And fayre befalle who in this halle repair
> in courtesie.
> From morn to nighte be't dark or bright we
> banish dole and dree.
> Come sit besyde our hearth; tis wide for
> gentylle companie.

When we purchased the place there were many apparent disadvantages. On the west, the beautiful park now called Macdonald Gardens, was then a disused cemetery which was overgrown with shrubs and bushes; and in the evenings was sometimes the resort of very undesirable characters. Eventually this was converted into a park and placed under the supervision of the Ottawa Improvement (now the Federal District) Commission. It was proposed to give this park my name; but I suggested that it should bear the name of Sir John A. Macdonald who was not otherwise commemorated in Ottawa.

I wrote to the Baroness Macdonald and she cabled her glad acceptance of the proposal.

The street was in terrible condition; there was an Infants' Home on the north, a scraggly spruce hedge along the front, and the southern part of the property was grown up in field grass. My wild garden was then a mere jungle. There were no flower beds, herbaceous borders or rose-garden. At the back of the ell the soil had been so much washed away that people prophesized the fall of the house into the Rideau river. There was no porch except a sort of storm-porch, unheated. The door of this porch was immediately opposite the front door; and icy blasts chilled the in-dwellers whenever the front door was opened in winter.

On the north the large dining-room was heated merely by a tiny radiator under each window-seat. We put in three large radiators; but even so one of the window-seat radiators froze and exploded during our first winter; and another went the same way during our second winter.

We have made numerous structural additions and other improvements and have lived very happily and comfortably in the house for twenty-seven years, especially during the last twelve years since I succeeded in emerging from public activities.

I remain, dear Sir, Yours faithfully,

May 12, 1933

SCHOOL-GIRLS ON TRAIN – AESOP'S FABLE

Sir,

Just a month ago today I was returning to Ottawa, having attended a board meeting of The Crown Life Insurance Company in Toronto. A number of girls, returning for the Easter vacation from some Toronto school, gave an extraordinary exhibition of which apparently they were rather proud. In manner they were loud, noisy and blatant. They took possession of the smoking-room and rent the air with instrument and voice, producing a vile cacophony to the vast disturbance and indignation of the other passengers. In truth they did little credit to their school or their training. Incidentally they brought stools from the rear of the train and practically blocked up the passage way along the centre of the car. In endeavouring to reach the rear of the car on one occasion, I unfortunately and inadvertently projected my left foot with some vigor against the leg of one of the stools with the result that the young lady who occupied it was deposited gracefully into the lap of her companion just opposite. I made elaborate apology but I rather hoped the incident might not be without salutary effect.

It was apparent that these girls were endeavouring not only to ape but to surpass the antics of young men on such an occasion; and it did not seem that the effort was worth while. One might have recalled, to their advantage, Aesop's fable of the donkey that sought to please his master by imitating the playfulness of the lap-dog.

I remain, Sir, Yours in sympathy,

May 28, 1933

JOURNEY BY AEROPLANE

Sir,

I first saw a flying-machine in the air near Montreal when Count de Lesseps gave an exhibition. Some twenty years later he was to find his grave on or near the rockbound coast of Labrador or northern Quebec.

After the first reaction it seemed to me perfectly natural that the machine should be skimming through the air; and I was quite devoid of that feeling of continued surprise which I had anticipated.

During the war I never was in the air, although it was the regular means of communication for my colleague Bonar Law who frequently flew between London and Paris. I sometimes had a half-formed intention to journey from Paris to London by air; but I was always deterred by the extreme uncertainty of the English weather.

On May 6, 1933, I was to leave Echo Beach for Ottawa; and I proposed to travel by motor. My friend Rhodes[2] told me that he expected an aeroplane that morning and invited me to accompany him. He had arrived with Colonel Eric MacKenzie a few days before; and MacKenzie, who was most reluctant to make the journey by air, told me that he had closed his eyes when the plane rose over the Ottawa river and had not opened them again until they reached Echo

2 Hon. E.N. Rhodes – a fellow member of Echo Beach and at that time Minister of Finance.

lake. Expecting a somewhat similar experience, I first closed my eyes as we rose from the water, but very soon I opened them and found that I was neither nervous nor giddy. This was quite a surprise, as ordinarily I dread any considerable height and am much relieved to reach *terra firma* once more.

We made the journey in thirty minutes which was a little longer than usual. I found the experience most enjoyable and surveyed with interest the country through which we were passing, noting the innumerable lakes and finally observing Ottawa which semed flatter than a pancake as we neared the river. The tallest trees looked extremely diminutive from our height of five thousand feet, the houses less than doll-houses and the roads like strips of tape. Throughout the trip, I had the sensation that the machine was motionless, that we were practically suspended in the air. Previously I had not heard of this reaction but afterwards I found that it is very usual.

We descended easily and gracefully upon the waters of the Ottawa river; and I reached my house early in the forenoon.

Ascertaining that my wife was not at home and that she was to lunch with Mrs Desbarats, I left a telephone message for her to call me at our house. When she telephoned, she inquired first of all where I was. I told her I was at Echo Beach; and she expressed surprise that I could telephone from there. I explained that we had a new line installed of which she had not heard. She wanted to know why it was that she could call me at our house and get in touch with me at Echo Beach. I explained that I had arranged for an immediate connection as soon as she would call the house. I told her that affairs at Echo Beach were in good condition, that I thought she would like to hear from me; and I asked how affairs were proceeding at our home. She was most appreciative of my having taken the trouble to call from that distance; and going back to the luncheon, she explained that she had just been speaking to me on the telephone at Echo Beach. Later in the afternoon she reported the incident to a lady whose husband was also at Echo Beach. This lady was quite concerned that her husband had neglected to call her.

When Laura [Lady Borden] reached home that evening I was waiting for her at the door; and she used graphic language to describe the 'grin' which pervaded my countenance. Very graphically also did she express her sensation; 'Of course I was glad to see him, but at the moment I could have killed him.'

My second air journey was on May 18, (1933) when Rhodes and I flew from Ottawa to Echo Beach in twenty-six minutes. Again the trip was thoroughly delightful and enjoyable.

Subsequently, I endeavoured to arrange with Canadian Airways for the journey on my own account; but as they have no aeroplane based on the Ottawa river, they would have to charge me from Montreal to Echo Beach – their estimate of the cost being over one hundred and eighty dollars. I told them that such a price was absurd; and I felt that their management was not very enterprising.

I remain, Sir, Yours in sympathy,

June 10, 1933

SUNRISE

Sir,

One sleeping in the open and waking at dawn or earlier sometimes sees glorious visions of the sunrise. First there is the faintest radiance in the east as *rododaktulos eos erigeneia* begins to open the portals of the dawn. If there are clouds above the eastern horizon they are flooded with an indescribably beautiful rose tint which gradually deepens into the full splendour of the sunshine bursting into a June morning.

Not long ago I saw island cloud continents in the eastern heavens; and just at sunrise they were touched with a radiance that had not yet reached the earth. One might imagine these island cloud continents to be the abode of the 'Shining Ones', for whom time has no meaning, who still behold the dawn of creation while they see our little planet whirling along in endless movement – keeping time with sister planets and attendant upon her lord and life-giver the Sun who obeys the urge of some greater centre – in fulfilment of a divine and eternal purpose that human intelligence has not yet comprehended or even imagined.

I remain, Sir, Yours in sympathy,

June 20, 1933

REMINISCENCES OF HOUSEHOLD PETS

Sir,

The recent advent of a half-starved cat, which has evidently been thrown upon its own resources by some householder on vacation and which now comes regularly to entreat a draught of milk, reminds me of our days at Pinehurst when Lady Jane the cat and Taffy the St Bernard were with us.

Lady Jane was a most interesting and intelligent animal. She did not at all care for the kitchen which she seldom visited except for food or when her family of kittens required direct superintendence. She would follow us like a dog in our walks around our little place of four acres; and she was on terms of friendship, even of affection with Taffy. Indeed they were such sworn comrades that when a family of kittens arrived, Lady Jane took great delight in bringing one of them with much pride for Taffy's inspection. She would place the little thing between Taffy's huge paws and he would fairly sigh with delight and excitement. On one occasion she forgot the kitten which Taffy proceeded to lick until it was practically unrecognizable. Laura arrived just in time to rescue the kitten in a condition of complete saturation.

Taffy was a great lumbering animal and he had the most extraordinary confidence in and affection for Laura. It was wonderful how so huge an animal could wander around our little drawing-room without overthrowing the small tables and bric-à-brac with which women delight to encumber the smallest of drawing-rooms; equally is it their delight to establish in windows, designed for admission of light and air, in the first place curtains, but more especially vases of growing flowers, so the unwary male, desiring to admit the air from outside, is prone to commit unexpected devastation.

On several occasions I had to speak sternly to Taffy and threaten him with punishment. On such occasions he always backed to the immediate vicinity of Laura, and close up against her he seemed to feel comparatively secure, thoroughly relying on her protection.

Once his neck was badly cut, evidently by barbed wire. Laura noticed that he was continually scratching and discovered the wound which was in a very serious, even dangerous condition. She immediately sent for a veterinary surgeon and he said that the scratching must be stopped or the wound would be fatal. He cleansed and dressed the dog's neck and encircled it with bandages of absorbent cotton firmly fastened with linen bandages. The vet had hardly reached his office before the dog's hind leg had completely demolished both linen and cotton; and once more the wound was being opened and perhaps infected. Laura telephoned to the vet who declared that nothing further could be done, that the dog would certainly die and that he would come to the house and chloroform him. This proposal Laura indignantly refused and then her woman's wit came to her aid. She had the wound dressed again and then she swathed the dog's paw with great bandages of absorbent cotton and linen. This effectually prevented him from scratching and further convinced him that he was very lame, as he went around limping. From time to time the bandage required to be removed and a new one applied. He would stand quivering while this operation was being accomplished. However he would still follow our carriage and people were amazed and sometimes distressed to see a dog following on three legs, evidently suffering intense lameness. The wound healed and Taffy was as well as ever.

Notwithstanding his size, he was a great coward; and every cur in the neighborhood, knowing his indisposition to fight, delighted to snap at his legs as he followed the carriage.

Eventually he died while we were in Ottawa. The news reached me in the afternoon but, knowing that Laura would spend a sleepless night if I told her of his death, I did not give her the news until the next morning.

Taffy was succeeded by Bobs, as fine a greyhound as I ever saw. Laura purchased him in town and he signalized the first night of his confinement in the kitchen by rounding one corner of the kitchen-table and by chewing into unrecognizable shape the cook's bonnet which was hanging above it. Laura turned him out of doors but he returned the following day which was Sunday and gave us a taste of his spirit when, gracefully bounding on to the dining-room table he made off with a large, untouched cake. Again he was turned out; and again he returned. His movements were the embodiment of grace; and, unlike most greyhounds, he would fight any dog that came within his range. In the guest bedroom there was an eiderdown on the bed which he greatly affected. Whenever he could seize the opportunity he would enter the bedroom, circle gracefully in the air, alight upon the eiderdown and enjoy refreshing slumber.

He had beautiful eyes and was extremely intelligent. One spacious arm-chair in our sitting-room was his especial delight. Sometimes when I was sitting in this chair he would come, put his head on my knee and gaze at me with the most appealing expression in his beautiful eyes. To my shame be it said that on occasion I was foolish enough to relinquish the chair which he would immediately occupy.

One afternoon a lady who was calling upon my wife was sitting in this capacious chair. Bobs who had been lying on the rug went over, put his head on her knee and made the appeal which he had found so effective in my case. The lady was quite touched by this evidence of warm affection. She moved forward in the chair and put her hand on his head to caress him. As she did so, Bobs leaped gracefully into the air and alighted between her back and the back of the chair, thus suddenly and disastrously dispelling her illusion as to his affectionate nature.

The stretch of road over which we were accustomed to drive to town was frequented by numerous curs who had enjoyed themselves vastly in the pursuit of Taffy. Recognizing our carriage, they attempted to indulge in similar antics with Bobs whose lightning-like responses to their advances left a trail of yelping curs throughout the length of Quinpool Road [a street in Halifax].

His swiftness was amazing. One Sunday morning he was following our sleigh when the coachman was driving us to church. On the north common, a huge St Bernard crept up to seize Bobs unawares while his attention was occupied with some attractive object. If his huge assailant had fastened on his back, probably Bobs would have come to an untimely end. He saw the danger just as the St Bernard was upon him, threw himself to one side with incredible speed, caught the St Bernard by the throat, shook him, left him dazed and amazed in the middle of the road and sped after us.

During our absence in Ottawa he contracted, through loneliness, a habit of roaming around the city; and eventually we were obliged to give him to a friend. Finally he came into the ownership of some gentleman in Moncton.

I remain, Sir, Yours in sympathy,

July 6, 1933

SEVENTY-NINTH BIRTHDAY

Sir,

As one grows older one learns more and more to marvel at the glories and wonders of nature in her myriad manifestations. One night in June after a heavy thunder-storm had rolled away to the south, I watched, after I had retired to my outdoor bed, a scene which continued for nearly an hour. The storm was so distant that one could not hear the roll of the thunder; but above the southern horizon was an almost constant lambent radiance through which played, practically unceasingly, shafts and tongues of intensely white flame followed from time to time by the forked lightnings of the storm. It was a scene never to be forgotten.

Since my last letter I have passed the seventy-ninth milestone of my life; and I was overwhelmed with congratulations. Lord Bessborough sent me a telegram from Anticosti; and friends from Atlantic to Pacific did not fail to remember me. The most characteristic and amusing message was from George P. Graham as follows:

'Family bible birth record unreliable congratulations.'

My memory extends over at least seventy-five years. I remember very distinctly my grandmother's sister, Frances Brown, who was born in 1780. What tremendous events have occurred and what wonders have arisen in that period of a century and a half, just a moment in the history of the world!

My wife tells me that I should have a birthday not more than once in three years. She informs me that up to a certain period a woman is accustomed to understate her age; afterwards she acquires the habit of overstating it so that she induces admiring friends to say: 'What a wonderful woman she is for her age.' Possibly this vanity is not confined to the fair sex.

On February 19, 1904, Sir Wilfrid Laurier and I attended in the Senate on the occasion of an address to Senator David Wark on his hundredth birthday. Sir Wilfrid spoke briefly and I followed. Senator Wark spoke in reply for twelve or fifteen minutes as brightly and clearly as if it were his fiftieth, instead of his hundredth birthday. He lived to be nearly one hundred and three. It is said that when he was about ninety-five he made a vigorous protest against delay in advancing the work of the session, declaring that he, in common with many other members, was anxious to return home and attend to his business affairs.

In returning with Sir Wilfrid from the Senate on that occasion he said to me: 'Borden, I should not care to live a hundred years.' And indeed there was good cause for that thought. Loneliness must cast a shadow upon one who lives so long that all the friends, not only of youth and middle-age but of old age as well, have passed on before him. Sir Charles Tupper, in speaking of himself, used to quote Dr Samuel Johnson: 'Superfluous lags the veteran on the stage.' But up to the end, both he and Lord Strathcona took an intense and active interest in life; and I could never observe any sensation of loneliness.

I remain, dear Sir, Yours in sympathy,

August 23, 1933

DEFEAT OF HARRINGTON GOVERNMENT IN NOVA SCOTIA – REMINISCENCES OF HALIFAX

Sir,

Although I am secluded from the activities of public life and although my interest in party success or disaster has been diminished to the vanishing point since my leadership of the Union government, yet I felt grieved and disappointed at the defeat of the Harrington government in Nova Scotia yesterday.

My chief experience with Gordon Harrington was during the war. Physically unfit to go to the Front, he found his metier in the organization of the Canadian Overseas Ministry. Both Sir George Perley and Sir Edward Kemp formed a high opinion of Harrington's character, ability and devotion to duty. He rendered to our country a service that could hardly be overestimated.

Since his accession to the Premiership of Nova Scotia he has given to that province excellent government; and indeed his record has never been surpassed. During these terrible years of depression he maintained the financial position of the province at a higher standard than elsewhere in Canada. And withal he is a gentleman of the old school, chivalrous, courteous, broadminded, harbouring no resentments and intent only upon the welfare of his country.

Notwithstanding this record and these attributes he was overwhelmingly defeated through causes which, no doubt, were complex but some of which can easily be guessed. Among them was the press influence exercised and funds provided by a recreant Conservative whose mental equipment, beyond a keen aptitude for money-making, is of the scantiest, whose service in public life would hardly be called respectable and whose chief characteristic is vindicative spite which he attempts to cover by a shallow pretense which deceives nobody.

To speak of Harrington recalls memories of the past. When I came to the bar in 1878, or rather when I began practice in Halifax in 1882 as junior member of Graham, Tupper and Borden, the four outstanding counsel were Wallace Graham, Hugh McDonald Henry, Robert Sedgewick and Charles Sydney Harrington (the father of Gordon Harrington). The three first named were elevated to the bench and such should have been the fortune of Harrington; but in this respect fortune was not kind to him.

From my memoirs I extract a description of C.S. Harrington's early activities as a public speaker; and I attach also a copy of a letter which I wrote in March last to the Nova Scotia Barristers' Society in which I recalled memories of the delightful days of old when I resided and practised in Halifax.

I remain, dear Sir, yours in sympathy

PS I have never met Mr Angus L. MacDonald, leader of the Liberal party, who gained a notable victory in this contest. He seems to be held in high regard by his party; and the *Halifax Chronicle* ascribes to him transcendent ability and every imaginable virtue. If, however, his quality is to be judged by his pronouncement on the evening of his victory, my native province is in for a rough journey. In that pronouncement he posed as the successor of Joseph Howe and as a protagonist of responsible government which as he claimed, had been challenged in the contest which had just concluded. So far as my knowledge goes, no more fatuous or absurd claim was ever made by a public man in his position.

EXTRACT FROM *ROBERT LAIRD BORDEN: HIS MEMOIRS* (PAGE 23)

Harrington was a leading counsel for many years and unsuccessfully contested the County of Annapolis against the Attorney-General J.W. Longley. He was an excellent after-dinner speaker and equally effective on the hustings. While still a very young man he met Hon. A.G. Jones who had been a member of Alexander Mackenzie's cabinet, a man of great ability and an impressive speaker but with a curious habit of seeming to close his eyes while speaking. Harrington, with ready wit and irreverent disregard of Mr Jones' high position, took full advantage of this peculiarity. He concluded an excellent speech as follows:

> 'Mr Jones will attack my arguments and contravert my facts. Do not believe him. I will give you a sure test. Whenever he shuts his eyes he is lying.'

There was wild outcry whenever Mr Jones was unable to resist the habit of apparently closing his eyes.

March 11, 1933

Dear Mr Inglis,

I am greatly touched by the very kind invitation to speak at the Annual Dinner of the Nova Scotia Barristers' Society and by a letter which I received by the same post from my valued friend, Hector McInnes, KC.

To my great regret circumstances prevent me from accepting the invitation which has vividly recalled the days of long ago when I had the honour first to be a member of the council and afterwards President of the Society during an extended period.

I have a very happy memory of the annual dinners which, in those days, were usually held at Bedford during the winter months. Among those who assembled on such occasions, who have since passed away and with whom I was then in intimate association, I recall many brilliant after-dinner speakers; James Norbeck Lyons, Wallace Graham, Robert Sedgewick, James Wilberforce Longley, Hugh McDonald Henry, Charles Sydney Harrington, Arthur Drysdale, Charles Hibbert Tupper, Benjamin Franklin Pearson and others.

Doubtless the same spirit of comradeship that prevailed in the Halifax bar in those days still continues. Our agreements as to matters or arrangement in our practice were usually oral; and from first to last I do not recall an instance in which the oral understanding was not respected. Sydney Harrington gave expression to a view, which indeed we all shared, that if question arose as to the exact meaning of the arrangement or agreement one should always give to one's adversary the benefit of any doubt.

Every member of the Supreme Court during my active practice has since passed away. Among them were two men in whose office I had studied, Robert Linton Weatherbe and Wallace Graham. I retain a vivid recollection of them, as well as of James McDonald, Hugh MacDonald, Samuel Gordon Rigby, John Sparrow David Thompson, Joseph Norman Ritchie, Charles James Townsend, Alexander James and Nicholas Hogan Meagher. I speak only of those before whom I practised.

For seven years I was a partner in business of Wallace Graham and I revere his memory. No man could have been kinder, more considerate or more generous than he was to me as a junior partner.

But besides those who have passed over to the Majority, there are others, now or recently upon the bench, with whom I had happy association; Mr Justice Russell, Mr Justice Mellish and Chief Justice

Chisholm my valued associate in business for many years.

I beg that you will convey to the President and members of the Council my very warm thanks for the invitation which indeed I greatly appreciate. Perhaps on some future occasion I may have the opportunity of speaking to the members of the bar in Halifax which I would regard as a distinct privilege. Many of the happiest years of my life were spent in the practice of my profession.

To the members of the council and to the members of the Society generally I send my very warm regards and best wishes that health and happiness may attend them in all the years that lie before them.

I remain, dear Mr Inglis, with warm personal regards,

Yours faithfully,

September 7, 1933

A GRAVE EXPERIENCE

Sir,

From August first to fourteenth, Henry and Jean Borden, Philip Bill and I spent a most enjoyable two weeks at Echo Beach. While there I bathed in Home Lake and enjoyed a sun-bath every morning.

On my return I seemed in excellent form; but apparently I engaged too strenuously in many activities. As a result I had an extraordinary and rather grave experience on August 24. About 11.30 am, as I was sitting in my library, my right arm became numb and useless and I rapidly grew very dizzy. With great difficulty I tottered to my bedroom and after undressing I rang for the maid who brought me a glass of brandy. My speech was quite affected for about two hours. Dr Hugh Laidlaw, who arrived very shortly, told me that such an attack was not unusual. He came again in the afternoon when I seemed to be almost normal. He said the attack was due to the failure of my nervous system to regulate the flow of blood and as a result the circulation had become too slow in some part of my brain. He did not fail to impart advice which he put in the form of a serious warning to materially curtail my activities.

I have endeavoured to follow his advice; and when the Canadian Bar Association met at Ottawa on August 30, I asked Mr Rowell to read the address which I had intended to present myself.

Thereafter I began moderately to resume my activities; and I attended the Canadian Seniors' Golf Tournament at Lucerne-in-Quebec for one day on September 6.

I remain, Sir, Yours in Sympathy,

September 20, 1933

BRITISH COMMONWEALTH RELATIONS CONFERENCE - TORONTO

Sir,

I returned a few days ago from the British Commonwealth Relations Conference, which opened in Toronto on September 11, at which I delivered the address of welcome and remained thereafter until September 14.

There was a strong delegation from every dominion (except the Irish Free State) and from India. The most outstanding figures from abroad were Viscount Cecil of Chelwood and Sir Herbert Samuel from Great Britain; Honourable W. Downie Stewart from New Zealand; Senator Malan from South Africa; Professor Charteris from Australia; and Diwan Bahadur Ramaswami Mudaliar from India.

During my visit there were several interesting and useful speeches but I felt that too much time was wasted in idle discussion upon relatively trivial matters. Accordingly, on September 13, I spoke in this sense and pointed out that legalistic refinements and ultra-technical considerations would play no part if, unfortunately, war involving the British Commonwealth should break out. They would escape notice in the reaction of the tremendous forces then aroused and would be no more heeded than 'seven seas would heed a pebble cast.' After my departure, my friend Rowell[3] informed me that the discussion had become more useful and constructive. It is doubtful however whether such a conference serves any better purpose than the intimate association, the fuller understanding, the human touch, which it creates.

At the dinner on the evening of September 11, I sat between

3 Hon. Newton Wesley Rowell of Toronto, who resigned the leadership of the Ontario Liberal party in 1917 and joined Sir Robert's Union government. The two men became close friends.

Lord Cecil and Senator Malan. Cecil, I believe, does not concur in my view that the peace of the world cannot be maintained by use or manifestation of force, nor does Rowell; but my strong belief to the contrary has not been in the least affected. Humanity, if it is to be saved at all from the unspeakable horrors and savagery of war, must be saved in the domain of the spirit.

I was much attracted by the Indian delegates to whom in my address I made an earnest appeal, declaring that, while each dominion had a great task before it, India had the most majestic task of all. And I warned them that nationhood cannot be conferred by statute, order-in-council or formal document; it could only emerge through acceptance and fulfilment of responsibility and through achievement.

One of the most interesting among the Indian delegates was Mir Maqbool Mahmood with whom I had intimate conversation and who gave a luncheon at which I was the guest of honour.

The future only can tell us whether any useful results will flow from the Banff Conference of the Institute of Pacific Relations and the British Commonwealth Relations Conference.

As for me, more than ever I am convinced that it will be the part of wisdom to abjure all such conferences in future. In this I am sustained by the opinion of my physician who came this morning for consultation as to the physical condition of my wife and myself. He was unexpectedly cheerful and reported that her blood pressure was more normal than it had been for some time, and that mine was excellent. But he advised me that the attack which I sustained on August 24, was not to be disregarded as it constituted a grave warning. He advised me to engage in reasonable activities but to avoid excessive fatigue; and he declared, what is very true, that the preparation and delivery of important speeches greatly exhaust my vitality.

I remain, dear Sir, Yours in sympathy,

PS I venture to inflict upon you a copy of my address of welcome to the Conference and my observations made on the 13th and 14th.

SIR ROBERT BORDEN – ADDRESS OF WELCOME TO THE DELEGATES TO THE BRITISH COMMONWEALTH RELATIONS CONFERENCE, TORONTO, SEPTEMBER 11–21, 1933

You are already assured of a warm welcome to Canada; and as Honorary President of the Canadian Institute of International Affairs, it is my privilege in bidding you doubly welcome to say how highly honoured is our Institute by your presence. Distinguished in public service, you have come from Great Britain and from sister nations of our Commonwealth, India among them, to sit in this informal council, and taking into account a long series of developments, to consider and estimate the nature and permanence of the relations that have ensued, the most acceptable means of increasing their efficiency and the probable tendencies of the future.

Perhaps as much as any living man I have striven for the right of full nationhood which the dominions now enjoy and toward which a great step was taken in the constitutional resolution of 1917. In Great Britain eminent statesmen, unrivalled in ability and experience, whose opinion commanded fullest consideration and respect were at first perplexed and alarmed by a development that was inevitable. To one of them who imparted to me at Paris in 1919 grave fear that the path we were pursuing would lead to the disintegration of the Empire, I replied with complete sincerity and equal earnestness that along this path and not elsewhere would be found its permanent and real unity, than which nothing was or is dearer to my heart. On the other hand, perhaps we of the dominions did not at first fully realize that nationhood can only be consummated by acceptance and fulfilment of its attendant responsibilities.

In endeavouring to foresee the tendencies of the future we may perhaps be assisted by study of the past. In that retrospect one cannot fail to be impressed by the influence of constitutional convention and by its power to mould effectually inter-Imperial relations. Let one illustration suffice. Not by statute, order-in-council or other formal act, but by the establishment of a recognized convention Canada was first endowed with the faculty of self-government. Upon the firm foundation of that convention the stately structure of the Commonwealth has been raised. Even upon the written constitution of United States the influence of convention, coupled with extraordinary subtlety of interpretation, has been remarkable. An ex-Solicitor-General of United States (Honourable J.M. Beck) has recently declared that, in striking contrast to the desire and intention of the framers of its constitution, that country is tending more and more to become a unitary rather than a federal state. It would be difficult to illustrate more vividly the incapacity of human intelligence to foresee or to estimate the play of future forces upon the most ingenious safeguards and devices that can be enshrined in a written constitution. And I venture to believe, that notwithstanding the Statute of Westminster, convention will continue to exercise an important influence upon the relations between the Commonwealth's self-governing nations.

May I diverge for a moment to remind you that the designation

'British Commonwealth of Nations', which I thought of very modern origin, was employed by a distinguished statesman, the late Lord Rosebery, nearly half a century ago. The expression has been challenged as illogical but it has persisted.

The present constitution (I use the word in its widest sense) of our Commonwealth is a tremendous experiment in governance. To imperil its unity would invite disaster to humanity; for how can the League of Nations, in whose service to the world I am a resolute believer, how can such a League survive if our Commonwealth may not endure? Is not its continued existence the most vital of all considerations affecting our future destiny?

In a recent instructive study of the period and personality of Metternich, Algernon Cecil refers to a truth which Metternich recognized and Lord Acton later emphasized that a commonwealth raised upon a diversity of racial genius is especially endowed with the rationale of a high civilization. In its diversity of race, language, creed, custom, interest, outlook, our confederation of nations, at first sight a phenomenon verging upon the impossible, is invested with a significance of vital moment to the wider community of the world's nations.

In the spirit of our discussions and in the principles to which we shall give adherence may it be our endeavour to consolidate, or, as Mr Gladstone once expressed it, to 'corroborate, the Empire's essential unity, the inspiring unity of its infinite diversity.' In these troublous times the conception which it presents of liberty and cooperation, united by goodwill in the pursuit of peace, is more than ever a priceless possession not only to its scattered nations but to the world. Let it not fail.

I pray that your deliberations may be fruitful. And I trust that they will not conclude without our heartfelt tribute to the late Viscount Grey, elder statesman of the Empire, servant of humanity, whose passing we so deeply deplore.

SIR ROBERT BORDEN'S ADDRESS AT THE BRITISH COMMONWEALTH RELATIONS CONFERENCE, SEPTEMBER 13, 1933

I wish to say a few words and as I am obliged to leave tomorrow, perhaps you will pardon me if my remarks should be a little discursive and possibly not quite relevant in every aspect to the very interesting and important speech to which we have just listened from the rapporteur.

We are engaged here in a very worthy purpose. Apart from any concrete results that may ensue from our deliberations, the very fact that we have come together to exchange ideas and get into touch with each others' views is of itself important. Perhaps we can be regarded as preparing the drawings for the architectural design of an improved structure of the British Empire. Any improvement is, of course, desirable. Not by way of advice, because advice is very seldom taken although it is very often given, but purely by way of suggestion, I think we should not put out of mind the fact that the British Empire was not built, but that it grew.

There has been much said about the difficult strategical positions of the various dominions. I shall speak of that generally for a moment; and later I would like to say a word with regard to Canada in particular. There is the great continent of Australia, dominating in certain respects the Southern Pacific Ocean. There is the adjoining dominion of New Zealand. There is South Africa with an immense task before her in the future. I do not doubt that in each of these dominions the task which they have before them will be approached in a worthy spirit and will be worthily fulfilled. But may I suggest to these dominions, as well as to those of the north, and to India, that in the very difficulties of their situations lie their splendid opportunities. That I am sure has been the case in Canada; and that I am confident will be the case in other dominions. The pine tree grows strong through the intensity of its effort to resist the tempest.

I am not in the least depressed by the proximity of Canada to the United States. It is fortunate for Canada that the dominance of the United States upon this hemisphere has tended to develop a strong Canadian nationality. Something has been said about the Monroe Doctrine. This is merely a canon of foreign policy of the United States which of course must be treated with the utmost respect; but it is not a doctrine of international law. Reference has been made to the supposed reliance of Canada upon the United States' Navy. I do not join in that feeling because if we really were forced to depend upon the United States' Navy, I should venture to suggest that we ought to contribute to it. We have never gone very far in our contribution to the naval forces of the Empire; but that is a subject upon which I am not disposed to dwell at the moment. A member of the Canadian House of Commons said after the London Naval Conference that Canada was the only nation which had emerged from that conference with her naval forces absolutely unimpaired.

We have learned something from the United States in the past. We have been inspired by the splendid spirit of self-reliance, by the strong belief in their institutions and in their destiny which have always characterized her people. They have taught us more than one important lesson. But I venture to suggest that our great neighbour, with whom we are on close terms of friendship and association, may in some respects have something to learn from us. Among others, I mention respect for the law, the administration of justice, and, in some aspects, the stabilizing of our economic institutions, especially our banking system. We shall continue on terms of good relationship with our neighbour. Sometimes, with that self-conceit which is so characteristic of Canadians, we have thought that possibly we might be a helpful medium of interpretation between the great republic and the mother country beyond the ocean.

I have listened to many attempts to forecast the future. We have been told, quite rightly, that we must deal with realities. I entirely agree with that, but again by way of suggestion and not at all by way of advice, I venture to say that we must be perfectly sure that we know just what the realities are. I have never been impressed with the ability of men to forecast the future and any little faith I may have had in that regard has been completely dissipated by events during the last four years.

To show how fallible human intelligence is. In 1918, I was a member of a remarkable committee of the British War Cabinet. It consisted of the Prime Minister of the United Kingdom and the Prime Ministers of the dominions, General Smuts representing General Botha. Our duty was to arrive at certain conclusions as to further effort necessary to win the war; where should the decisive blow be struck; when could it most effectively be delivered. We conferred, we had generals and chiefs of staff to advise us; we had commanders from the western front and from Italy; we had all possible available information for the purpose of our report; and from first to last, there was never a single man, soldier or civilian, who dreamed that the war could be brought to a successful conclusion in 1918. A distinguished statesman, whose name is a household word throughout the Empire, said that he did not believe it could be brought to a conclusion even in the following year, 1919. The greatest soldier who advised us thought the Allies might perhaps hold their own until the middle of the following summer. In that incident there is an illustration of how little we may be in touch with realities. The morale of the German people behind their army had broken and we did not know it.

I give you another and more modern instance of the futility of human intelligence in determining the future. In New York, in April 1929, I was present at a meeting where were assembled more than twenty of the ablest men in United States, men prominent in finance, in banking, in transportation, in industrial affairs, in electrical development. They were all outstanding men; and not one of them at the round table conversation which took place had even the faintest suspicion of what was before us in the immediate future.[4]

As is natural, I am living more in the past than in the present and I have come to the conclusion, after listening to the deliberations of this conference, that we are exercising too greatly our ingenuity in conjuring up difficulties and inventing problems. The nations of the British Commonwealth seem to have a certain practical ability to meet emergencies. I was impressed by the Chairman's observations, day before yesterday, that in our deliberations we have been thinking too much about war, too little about the preservation of peace.

The great significance of the British Commonwealth to its people and to the world is to be found in the fact that it does ensure peace within one-fourth of the world's territory and between four hundred millions of its people. Is or is not the continuance of that condition something upon which we should concentrate our best endeavour? I do not think you have any doubt as to my own opinion.

May I say one final word to the men of India whom I am so glad to see among us and with whose fellow-countrymen it has been my delight and my opportunity to cooperate in the past. I refer to the late Lord Sinha, eminent in character, ability and good judgment, and to Mr Sastri, whose cooperation as a colleague at the Washington Conference[5] I so greatly valued, to whom I hope my friends will give my kind regards and affectionate greetings.

Each of our dominions has a great task before it but India the most majestic task of all. Let us not imagine that a nation can be created by act of parliament, by order in council, by any formal document; a nation can only be created by acceptance and fulfillment of responsibility, by achievement. The task that lies before your country, my friends from India, is the most majestic task within our Empire. I hope and indeed I believe that this tremendous task upon which the future of the Commonwealth so greatly depends will be splendidly and worthily fulfilled.

4 This reference is to the world-wide depression which started in October, 1929.

5 The reference is to the Washington Disarmament Conference Nov. 1921–Feb. 1922 at which Sir Robert represented Canada.

SIR ROBERT BORDEN'S ADDRESS AT THE BRITISH COMMONWEALTH RELATIONS CONFERENCE, SEPTEMBER 14, 1933

The discussion has been quite interesting and I have listened attentively to the legalistic refinements and considerations that have been presented from time to time with marked ability by various speakers. But is it probable that our discussion is of much use in forecasting the situation that will arise in the terrible eventuality of another war? The action of the nations of the Empire will not then be determined by legalistic distinctions or technical aspects; it is impossible for us sitting here to forecast in any measurable degree the play and reaction of the tremendous forces that would then control and dominate. The situation will provide its own solution; and it will solve itself in a way that we cannot anticipate with any degree of certainty. Who among the European continental nations, or even within the Empire, had any conception of what the Empire's response would be in 1914? A Canadian officer captured by the Germans had this question propounded to him: 'What did Great Britain offer you Canadians to induce you to come and fight for her?' Such was the German outlook. It is desirable no doubt to consider relevant aspects; but I venture to submit that in devoting so much attention and debate to legalistic refinements and technical considerations we may be wandering a little into dreamland.

September 28, 1933

LORD MACMILLAN – OTTAWA CANADIAN CLUB – CONTRAST WITH SIR HERBERT SAMUEL

Sir,

Today I listened to a really fine address by Lord Macmillan[6] to the Canadian Club of Ottawa. I was very happily situated on the right of Lord Macmillan, with Sir Charles Addis at my right.

During the course of the luncheon Macmillan told me some very amusing incidents of our profession in Scotland.

In the early part of his speech he made reference to economic

6 Then chairman of the Canadian Royal Commission on Banking.

conditions and declared that our highest hope lies in the fact that our present difficulties have arisen not from some outside and controlling force but from our own lack of capacity and foresight. In this connection he told a story of a Scottish Divine who preached very devastating sermons. After one of these, a parishioner asked: 'How can you believe that a God of mercy could be so terribly cruel as you declare?' To this the preacher replied: 'We must always distinguish between what God would do as an individual and what he is obliged to do in his official capacity.'

He paid a great tribute to women, saying that he had known of no man who had accomplished great things in public life who had not been dominated by the influence of some woman, wife, sister or mother.

He quoted interesting passages from Jefferson and Adams; and he spoke of the Eastern proverb:

> If it can be done, it is done. If it cannot be done, it shall be done.

This he thought might be a real inspiration to statesmen at the present time.

In alluding to his ancestry he related this anecdote. The conversation took place between an English tourist who happened to wander to the vicinity of a graveyard and a grave-digger. The conversation in abbreviated form is as follows:

ENGLISH TOURIST Well it is very silent around here.
GRAVE-DIGGER Not more than they.
ENGLISH TOURIST Do people die frequently here?
GRAVE-DIGGER Only once.
ENGLISH TOURIST Have you lived here all your life?
GRAVE-DIGGER Not yet.

Then Macmillan gave a most inspiring account of the origin, functions and duties of the Judicial Committee of the Privy Council. These all sprang from the primitive idea that the king is the fountain of justice and dispenses justice to every subject who is wronged. He spoke of the committee's jurisdiction over one-quarter of the earth's surface and of the immense number and startling variety of the judicial systems with which it had to deal. In passing, he paid a fine tribute to Chief Justice Duff [Rt. Hon. Lyman P. Duff (later Sir) then Chief Justice of the Supreme Court of Canada]; and it was received with tremendous applause. In this part of his speech he told of an English traveller in some remote part of India who had come across a shrine at which natives were worshipping. He inquired to what god the shrine was dedicated. 'We do not know this god, but he is a wonderful god, because he has restored to us our temple.' Upon further inquiry he was told that, so far as they were aware, the name of this god was 'Judicial Committee of the Privy Council.'

I have never seen a more appreciative audience.

Lord Macmillan's speech was in marked contrast to that of Sir Herbert Samuel[7] on September 23, as to which I had correspondence, copies of which are appended.

In conversation with Macmillan, he said he had heard of Samuel's indiscretion and attributed it to his lack of any sense of humour; but in my opinion there was lack of something more.

...

I remain, Yours in sympathy.

EXTRACT FROM LETTER FROM HON MARTIN BURRELL, DATED SEPTEMBER 24, 1933

I tried to find you after the Club lunch yesterday as I was curious to learn your reactions to Samuel's speech. Some one should have tipped him off that the Canadian Clubs were not the place for partisan remarks on controversial questions? He intimated that he was going to be 'reticent.' My Lord! if that is his conception of reticence, what would it have been had he been frank?

COPY OF SIR ROBERT BORDEN'S REPLY TO HONOURABLE MARTIN BURRELL, DATED SEPTEMBER 25, 1933

My dear Burrell,

You inquire as to my reaction to Samuel's partisan utterances. The main part of his speech was excellent; but I thought his attack upon the Ottawa Economic Conference and his sneers at protection were not only in extremely bad taste but rather narrow and stupid. I asked him at the conclusion of his address whether he realized that in Canada, with less than one-quarter of Great Britain's population, we have half as many unemployed. In Great Britain there are 2,400,000, according to Samuel; in Canada they number 1,200,000. My

7 Then leader of the Liberal party in the British House of Commons.

inquiry was apropos of his lamentation that Canada was benefiting at the expense of Great Britain.

The Ottawa Economic Conference seems to have had the same effect upon Samuel as King Charles' head had upon Mr Dick in *David Copperfield.* It so continually obtrudes itself upon his inner consciousness that it results in spoiling what would otherwise be a really fine speech. The fanatical British Free Trader has about the narrowest vision that could be imagined.

I entirely agree that channels of trade which are presently blocked by absurd tariffs and other devices ought to be cleared; and I have said so very distinctly and emphatically on two public occasions within a year. But to suggest that we should throw open our markets to the manufacturers and producers of United States, drive tens of thousands of Canadians out of employment, and in the result render ourselves no more than an appanage to that country, is manifestly absurd.

Thirty years ago I heard from a Toronto workman the shortest and one of the most cogent protectionist speeches I ever listened to:

> We were getting fairly good wages and had comfortable homes. I was working in a furniture factory when about 1877, United States dumped furniture into Canada and shut up our factory. We walked the streets and ate in soup kitchens. The factory in which we had worked was converted into a warehouse for storing furniture imported from United States.

I remain, Yours faithfully,

SIR ROBERT BORDEN'S LETTER, DATED SEPTEMBER 25, 1933, TO DR J.H. LAIDLAW, PRESIDENT OF THE CANADIAN CLUB OF OTTAWA

Personal

Dear Dr Laidlaw,

I really think that people of a certain temperament should be warned that the Canadian Club is not a forum for the dissemination of partisan theories. I was greatly surprised that the usual amenities of such an occasion did not deter Sir Herbert Samuel from giving the exhibition of bad taste to which he treated the Canadian Club on Saturday last.

For your information, I enclose an extract from a letter just received from my friend Martin Burrell, as well as a copy of my reply.

Faithfully yours,

DR LAIDLAW'S REPLY
TO SIR ROBERT BORDEN,
DATED SEPTEMBER 27, 1933

Dear Sir Robert,

Your letter of September 25, 1933, re Sir Herbert Samuel's address at the Canadian Club, was duly received, also copies of Mr Burrell's note to you and your letter in reply thereto for which I wish to thank you.

On July 31st, 1933, the Secretary of the Club, at the request of the executive, wrote to Sir Herbert extending him an invitation to address the Club. In this letter it was stated definitely that the Canadian Club of Ottawa was non-political and that its members included the Prime Minister and his Cabinet. We are careful in all invitations to call attention to this fact and very rarely has any speaker failed to observe the amenities expected of him when such information is given. I agree with you that 'The Canadian Club is not a forum for the dissemination of partisan theories'; however, despite the care which the executive exercises in the matter of trying to keep discussions within the unwritten law of good taste, on occasion our vigilance may be defeated.

I appreciate your writing me and your comment.

Sincerely yours

SIR ROBERT BORDEN'S FURTHER LETTER
TO DR LAIDLAW DATED, SEPTEMBER 28, 1933

Personal

Dear Dr Laidlaw,

My best thanks for your letter of yesterday. Evidently you explained the situation very clearly to Sir Herbert Samuel. That gentleman, however, does not appear to be endowed with certain qualities that one would expect in a person of his position and experience. I refrain from giving harsher expression to my impression of some of his characteristics.

It is evident that great care will have to be exercised in future. A Canadian Club might easily be brought into disrepute through such an incident and its results. The next speaker to address your club might have been a person strongly resentful of Samuel's diatribe and determined to answer it in the same forum.

With renewed thanks and best wishes, I remain, dear Dr Laidlaw,

Yours faithfully,

October 28, 1933

ARRIVAL OF WINTER – DINNER AT THE RIDEAU CLUB (OTTAWA)

Sir,

On October 24, winter paid us what I hope will be a flying visit. January weather arrived and still continues; but we hope for a short intermission before she makes her abode with us for the next four or five months.

The thermometer descended to 14; nearly a foot of snow fell; and for the first time in my life I saw brilliant autumn leaves drifting down upon a carpet of newly-fallen snow.

The winter scene has continued until today; and we are promised colder weather tonight.

It appears that the vagaries of our climate during the present year are attributable to a decrease of sun-spots. We earnestly hope that old Sol's countenance will be properly decorated before another season.

Last evening I attended a dinner at the Rideau Club to meet Dr F. Schoenemann, professor of American Literature and the History of American Civilization at the University of Berlin. He is a most attractive speaker, earnest, thoroughly at home in English, moderate, enthusiastic and very plausible in all cases where he did not have a satisfactory reply to questions showered upon him.

At the time of the German Revolution, the Russian representative intervened with financial assistance to the German Communists and Dr Schoenemann believes that Russian propaganda still persists in Germany but is quite unable to make headway against Hitler.

The Professor was not a member of Hitler's party, although now he supports the movement which Hitler embodies, because he believes it has united and inspired the German people. I asked him for a comparison between Hitlerism and Fascism. He contends that Hitlerism has a fundamental democratic basis which Fascism lacks. All parties, except Nazis, have been placed beyond the pale in Germany so that there may be no party conflict. Nevertheless, the great policies of Hitler's government are submitted to the people for their approval or rejection. At the approaching election on November 12, all the adult population of Germany will be entitled to vote.

So far as religion is concerned, Dr Schoenemann emphasized and strongly approved Hitler's action in uniting some fourteen or fifteen Protestant Lutherans separated by minor differences of creed or ritual. The Protestant element constitutes about 60 per cent of the population, the Roman Catholic about 40 per cent, and the Jews about 1 per cent.

Then he spoke with strong commendation of Hitler's successful effort to create good relations with the Vatican. In the result a concordat had been established which contains provisions satisfactory to the church and to the state.

The trade unions have been abolished and their place has been taken by commissions upon which both employers and employed are represented, with power of control vested in the state so that, under present conditions, there can be no strike menace in Germany.

He declared that the Jews had exercised an undue, and in many instances a malign influence in Germany. They dominated the bar and in considerable measure the bench. In finance and industry their influence was also predominant. And he declared that Jews possessed of immense power do not fail to make extreme use of it.

As to war, he insisted that Germany is entirely unprepared and has no desire other than to maintain her claim of equality with other great nations, and to give her undivided attention to the healing of internal wounds. The marchings and demonstrations, much noised abroad, are due to the need of keeping the lethargic German people aroused to a sense of their need.

He deprecated the efforts of France to control the small nations of eastern Europe and to create among them a spirit hostile to Germany. Danger of war, he claimed, comes not from Germany but from France. He admits there is strong desire in Germany (and among the majority in Austria) for *anschluss* (union). But, in his opinion Hitler is not presently anxious for this. Vienna is predominantly Jewish and this might create embarrassment. Further, Italy might view with alarm a union of Austria with Germany.

Dr Schoenemann, however, favours economic cooperation between Germany, Austria and Hungary; and he thinks this will come about.

He admitted that the campaign against the Jews had been excessive and in his belief harmful; but it was absolutely necessary that Jewish influence should be curbed. In the not distant future he said there will be a *modus vivendi* with the Jews which will lead to better relations. In the meantime, the Jewish elements in various countries will probably over-reach themselves and lose sympathy through the extreme fierceness of their attacks.

He was questioned about restrictions upon the liberty of the press, expulsion of foreign correpondents; and perhaps he gave less satisfactory replies than upon other topics. He claimed that the expelled correspondents had been in close touch and sympathy with dangerous communistic elements from whom they had derived their inspiration; and generally speaking he took the ground that in the effort to unite the German people, to inspire them with a new self-respect and to obliterate the spirit of defeatism, it is necessary, at present, that full control of the press shall be established. The control and domination exercised by Hitlerism are mild, he claims, compared with the tyranny of the Communists if they were vested with power.

The political policies, domestic and foreign, are presently guided in Germany by its youth. It is the enthusiasm of men, from 25 to 35 years of age, that controls the situation. Dr Schoenemann admits that they have made, and being mortal will make, mistakes; but he believes that wonderful progress has been made in reconstructing the nation to take its part in the world's progress and development. Among other tendencies, he noted migration from urban to rural communities. This is being developed and encouraged by the division of great estates no longer capable of being maintained. The small farm is dealt with as if it were an institution to which a citizen may be attached. If he makes good, all is well; if he fails, then must he vacate.

Dr Schoenemann is to speak in Montreal and Toronto, after which he has a task of some thirty addresses in United States. Among these will be an interesting encounter with a Jewish Rabbi before the Foreign Policy Association of Philadelphia.

In private conversation, Dr Schoenemann defended Germany's withdrawal from the Disarmament Conference upon the ground that the allied nations were really paltering with a solemn engagement into which they had entered; withdrawal from the League he attributed to the need of impressing upon the world the German claim and demand for equality.

He speaks not of 'Hitlerites', but of 'Hitlerism', which he describes as 'not a party' but a 'movement'; and he is convinced that it will survive Hitler.

I remain, Sir, Yours in sympathy,

December 6, 1933

APPRECIATION OF SIR ARTHUR CURRIE

Sir,

The untimely death of Sir Arthur Currie on the morning of November 30, has stirred all Canada with emotion. He made a wonderful fight for life.

My tribute to him was expressed in these few but very sincere words:

> In Sir Arthur Currie has passed a great Canadian whose service to Canada and to the Empire was conspicuous and will never be forgotten. As a soldier he won high distinction during the war not for himself alone but also for the Canadian Corps under his command. I was brought into very intimate touch with him during the agony of that conflict and my high regard deepened into sincere affection and warm admiration. Since the peace his service has also been notable as principal of one of our greatest universities. Not only in achievement and example but in penetrating thought devoted to our country's welfare and couched in eloquent expression has he given of his best to Canada and to the Commonwealth. Deeply and sincerely he will be mourned by all true Canadians but especially by those who on the plains of France and Flanders learned under him to know the true meaning of comradeship and sacrifice.

I first met Sir Arthur at Valcartier in 1914. A few days before the division was to embark I addressed each of the brigades; and I was impressed by Currie's reply. He spoke with evident emotion, with apt expression and in thorough appreciation of the duty that lay before him and his men. From the first, he was an outstanding commander among the Canadians; and in November 1915, he took over command of the 1st Division.

Currie had no great appreciation of General Alderson; but he had deep admiration and affection for General Byng. Under Byng, the Canadian Corps was thoroughly trained and eventually developed into a fighting unit unsurpassed in striking force by any unit of equal numerical strength in either of the opposing armies. The capture of Vimy Ridge in April 1917, gave proof of this. There had been several unsuccessful attacks attended with disastrous losses. To Canada belongs the honour of hurling back the Germans from the summit of that Ridge.

There were many attempts to carry Passchendaele in the autumn of 1917. First the British and then the Australians attacked without success. Currie (who succeeded to the command of the Corps in 1917) was asked whether the Canadians could carry the position. He replied, 'Yes, with a loss of fifteen thousand casualties.' He insisted upon adequate artillery support and other essentials. The Canadians made the attack and carried the position.[8]

Currie told me that the venture was by no means worth the cost and that it was won to save the face of the British High Command, who had undertaken, all through autumn, unsuccessful and highly disastrous attempts. After Currie's return to Canada he expressed an entirely inconsistent view, which perhaps was occasioned by learning at the Paris Peace Conference that some such venture was necessary to hearten the French Army in which mutiny had broken out.

The following extract from a cable to the Acting Prime Minister, dated June 15, 1918, sets forth my appreciation of Currie at that time:

> By reason of information which reached me from various sources I thought it desirable to send for General Currie who came to town on Wednesday and with whom I discussed the campaign of last year, and especially the German offensive during the past three months. The report which he gave me was very depressing and I am convinced that the present situation is due to lack of organization, lack of system, lack of preparation, lack of foresight and incompetent leadership. If the British Army Corps had made the same preparation to meet the German offensive as did

8 Sir Robert's cousin, Robert Clarence Borden, then a corporal, took command of his platoon when his sergeant fell and fell himself as their objective was carried.

General Currie, and the officers and men of the Canadian forces, the German offensive could not possibly have succeeded as it did. Their losses would have been so appalling that they would have been obliged to stop. The British offensive of last year was obviously a mistake. Robertson and Haig urged it against the protests of the cabinet. I have read the records of the cabinet meeting of 21st June, 1917, at which Lloyd George examined with great ability the reasons pro and con and stated the opinion of the cabinet that no such offensive should be undertaken. He said, however, that they must be guided by their military advisers and would defer to them if, after hearing all that was urged, they still thought the offensive should be undertaken.

It will be remembered that the Canadians took Passchendaele at a cost of 16,000 men, at the end of the offensive. Currie tells me, and I believe he is right, that it had no useful result, as the British Army immediately went on the defensive and the campaign ceased for the year. No advantage in position was gained and the effort was simply wasted.

Currie reports that the conditions in front of Passchendaele, when the Canadian Corps were ordered to take it, were simply indescribable. I cannot enter into the particulars which I placed before the War Cabinet on Thursday, but when you hear them you will realize that we are being defeated by our own methods.

The Canadian Army Corps is admittedly the most formidable striking force in the allied armies. Probably it is the best organized and most effective unit of its size in the world today. It has come on wonderfully since last year and this is due not only to the courage, resourcefulness and intelligence of the men, but to the splendid and unremitting work of the officers, and to Currie's ability. I believe he is the ablest Corps Commander in the British Forces; more than that I believe that he is at least as capable as any Army Commander among them.

To give you an example of what work will accomplish and what casual indifference and indolence will leave undone; the Canadian Corps put out last autumn and winter 375,000 yards of barbed wire entanglements by which every trench and all supporting trenches were thoroughly protected. These entanglements were co-ordinated with machine guns skillfully placed and concealed and strongly protected. At a conference between Currie and three other Corps Commanders, one of them (Portuguese) said that he had put out no barbed wire; one of the British Corps Commanders said that he had put out 30,000 yards, and the other Corps Commander had put out 36,000 yards. A British officer told Currie that his Corps had no barbed wire protection on any such scale as the Canadians and that the men were employed in laying out lawn tennis courts.

It appears that the younger members of Haig's staff recommended, in November last, that ten Corps Commanders should be dispensed with and replaced. They were kept on during the winter and about the time the offensive began eight of them were relieved. The British High Command believed that the Germans would not undertake an offensive. Three days before it began the Chief Intelligence Officer gave the Canadian Corps a tip that they need not expect an offensive from the Germans. Currie told me that the reports of the Chief Intelligence Officer at British Headquarters were so useless and misleading that when he recognized the signature he always tore them up and threw them into the waste-paper basket without reading them.

Of course there are many British Divisions well organized, highly trained and competently led, but there are enough otherwise to enable the Germans to strike, and the Germans always know just where to strike.

At Passchendaele last autumn, Currie refused to fight under Gough as he considered him incompetent.

It is possible that this estimate of Currie's ability as a commander may be somewhat exaggerated but the despatch sets forth what was my firm impression at that time.

The despatch above quoted refers to my address in the Imperial War Cabinet on June 13, 1918. Before speaking I had sent for Currie and, as Prime Minister, I directed him to put aside all considerations of military etiquette in replying to my inquiries on urgent and important matters. On the day following the interview I did not mince matters in speaking in the Imperial War Cabinet. Lloyd George sent for Sir Henry Wilson[9] who has alluded very slightly in his *Diary* to my charges of incompetency. Lord Milner, then Secretary of State for War, told me that I would be answered; but no answer was ever forthcoming for none was available.

I was informed that Currie might be 'sent to Coventry' by the British High Command for telling me the truth. I sent word to him that I should be informed if he should observe the slightest evidence of any such attempt and that I would then take care of the situation.

Being human, Currie had his weaknesses. He seemed to have no

9 Then Chief of the Imperial General Staff.

appreciation of the value of money. Perley had great difficulty in restraining his extravagance. In his personal affairs he had been careless in this respect; rumours of default in using for his business purposes moneys held in trust are still current. I received many complaints as to his conduct in this respect. ...

Further he was altogether too impulsive in his public statements and he was not always consistent.

In September 1924, in addressing the delegates to the Tax Conference and the Civil Service Research Conference at Montreal, he placed himself in a false position by absurd charges which may be summarized as follows:

> The government deliberately ignored expert advice in important problems of the war.
>
> Expert advice at the beginning of the war said that the Ross Rifle was no good, and it was not. Yet succeeding units came over to us armed with the Ross Rifle.
>
> Expert advice said that the Oliver equipment was not suitable, was of no use, and yet unit after unit came over equipped with the Oliver equipment.
>
> There were at least 100,000 men enlisted and sent over to us overseas, who were of no use to the army. The average cost of them was around $1,500., so, the total cost of them would be $150,000,000. Many of these men are still under government pay in our hospitals.
>
> I do not know all about the expenditure of the war, but I know that it cost hundreds of million dollars more than it should have cost or would have cost, if the expert advice that was available had been listened to.

At the time he made those charges I believe he had thoughts of a political career and expected to strengthen his position for that purpose. Important intriguers were then engaged in undermining Meighen with the intention of supplanting him by Currie. Knowing what I did of Perley's experience in endeavouring to keep Currie's extravagance within bounds, I was not only astonished but amused by his diatribe with regard to the extravagance of the government. I did not enter into any public controversy but I conveyed to the editorial staff of important newspapers a memorandum (copy attached) which I think thoroughly demolished Currie's contentions, several of which were manifestly absurd and even self-destructive.

But, on the whole, his speeches on public occasions, especially during his tenure of office as Vice-Chancellor and Principal of McGill University, have been all to the good.

After the Armistice, I thought that, as he had sacrificed his business interests, parliament should grant him a reasonable sum; but my colleagues and the caucus as well did not in the least favour the proposal, which had to be abandoned. At that time Currie was not highly popular either in the Canadian army or in Canadian public opinion. He grew in favour as the years passed by.

His funeral ceremony which took place yesterday was most impressive. Being confined to the house while convalescing from influenza, I was unable to be present but I was represented by my Principal Secretary during the War, Loring C. Christie, who accompanied me to Great Britain and France on no less than four occasions during the War, during my attendance at the Imperial War Cabinet and the Imperial War Conference, my visits to the hospitals, my visits to the Front, and at the Paris Peace Conference. The ceremonial was perhaps more elaborate than at any state or military funeral in the past history of Canada. Neither Sir John A. Macdonald nor Sir Wilfrid Laurier received such a tribute. The future historian will have to judge whether Currie's service was comparable with theirs.

I remain, Yours faithfully,

MEMORANDUM RE SIR ARTHUR CURRIE – REFERRED TO IN THE FOREGOING LIMBO LETTER

On my return to Ottawa my attention has been directed to recent public utterances of Sir Arthur Currie. Several of his charges against the government of which I was the head are rather stale and have been effectively answered in Parliament on more than one occasion. The rest consist of sweeping assertions of a general character for which there is little, if any, foundation. He avers that the government deliberately ignored and disregarded expert advice. On the contrary it sought expert opinion on every problem of the war and brought to Ottawa the most experienced authorities on every important question. When experts differed, as not infrequently happened – (as sometimes happened among military experts overseas, with respect to conduct of the war, as Sir Arthur Currie will remember) – the government was obliged to accept that opinion which seemed most reasonable and practical.

As to the Ross rifle, Sir Arthur Currie seems to forget that many years before the war that rifle was adopted, after very careful consideration, by Sir Wilfrid Laurier's government, of which Sir Arthur himself was a strong supporter. The action of that government was ratified and confirmed by parliament and a factory for the production of the rifle was established. If Sir Arthur, who was then prominent in military circles, made any protest against the adoption of the rifle his voice did not reach the general public. When war broke out the Ross was the standard rifle of the Canadian army and the only rifle that could be manufactured in this country. Then and for long after the Canadian army must be armed with the Ross rifle or with none. For accuracy of shooting it was unsurpassed but its construction in some respects proved to be unsuited to the severe conditions of warfare in France. Also, a prejudice arose against the rifle by reason of the supply to the Canadian soldiers of defective or unsuitable ammunition. When these conditions were made clear to the government the Ross rifle was replaced by the Lee Enfield. But, in corroboration of Sir Arthur Currie's statement that he 'does not know all about the expenditures of the war', it may be of interest for me to add before I drop the matter, that the substitution of the one rifle for the other was at the expense of the British government, the British authorities accepting the Ross rifles turned over to them in payment for the Lee Enfields. Sir Arthur is as curiously astray with respect to waste in the supply of equipment. The British Army authorities, for obvious reasons, desired similarity in equipment in all like arms of all services fighting under the supreme British commander. In the beginning it was impossible to achieve, instanter, this aim, but in the course of time it was achieved – at the expense of the British government, and not in the wasteful way that Sir Arthur charges. It cost not an extra dollar to Canada, and the substitutions, by the way, implied convenience and not unsuitableness or inferiority.

The simple fact is that Sir Arthur Currie in dealing with such matters is invading what is to him an unknown field. His business, excellently performed, was to get the best out of the best men and equipment that others could supply to him. He imperils his high reputation when, for any reason, with whatever inducement, he undertakes to deal with matters concerning which he can, and does, know nothing.

As to his assertion that one hundred thousand men were enlisted and sent overseas who were of no use to the army – if this statement was made as reported it is a very serious exaggeration. No men were sent over except such as had passed such medical and other expert examination as the regulations required to enable assignment to the particular arm of military or other service for which the men were intended. Many thousands of men were sent to Great Britain and to France in forestry, railway, construction and labour units who were not intended for service in the field, but for other service that was absolutely essential to sustain the front, to ensure lines of communication, and to carry on all the subsidiary activities necessary to the success of an army in the field. So vital were these subsidiary services that, at the urgent request of the British government, who represented the need as imperative, the Minister of Overseas Service on one occasion permitted men of A class to be drafted temporarily into forestry units. It is surely a striking circumstance that if one man in four of those sent overseas were 'of no use to the army' the various commanders of the Canadian Corps in the field, whereof Sir Arthur Currie was the last, were so derelict in duty as to omit expression of the fact to the proper authority. There was no such expression. And besides, no army whereof one man in four is useless could have performed the glorious exploits with which the Canadian army under Sir Arthur Currie, no less than under the commander who preceded him, was distinguished. I am quite aware that in the competition to fill up as speedily as possible authorized battalions, medical officers were sometimes careless and permitted unfit men to be enlisted. As soon as this was brought to the attention of the government every precaution was taken to prevent its recurrence. Notwithstanding, the proportion of ineffectives, not casualties, officially reported from England in 1917, was less than two per cent of the total forces sent over. These ineffectives included all fit men who were ill or incapacitated from any cause except wounding in war. The deserted, discharged and resigned, at the same time (including those discharged on account of wounds and illness) formed less than six per cent of the total sent over. The conditions would not be materially different in 1918. The soldiers supplied to Sir Arthur Currie's command were efficient and were supplied under an efficient system. Necessary reinforcements were always ready and these of a calibre always high. Even after the attack on Passchendaele where the Canadian Corps suffered 16,000 casualties, so thorough was the system of supply and so adequate the arrangements for all arms of the service that during the last year of the war the Canadian Corps was undoubtedly the most formidable fighting force of anything like its numbers that could be found in any of the belligerent armies. The splendid gallantry, the undaunted spirit and the unfailing resourcefulness of our men had made this possible.

Doubtless there was waste and extravagant expenditure during the war, especially in its early stages, but the government took every available means to check and prevent it, and I am confident that in this respect Canada has as good a record as any of the nations of the British Commonwealth. The Ministry of Overseas Service found difficulty even during the last two years of the war in checking extravagant and wasteful expenditure at the front (especially by certain generals, and I am informed that none was a greater sinner in this respect than Sir Arthur Currie himself). He is to be commended for insisting upon efficient and economical administration of public affairs but I suggest that he poorly serves his purpose by resort to careless misstatement and thoughtless exaggeration.

George Eulas Foster (later Rt. Hon. Sir George) was born in New Brunswick in 1847. He was elected to the House of Commons in 1883 and became Minister of Marine and Fisheries in the government of Sir John A. Macdonald in 1885. He was defeated in the election of 1900 and consequently was not a member of the House of Commons in 1901 when the Liberal-Conservative members of the House and Senate elected R.L. (later Sir Robert) Borden as leader of the party. It was not until 1919, when Mr Mackenzie King was elected leader of the Liberal party following the death of Sir Wilfrid Laurier, that the practice of holding a convention of party delegates from across Canada to select the party leader came into vogue. Hitherto the leaders of the two political parties had been selected in the manner in which Sir Robert was in 1901.

Sir George died in 1931 and his *Memoirs* were published in 1933 by the late W. Stewart Wallace, at that time the Chief Librarian of the University of Toronto.

The following Limbo letter was written following Sir Robert's reading of these *Memoirs*.

Appended to the letter is a copy of a newspaper article *Political Secrets Exposed* published in late 1933.

December 8, 1933

ESTIMATE OF SIR GEORGE FOSTER

Sir,

I have recently read with great interest the rather meagre *Memoirs of Sir George Foster* by Professor W. Stewart Wallace. In many respects the book is useful and instructive, especially in the incidents of Foster's successful struggle to acquire an education, in which he displayed the great qualities which afterwards raised him to the forefront of public life.

Foster was endowed with brilliant parts, high ideals, untiring ambition, fierce energy and unflagging industry. He was handicapped by lack of tact and sound judgment, and by various inconsistencies and obsessions which probably debarred him from attaining the Premiership to which his outstanding qualities seemed to entitle him.

When I was reluctantly obliged to assume leadership of the Liberal-Conservative party after its second defeat in December 1900, Foster, by reason of his distinguished ability, his twenty years' experience in public life and his commanding position should, in the ordinary course, have been selected as leader. He had not, it is true, a seat in parliament but one could easily have been provided for him. Outside of John Haggart,[10] hardly a voice was raised in his favour. This was due to distrust of the soundness of his judgment. His brilliancy was acknowledged; but men doubted his possession of a leader's qualities.

After an unsuccessful attempt in 1903, Foster came into the House at the general election of 1904. I had been defeated in Halifax and was without a seat in parliament. Why Foster was not selected for the position which I had held is unaccountable, except for the reasons I have indicated. Of course, in the meantime I had put up a strong fight in the House and in the country. There was the force of warm party loyalty and Conservative members of parliament apparently thought a change undesirable.

When it was proposed between 1901 and 1904, to provide a seat for Foster, I was asked whether I had any objection. This question I fiercely resented, because it was apparently based upon the idea that I might fear so brilliant a colleague. With considerable warmth I replied that I would welcome Foster or any other as my colleague and that if he should develop qualities that made my supersession desirable I should willingly give way.

The relations between Foster and myself were always cordial, although on occasion his maladroitness and tactlessness placed the party in an unfortunate position. Never was he party to any of the intrigues that were raised against me while in opposition. Naturally he must have felt that I had usurped the place to which he was entitled.

10 Hon. John G. Haggart, Conservative member for S. Lanark, Ontario, for many years. A member of the Conservative governments in Ottawa from 1888 to 1896 and a colleague of Foster in those administrations.

But I never observed any appearance of jealousy, much less any overt act. In 1917, when in the public interest I offered to resign and serve under him, he declined in caucus and paid a warm tribute to my leadership.

On the other hand, I always endeavoured to treat him with the consideration due to his distinguished ability and experience. Upon my recommendation he was created first KCMG, and afterwards GCMG and was appointed a member of His Majesty's Imperial Privy Council; so that he received all the honours that were accorded to me as Prime Minister.

The following qualification should be made to the foregoing paragraph. When we came into power in 1911, I was convinced that Foster's resumption of the finance portfolio would be unfortunate not only for the party but for himself. It was essential that the government should include some outstanding Liberal who had joined in our campaign against the Reciprocity Pact. A brilliant and outstanding Liberal was available in the person of W.T. (afterwards Sir Thomas) White. I had to put the situation as it lay in my mind before Foster with complete frankness. He was greatly moved and strongly urged his right to resume his former portfolio, declaring that otherwise he would be humiliated. However, I remained firm; and he accepted the Department of Trade and Commerce.

Professor Wallace barely does justice to Sir George's wonderful powers as a debater and public speaker. In the House of Commons, when I first entered it, I regarded him as *facile princeps* in many aspects, although Laurier was more eloquent, tactful and plausible and Cartwright and Tupper were very hard hitters. Foster's gift of striking expression, his remarkable powers of keen analysis, his fund of biting invective and cutting sarcasm made him a commanding debater.

John Haggart, a most capable judge, regarded Foster as the most powerful debater he had ever known in parliament; and he declared that the greatest speech Foster ever delivered in his hearing (at some small meeting in rural Ontario) was never reported. Liberals who were present at Foster's speech on nomination day in St John in 1900, have told me that he really hypnotized his audience on that occasion and that, if the vote had been taken immediately after his speech, he might have been elected.

But I never regarded Foster as a skillful platform speaker. Sarcasm and invective when employed as he knew how to use them always evoke the warm plaudits of partisans, but they do not often appeal to those whom a speaker should seek to reach and influence, men of moderate opinions who vote now with one and now with the other party. Such attacks always arouse intense bitterness and resentment among opposing partisans and stimulate them to forget their grievances and to put forth intense effort.

The late J.W. Longley[11] told me that in 1900, the Liberal party in Halifax was so discouraged, dissatisfied and resentful of its leaders that the loss of both seats seemed inevitable. The party workers were sulky, inert and inactive. Foster came to Halifax and at a great public meeting made so bitter an attack that the Liberal ranks closed up forthwith and joined battle with fierce energy. Russell was sent to Hants, as he had become impossible; and Roche, nominated in his place, was elected.

His biographer speaks of his success as an administrator. Among his colleagues in my government he was not so regarded. Undoubtedly he worked very hard; but he was systematically unsystematic. I was told that the appearance of his office was astonishing. Tables and desks were piled with files that should have been kept in their filing-cabinets; these files and other documents over-flowed the tables and desks and littered portions of the floor. He had a passion for keeping documents in his immediate possession. Despatches which I sent to him while he was Acting Prime Minister he carried away, although they should have remained as they were official and he had no right to retain them.

His lack of system was illustrated by his omission to take his code-book when he embarked upon the long journey to New Zealand, Australia and Japan, described in his biography. We sent cables in code which he was utterly unable to understand; eventually we were obliged to communicate *en clair*.

He had a passion also for extending the jurisdiction of his department in every possible direction, although its original scope was quite sufficient to absorb his whole energies. He was pervaded with an obsession to travel abroad, especially to spend many months as member of this or that commission, when his energies could more usefully have been employed in the duties appertaining to his department. I am quite convinced that he would have been willing to add to his department a very large proportion of matters appertaining to all the departments of the government, in which case he would still have been eager to journey abroad on occasion. While we were in opposition, he was made chairman of our parliamentary

11 Hon. James Wilberforce Longley, prominent member of the Liberal party in Nova Scotia, member of the bar and subsequently of the Supreme Court of Nova Scotia.

committee on organization. He gladly accepted the appointment with results that were absolutely negligible, indeed wholly invisible.

Undoubtedly he was a man of high ideals, thoroughly conscientious but, like many other men, he could find more excuses for himself than for his fellows. He had placed his standards and ideals of public and private life on a wonderfully high plane in his public addresses immediately before the scandal respecting his activities in connection with the Independent Order of Foresters and the Union Trust Company in 1906.[12] This undoubtedly contributed to the strong feeling aroused by the discussion that ensued. A powerful group of our parliamentary following urged the necessity of Foster's retirement and threatened to repudiate him. This would have been disastrous, and I succeeded in making such a fight and obtaining such support as held them in line. Thereupon, without consultation with me and against the opinion of his friends, he plunged into and lost a libel action against the *Toronto Globe*. This made his position infinitely more difficult. He was continually on the defensive.

There is no doubt that the attack which Shepley[13] (under Aylesworth's[14] direction) launched against Foster was intended to effect his political destruction. I was placed in possession of evidence which I could not use but which convinced me that Aylesworth decended to disgraceful methods for the purpose of destroying Foster's future usefulness. I do not say that the members of the commission were privy to this conspiracy but one cannot be blamed for suspecting it.

Sir George was the most emotional man I have ever known in public life. This quality undoubtedly contributed to his great oratorical power. When I entered the House of Commons I shared the prevailing public opinion that he was cold and unsympathetic. But in truth Laurier was of a much colder and more calculating temperament. In some respects his nature was quite the converse of Foster's. I have seen Foster so overcome by emotion during a tribute to a personal friend that he was obliged to leave the Chamber; and I remember how greatly he was moved by a passage in my speech on May 18, 1917, when I announced conscription.

In 1912, at his earnest request I appointed Mr A.B. Morine chairman of the Public Service Commission established in 1911. Without waiting for communication of the minute to the Governor-General, Foster dashed off a telegram to Mr Morine who, forthwith,

12 This matter is dealt with by Sir Robert in some detail in his *Memoirs* – Vol. 1, pages 169–171.

13 George F. Shepley, chief counsel for the government.

14 Mr (later Sir) Allen Aylesworth, then minister of justice.

astonished newspaper editors in Toronto by appearing on the scene with typewritten enumeration of his qualifications for a position of which they had heard nothing.

Similarly in England, in 1912, he aroused strong feeling in members of the British (Liberal) government through his close touch with opposition members and his residence at a Conservative Club. The feeling was so strong that I was obliged to intervene.

Speaking in 1900, upon my motion respecting the Brockville and Huron election scandal, he made a tactless suggestion which Laurier skillfully used to hold his party in line and escape from an extremely difficult situation.

In 1911, when I was endeavouring to hold my following together in caucus for the purpose of fighting the Fielding Reciprocity Pact, Foster, maladroitly, declared that his heart had gone down into his boots when he heard Fielding's announcement.

With regard to political strategy he was useful to us in a rather unusual sense. His emotional temperament made him a most unsafe guide. When any such question arose for discussion, several of my colleagues (notably Dr Reid and Martin Burrell) listened carefully to Foster for the purpose of recording their votes in the opposite sense, as they firmly and invariably relied on the unsoundness of his judgment.

In 1900, he might well have challenged Blair[15] to come into York, in which case not Foster but Blair would have been defeated. Instead of this he made a public announcement that he would wait until Blair selected his constituency and would meet him there. Blair made no announcement until after he had established his organization and laid the train for victory in St John. In this way, Foster prepared victory for Blair.

The thorough unsoundness of Foster's political judgment was illustrated in the following incident.

On February 19, 1907, George W. Fowler, roused to fury by charges made against him in respect of his personal affairs, declared in a famous outburst that if his private business was to be discussed in parliament, he would take opportunity to discuss the private character of members of the administration and their supporters.

> I shall call a spade a spade ... I shall discuss the characters of honourable members opposite whether they be Ministers or private members and their connection with wine, women and graft.

15 Hon. A. G. Blair, Minister of Railways in Laurier's government.

Mr Bourassa,[16] after alluding to this incident on February 21, initiated on March 26, a lively debate and concluded with a long motion in which he set forth the attacks upon Messrs Foster, Fowler, Bennett, Pope and Lefurgey, the observations of Messrs Carvell, Ross and Devlin to the effect that the four gentlemen named were unworthy of seats in the House, and the remarks of Mr Fowler quoted above. Declaring that these statements had become a matter of general comment and a scandal throughout the country, Bourassa urged an immediate inquiry and moved for an investigation by a special committee.

Mr Carvell, evidently by arrangement with his leader [Sir Wilfrid Laurier], followed in a speech devoted chiefly to discrediting his political opponents.

In announcing the attitude of the government, Sir Wilfrid Laurier declared that mere rumour was no ground for investigation and he denied Mr Bourassa's statement that there was a 'saw-off' between the two parties.

Replying to Sir Wilfrid, I recalled his promise of February 21, that the session would not pass without the subject receiving the attention of the House. Then I concluded as follows:

> I have pledged myself to two things in this House and I propose to stand by them to the end. I have pledged myself that I have not made and that I would not make any arrangement with hon. gentlemen on the other side of the House upon any matters touched upon in the discussion during the past session which have been commented on by the Hon. member for Labelle and I have pledged myself also that if any hon. gentlemen in this house took steps to forward an inquiry touching the position of hon. gentlemen on this side of the House, who are my colleagues and associates, I would give my best efforts to probe the matter of that inquiry to the bottom. Therefore, I am not disposed for the sake of any Parliamentary precedent, for the sake of any hair-splitting, or for the sake of anything that has been uttered by the Prime Minister, and especially in view of the construction which I put upon this resolution, I am not disposed to vote against this motion and I shall record my vote in favour of that resolution although I wish that the procedure suggested had been different and that the resolution had been couched in somewhat different terms.

16 Henri Bourassa, member of the House of Commons from 1896–1907 and known as 'the leader of the Nationalists.'

Foster was amazed and immensely disturbed by my proposal to vote for Bourassa's resolution. He said to me: 'Do you intend to support a resolution which, if carried, would expose me once more to the malice and cruelty of men eager to treat me even worse than I have been treated during past months; men who would unhesitatingly use their power to persecute and destroy me?' To this, I replied: 'I am supremely confident that you will be able to vindicate yourself; and if I and my followers should vote against the proposed investigation, your prestige and your influence would be infinitely lessened, because it would be charged, with some show of reason, that between the two political parties there was an understanding that the truth should not be revealed.'

At this time Foster had been seriously discredited by very grave charges levelled against him and by the complexity of his explanations which absolved him from any moral lapse or improper purpose but which were not clearly understood by the people. Had I voted, as he desired, against Bourassa's motion, his position would have been so impaired that I might have been obliged to dissociate him from any important position in the counsels of the party.

The course which Foster desired would have convinced the public that the two parties were in collusion to prevent scandalous exposure and would have sealed his political death warrant. Moreover, the brunt would naturally have fallen upon the Conservative party which would have lost caste at a time when the integrity of its leaders was one of its most important assets. That Foster failed to realize this and urged me to oppose Bourassa's motion, illustrates vividly his utter lack of political sagacity.

After the debate had concluded and the motion was lost he acknowledged that I had been right and that his judgment was mistaken; and he thanked me for the course I had taken.

Foster was, assuredly, a creature of inconsistencies. Upon my entry into Parliament (1896), I looked up to him with profound admiration and respect as the exponent of careful finance. Sir Charles Hibbert Tupper told me that Foster had accumulated $100,000 by judicious investment in mining stocks. So, when Sir George invited me to subscribe for shares in a mining company of which he was president, I accepted the invitation with alacrity and acquired three thousand shares at eighty cents on the dollar. I was particularly impressed and attracted by his statement that the company was paying dividends at the rate of one percent per month. After receiving my contribution of $2,400 the company paid only one dividend ($30) which was accompanied by a notice that dividends were suspended for the future. Sad to relate they were never resumed. My contribution of $2,400 was used to pay that dividend. At the annual meeting, under cross-examination by the late Senator Clemow, Foster, thoughtfully stroking his beard, was obliged to admit that, from first to last, the company had never made more than its operating expenses. Dividends had been paid out of monies received from unfortunate subscribers of whom, alas, I was one. The sum of $2,370 which I thus contributed still remains a permanent investment. From that day to this I never heard a word on the subject from Foster or his company.

This incident does not alter my opinion as to Foster's fine idealism and perfect honesty. He seemed absolutely incapable of judging his own actions by the same standards which he applied to those of other men. But how he would have thundered against such a transaction if it involved one of his political opponents!

Being human, he had his imperfections, some of which I have noted; but Canada has reason to hold him in grateful memory.
I remain, Yours faithfully,

PS Immediately after his death, I gave to the press the annexed tribute.

TRIBUTE TO SIR GEORGE FOSTER

Even at Sir George Foster's very advanced age, the tidings of his death come as a great shock. For half a century he gave unstinted and distinguished service to Canada. From the very first his preeminent ability placed him in the forefront of parliamentary debaters and with little delay advanced him to cabinet rank as Minister of Finance.

For more than a quarter of a century I was closely associated with him in active public life and enjoyed the privilege of his intimate friendship. His splendid qualities need not be enumerated or recalled; they are known of all Canadians. Above and beyond all other considerations he stood for the unity of the British Empire. That was his constant ideal and no cause had a more forceful, ardent or valiant protagonist.

His wonderful gift of expression, his powers of keen analysis and the over-mastering force of his convictions were illustrated both in parliament and on the public platform in his commanding eloquence.

There were those who in his early days spoke of him as cold – a complete misinterpretation of his nature. In critical or solemn moments he was stirred to the depths of his being by such emotion as few men are privileged to feel. This was in some measure the secret of his remarkable power.

Canada is infinitely the richer by his great career and although the years had told upon him, she is the poorer for his loss. We who knew him best mourn him most deeply; but I feel that all Canada joins in mourning him as a great Canadian.

POLITICAL SECRETS EXPOSED

By FRED WILLIAMS [Toronto Journalist]

Do you know when political secrets cease to be regarded as confidential? It is a cardinal principle among newspapermen that information which comes to editors or reporters in a confidential way shall remain secret until such time as opportunity may develop in later days after the persons involved have passed from the earthly stage. There has never been, is not now, and never will be a newspaper correspondent at Ottawa, at any of the provincial capitals, in the financial district of any city, or on other beats, who does not know a good deal about things that are going on behind the scenes and writes nothing about it. Journalists have information about proposed policies, news of which would be News with a capital N, but they keep faith. They are talked to in confidence by statesmen and lesser politicians because they know that they will preserve that confidence, keeping their mouths shut and their pens dry, when, if they were unscrupulous they might get rich. Time and time again in my newspaper career I have been told certain things: in some cases I was justified in publishing them when the right time came; others have never been told, probably never will. Why? Because that is the ethics of the newspaper business. Preservation of confidence is the very rock foundation of our profession.

Why should not the same principle apply to biographies? I am forced to ask the question after having given very careful reading to '*The Memoirs of the Rt. Hon. Sir George Foster*' by Professor W. Stewart Wallace, recently published by the Macmillan Company of Canada. For the book itself I have nothing but commendation; it is a review of fifty years of Canadian politics, which will be of much value to the present and future generations. It gives us an insight into the motives which actuated the career of the New Brunswick lad who became one of Canada's political leaders. Regarded as such it should have a large circulation; certainly no student of our politics for the past half century can afford to neglect it.

But I must enter a strong protest against the inclusion in the volume of certain passages of Sir George Foster's diary concerning the formation of the first Borden cabinet in 1911. There is no doubt that Mr Foster wrote what he thought to be the facts; but I have my doubts whether if he were now alive he would have agreed to the publication of that particular portion of his diary yet. Those newspapermen who were in the Press Gallery at that time knew most that was going on; they knew of Mr Borden's difficulties; they knew of the pressure of the claims of this or that aspirant for a portfolio; but not even the most rabid Liberal of them wrote about those things. Some of the rumors that were then current in Ottawa would have made fine 'copy'; they were passed by, to be conserved in memory, simply because their publication would not have been according to the rules of the game.

Why then should those things be published now when the great man who was then, so fortunately for Canada, called to be Prime Minister is still alive? Why should his faithful wife be sneered at? Why should men who were afterwards Foster's colleagues and who are still with us, be pilloried? Why the mention of wire pulling, of 'opposition by financial interests'? Why the publication of the statement that the Prime Minister 'doesn't know his mind from day to day,' or 'was helpless on the surf'? George Foster was sincere when he wrote these things – no one ever doubted his sincerity – but years later he must have regretted having penned them, even within the pages of his private diary; and those who admired him most must regard their publication to the world at this time as most unfortunate. Perhaps they might have been fairly published when Sir Robert Borden had passed on. In my humble opinion they should not have been printed so long as the men involved are alive.

These few pages are the only blemish in an otherwise most valuable and interesting volume. Their inclusion appears to me to violate the principle laid down by Professor Wallace himself in his preface: 'It is no doubt a sound principle that one should not drag into the limelight those things, which, if published, would do more harm than good, or which, when reference is made to persons still living, would cause needless pain.' The author justifies himself by adding: 'The only exception to this rule would appear to be in those cases where justice to the memory of the dead demands that the truth should be revealed.' But I submit that 'justice to the dead' does not justify villification of the living, even if the libellor is dead. I may be old fashioned; I shall probably be accused of being too sensitive; but I am still of opinion that the long-established rule of the preservation of political secrets is a good one and should not be violated. At the same time I hope the biography will have a large circulation. As a history of our politics it deserves to have.

January 24, 1934

LETTERS OF LORD OXFORD TO A FRIEND, 1915–1922

Sir,

I have finished reading H.H.A. *Letters of Lord Oxford to a Friend, 1915–1922*. The book contains some interesting matter but on the whole it is rather thin, to use a common phrase.

Mr Asquith's relation to his correspondent seems to have been extremely intimate, although wholly platonic; and evidently a very close affection developed between them. Apparently her intellectual qualities appealed to Asquith and their tastes in art and literature were very similar. The intimacy seemingly was known to Lady Oxford who apparently approved of it. Probably Lord Oxford found a welcome relief in his association with a comparatively young lady who so greatly intrigued him. There must have been a very strong contrast between Margot's tempestuous temperament and the quiet, intellectual tastes of this nameless friend, a welcome change as well.

In referring to the publication of the Lloyd George–Asquith correspondence in the autumn of 1916, Lord Oxford makes the following comment, in which some of his natural and perhaps excusable bitterness is apparent:

> The only thing that will be new to most people is that L.G. insisted on Balfour going, and that I refused to part with him; for which I was rewarded by his being, two days after, the first of the Tories to go over to L.G., for whom he has jackalled ever since.

But neither Mr Asquith's comment, nor any other consideration would induce me to believe that Balfour's action at this crisis was inspired otherwise than by the highest patriotic motive.

The book contains an interesting account of a visit to Lord Rosebery during his last illness. This is relevant to my estimate of Rosebery which is to be found in my letter to you of March 6, 1933.

> Hardly less remarkable is the host; he has to be carried in a chair up and down stairs being almost half paralysed; but his brain is as active and individual as it was 25 years ago when I served under him as Prime Minister. No one has ever had the same advantages; a most definite and inimitable personality; extraordinary gifts of speech; a fine wit, both mordant and lambent; rank, wealth, cultivation: in fact everything both to allure and compel. And yet there he is – the most tragic example in our time of a wasted and ineffectual life.

At pages 154–55, he quotes a *bon mot* of Antoine's:

> The Germans have been for four years trying to win the war, and have failed: the Allies for four years have been trying to lose it, and have failed equally: who can say how it will end?

At page 167, is the following reference to Laski:

> He is a really clever creature and talked brilliantly and mordantly of Haldane and the Webbs: also of President Wilson of whom he saw a good deal, with eyes of ever-growing disillusion. He quoted a good remark of William James (brother of Henry) the Harvard philosopher, who said of Bryce, 'To him, all facts alike are born free and equal', a very good description of the accumulative and assimilative as distinguished from the originative and selective mind.

At page 198, is the following quotation from a sonnet of Spencer's:

> Her temple fayre is built within my mind
> In which her glorious ymage placed is
> On which my thoughts doe night and day attend,
> Lyke sacred priests that never think amiss.

He writes of a wonderful gem from the wit and wisdom of Marie Corelli:

> Thyself away art present still with me,
> For thou not further than my thoughts canst move
> And I am still with them and they with thee.

The great qualities of Mr Asquith and of his successor, Mr Lloyd George, have given to each of them an enduring place in history. They were of very diverse types and temperaments. The genius of Mr Asquith was more suited to leadership during peace than in war. On the other hand, the qualities of initiative, resourcefulness, optimism and imagination made Lloyd George a conspicuous figure and an immense asset to his country in war-time, although they did not contribute to the steadiness and stability which are so essention to a prime minister in times of peace. After the War, Lloyd George kept on firm ground so long as he had Bonar Law at hand to guide and control him.

In the second volume of Lloyd George's *War Memoirs*, there is a rather penetrating analysis of Asquith's intellect and temperament. Full meed of appreciation is given to his intellectual powers; but at the same time his lack of initiative and his tendency to wait and see are emphasized as contributing to his inefficiency as a war minister. As a peace minister his achievement was more impressive. But, to quote Lloyd George, 'For the deluge Noah was better adapted than Gamaliel would have been.' (Page 1007, Volume II.)

In his early life, Asquith was almost an ascetic in his habits. During his premiership and especially during the War he developed into a *bon vivant*. This must have had an unfortunate effect upon his intellectual powers and must have intensified his temperamental infirmities. In 1915, those who had the privilege of meeting him at dinner sometimes regretted that he did not cultivate a greater abstinence in the use of wines.

I regretted and resented the action of Lloyd George's government in securing his defeat in the autumn of 1918; and later in endeavouring to debar him from the parliamentary arena. His splendid career in public life, his patriotic service, his high character and ideals should have secured for Asquith an acclamation. When I took occasion to remonstrate with Bonar Law respecting this deplorable action of the government in which he was a leading figure, he told me that they had been unable to control local feeling against Asquith. It seemed to me that so powerful a government could have overcome this without difficulty.

I remain, Sir, Yours in sympathy,

January 27, 1934

OPENING OF A PUBLIC LIBRARY AND A CANADIAN CLUB LUNCHEON

Sir,

Recently I have had the privilege of attending two functions, the incidents of which I deem worthy of recording.

First, the opening of the branch library on Rideau Street. The building, quite spacious, is well designed for a bilingual library, as in this part of the city the mother tongue of a considerable proportion of the population is French.

The proceedings were of a formal character; and Colonel Marriott, who presided after Mrs Sears had said a few words, called upon me to make an introductory speech and to declare the library open. I discharged this duty with appropriate brevity and was followed by M St Jacques who spoke in French at very considerable length. Then followed Mr Jennings, Inspector of Libraries, who spoke at even greater length. His remarks, like those of M St Jacques, were much too prolonged and extremely discursive. The major portion of his speech was devoted to description and eulogy of John Ruskin's teachings. He omitted, however, to comment upon Ruskin's glorification of war.

There were several musical numbers; and as the clock showed the approach of 10.30, and, as I was extremely fatigued from three very active days in Montreal and Toronto, I had arranged to leave, just as Mayor Nolan was announced. My wife and I had put on our coats before he had begun to speak but we waited for the conclusion of his address. Without due consideration he launched forth into a description of the value of literature, with the result that his observations had a rather startling aspect. For example, he ascribed to Homer the great merit of having made the world acquainted with Alexander the Great; and later, he attributed to the literary genius of Ben Jonson, 'Rasselas'.

On the following day, he met my wife at a luncheon at the Women's Canadian Club, and he told her that he had been treated with incivility by the Library Board and that he had administered to them a sharp remonstrance. In his opinion, he and I should have been the only speakers and he should have followed immediately after my remarks.

At the Canadian Club luncheon, above mentioned, I sat on the left of Mrs J.A. Wilson (President) and on my left was Donna Adelina Colonna whom I had met at dinner at Government House on the previous Sunday evening. We had a long and interesting conversation on the political and social development of Italy. Donna Colonna has a profound admiration for Mussolini; and she told me that Italy, as I had known it in 1927, had greatly changed for the better.

On the day preceding the luncheon I had seen her and her husband, duc di Rignano at the opening of parliament, so I asked her how the ceremonial had impressed her. She thought that it was very beautiful; but, in her opinion, it was marred by one feature. The attire of the senators seemed to her incongruous. Those invited to seats on the floor of the senate were either in uniform or evening dress, while the senators themselves were garbed in lounge suits, not always of attractive appearance. She said that in Italy this would not be permitted at a ceremonial, although during the ordinary business session of their senate no especial attention is paid to attire. Her view, in which I entirely agree, was that in the presence of the Sovereign's representative and on such an occasion when the attire of the others is *de rigeur*, the senators should appear in morning dress suitable to the dignity of the occasion.

Don Mario Colonna gave a very interesting and impressive address at the luncheon. He received from his audience the tribute of breathless interest and attention.

It has been said that this Italian delegation has been endeavouring to spread Fascist propaganda. On this occasion there was not the slightest indication of any such desire. The speech was particularly interesting in its description of conditions that supervened in Italy after the War.

I remain, Sir, Yours in sympathy,

February 27, 1934

WINTER READING

Sir,

During the winter, I have been re-reading Dickens and Scott with much enjoyment. *Nicholas Nickleby* and *Our Mutual Friend*, I found delightful, as well as *Guy Mannering*, *The Monastery*, *The Abbott*, *The Legend of Montrose*, and *Anne of Gierstein*. Also, I read *Sir Launcelot Greaves*, Smollett's rather fantastic and strained tale.

Every night after retiring, I read and re-read Shakespeare's plays, chiefly, *King Lear*, *Hamlet*, *Macbeth*, *Othello*, *Julius Caesar*, *The Merchant of Venice*, *The Tempest*, *As You Like It*, and *Midsummer Night's Dream*.

The snowfall has been excessive, the streets being almost impassable. It is difficult to get sufficient exercise, as drifts are so deep that it is impossible to maintain the paths as I usually do in winter. In addition, the cold has been so severe that one can remain in the open air with comfort for only a brief period.

I remain, Sir, Yours in sympathy,

March 30, 1934

INACCURACY OF THE PRESS

Sir,

Among the very numerous instances in which I have observed absolute inaccuracy in press reports of incidents within my personal knowledge, I note the following.

With considerable reluctance, I finally yielded to the strong, indeed insistent, urging of Sir George Perley and other Conservative friends to attend the Winnipeg convention during October, 1927. The outcome of that convention was the selection of Mr R.B. Bennett as Conservative leader. On the first day, I was called upon to speak; and I append a copy of my remarks on that occasion. I was not present on the afternoon of the second day, as my hostess, Mrs Gemmill, took me for a motor drive. During my absence, a fierce controversy arose between Arthur Meighen and Howard Ferguson which became the subject of extensive press comment from Atlantic to Pacific. As this convention was regarded as extremely important, many very prominent journalists attended. Among others was P.D. Ross, the proprietor of *The Ottawa Journal*, who contributed graphic reports of the proceedings and especially of the incident between Meighen and Ferguson. In this report, his imagination over-balanced his observation, as he described, *inter alia*, the expression upon my countenance as this violent controversy emerged. Having regard to my absence from the platform at the time when he described so vividly my expression of disappointment and dismay, I consider this a singularly notable illustration of inaccuracy in press reports.

On December 14, 1933, the following item appeared in the 'Forty Replies Column' of the Toronto *Mail and Empire*:

> A Rolls Royce – that's what Sir Robert Borden asked for when his ministers came to him when he was about to retire, and asked what token of remembrance and appreciation they could give him. Well, my wife wants a Rolls Royce.

I immediately wrote to the chief editor, F.D.L. Smith, informing him that there was not a shadow of foundation for the statement. He took up the matter and gave me an explanation from which it appeared that a rather silly girl in charge of this column had been the subject of a practical joke; and that 'she did not have enough common sense to see that she and the newspaper were being sadly put upon.'

Charles S. Hamilton, who was my senior by about ten years, was born at Grand Pré, Nova Scotia. His father, James Edward Hamilton owned a farm about half a mile from that of my father. I have a vivid recollection of the old man and of his brother, George Hamilton whose residence was within a few hundred yards of my father's.

James Edward Hamilton had a large family, two of whom I knew intimately – James Henry Hamilton, under whom I studied, was born in 1841; and in 1873, when I was in my nineteenth year, I went as assistant teacher in his school at Matawan, New Jersey. Charles S. Hamilton graduated from King's College, then situated in Windsor, Nova Scotia, and eventually was admitted to the New Haven bar where for many years he was an outstanding figure. During the summer months he spent his holidays at Wolfville, Nova Scotia, where he had acquired a small property.

In the *New York Times* of March 21, 1934, a very appreciative obituary notice of Mr C.S. Hamilton contained the following.

> He was born in New York City, son of Mr and Mrs James E. Hamilton. His father was a merchant in the West Indian trade whose summer home in Grand Pré later became that of his son, Charles.

This notice was inaccurate in the following respects:

1 He was not born in New York City, but at Grand Pré, Nova Scotia.

2 His father, James Edward Hamilton, was not a merchant but a farmer and never resided elsewhere but in Grand Pré. So far as I am aware, he was never outside his native Province of Nova Scotia.

3 James Edward Hamilton never had any connection whatever with the West India trade; and his activities were confined solely to the incessant labour and difficult task of making a living off a back-road farm at Grand Pré.

4 James Edward Hamilton never had a summer home at Grand Pré other than the above mentioned farm on which was situated an old house where I was occasionally a visitor.

The notice is also inaccurate in stating that C.S. Hamilton graduated from Acadia University.

Other illustrations of inaccuracy may be found in the obituary notice of the Honourable Nicholas Hogan Meagher, for many years a Judge of the Supreme Court of Nova Scotia, whom I knew intimately, and in an article in *The Dalhousie Review* (April 1934) in which the late Sir John Thompson is described as a 'Nova Scotian Scot'.

The above are but a few of many illustrations of press inaccuracies that frequently have come under my notice.

It is said that a great German historian, Ranke (if I remember correctly) while engaged in writing one of his notable works, was interrupted by a riotous disturbance just outside his window. Endeavouring to ascertain the cause of the incidents of this disturbance, he received so many inconsistent and indeed contradictory reports that he was inclined to abandon his historical labours. If he could not obtain a lucid and truthful account of an incident that had occurred just outside his house only a few minutes before he began his inquiry, how could he possibly expect that his history would present even a moderately truthful picture of the events he was describing?

I remain, Sir, Yours in sympathy,

October 10, 1927

The Winnipeg Evening Tribune

SELECT YOUR LEADER, THEN STAND BY HIM, IS ADVICE OF SIR ROBERT BORDEN

Select your leader, and when you have selected him, stand by him. Being human, he may not always be right, but perhaps it would be well for you to remember that you also are human, and that when you think he is wrong he may be right.

This was the message today of Sir Robert Borden to the National Liberal-Conservative convention opening.

Sir Robert's speech follows:

'This is the most harmonious convention I have seen up to the present time. I hope it will continue so to the end. I have had a good deal of experience of caucuses, and this is a sort of general caucus of the Liberal-Conservative party from all over Canada, but I wish to repeat that in all my experience I never saw anything so delightfully harmonious as this assembly this morning.

'That invitation that was just presented by the chairman seemed to me also particularly pleasant. He asked you all to remain seated and if there is anything that a man, in parliament, or in any assembly, desires it is to remain seated, so I think that is a very happy omen.

'Also your chairman has told you something of my selection as a leader 26 years go. I didn't intend to speak about it, but, as he has told you part I will tell you something more that has not been spoken in public up to the present time. I did not want the position as leader of the Liberal-Conservative party at that time, nor indeed at any time, for two reasons.

'In the first place I didn't think I was qualified for it, and in the second place I didn't desire it. Finally on the second night of the caucus I accepted, but for one year only. They came to me after the caucus was over. These gentlemen were too clever for me. They said 'If you make any announcement of that kind – as I had intended to make it – it will interfere with your authority as temporary leader, and therefore you had better not make any such announcement.

'I recall something said by a great Englishman about 300 years ago, "The sons of Zellulia be too hard for me." They were too hard for me on that occasion. I accepted for one year, and I remained leader for 20 years. And I had the unique distinction of leading a political party in opposition longer than, I think, any other man in Canada ever did.

'Sir Wilfrid Laurier made a pretty good record of nine years, but I went one better, and surpassed it by, I think it was, 18 months.

'Before coming to the few disjointed remarks which I wish to inflict upon you in this before-lunch speech, I would like to just make a slight addition to some words which fell from my friend Mr Baxter in his very eloquent speech. I should like to remind you that there is another great Canadian whom he did not mention, without whom this Confederation could never have been rounded out. I refer to Sir George Etienne Cartier.

'Without him Quebec could not have been brought into Confederation, and his memory should be on our hearts whenever we consider the past record of the great party to which we owe allegiance. Now, today, we bear the portrait of Sir John A. Macdonald upon our hearts, and as we bear his memory we have here on the platform his honored son. We have, I say, his honored son with us, known from the Atlantic to the Pacific, as Hugh John. Long may he live. And long live the great party which his father in effect founded.

'I really did not anticipate that I should have the pleasure of coming to this convention, nor that I should have the honor of addressing you. Now that I am here I am quite sure I cannot do any good, and it is my most earnest hope that I shall not do any harm.

'In 1916, after the Parliament buildings at Ottawa had been burned, we went on the next day to the Royal Victoria museum. We didn't miss a day at all. That wasn't a bad record, as you will admit. There are some curious inscriptions which had been established in that museum before we moved into it, and some scoundrel, whose identity has never been detected, took one of those inscriptions and placed it above the door of the room appropriated for the sittings of the senate.

'If this man had ever been discovered I am sure he would have been sent to the Tower for the rest of his life. There wasn't a tower at that time, but we would have built one.

'The words were, "Prehistoric Fossils." It was singularly inappropriate for the senate, but extremely appropriate for my appearance here today, because I come before you as a prehistoric political fossil and what can such a person say to such an assemblage as this, vibrating with life, energy and confidence?

'Well I don't know what I can say very much that will be of use. I can only say that it is the greatest convention, as has been said, the greatest political convention ever held in Canada and the first Liberal-Conservative convention ever held in federal affairs in this country. I don't think any words of congratulation could be too great for your splendid committee which has organized the convention, or to the chairman of that committee.

'This convention is invested with tremendous responsibility. Do you know that we have, in this country, as in all the British dominions, democratic government carried on by means of the party system. It is very easy to point out defects in the party system, but until someone can invent something that promises better I think we, in Canada, and in all the English speaking countries, will continue to follow the party system. And the highest ideal of that system would be two parties united in generous rivalry in the service of the state.

'Human nature being what it is we perhaps do not always attain that ideal in its highest conception, but we in the Liberal-Conservative party, I hope, will always continue to aim at that ideal. Now something has been said of the past record and traditions of the Liberal-Conservative party. That party has governed this country for more than half of the 60 years since Confederation. On two occasions, it least, it has led the people of Canada with the principle that under all conditions Canada at all times in the future shall control her own destiny. Canada has followed that leadership. The highest praise which could be given to a statesman of old was that he had deserved well of his country.

'And I say to you men and women, Liberal-Conservative delegates from all over Canada, that your party during these 60 years has deserved well of its country. But with that statement I would like to add something else. That is, that no party can live on its past record and its traditions, not on these alone.

'They are splendid inspirations and a stimulus to higher effort but one must look forward to further usefulness and certainly I, for one, do not in the least doubt the return of the Liberal-Conservative party to power. I should like to accompany that with this thought, that the mere attaining to power is not in itself success. It gives the party an opportunity of success in service to the country, but the mere attaining of power in the country is not, according to my conception, success. There are splendid opportunities for great service in Canada. Let us always have implicit confidence in our country and our destiny.

'Now as to this matter of selecting a leader. What have I to say? Just two words. Select your leader and afterwards stand by him. Being human, he may not always be right. But perhaps it would be as well for you sometimes to remember that you are also human and that, occasionally, when you think he is wrong he may be right.

'Then, I would suggest another thing, that you should go to the selecting of a leader bearing in mind that he ought to have something to say about the definition of policy.

'There are some great fundamental principles of course to which the Liberal-Conservative party has always been committed, and to which I hope it always will be committed. But when you come into detail and define a policy very much in detail, remember, pray, that this country is rapidly developing, that conditions are changing from time to time and that you must not forestall too much a leader who will be responsible to you and to parliament and to the country for the policy to be put before the people.

'I would say just one word with regard to policy. That is more an echo of what has been said before on this platform, more effectively than I can say it. Let your policy always stand for Canada's place as a fully autonomous nation within the British commonwealth of nations.

'This is, indeed, a magnificent convention. I hope it will give good service, bear glorious results. New questions that are already looming up in the future, we must approach, we must consider. The Liberal-Conservative party and its leader can approach them with a firm heart, having their inspiration in the desire to serve.

'Once more I say to the new leader, "Trust the rank and file." In my own experience as a leader for nearly 20 years, I found my highest inspiration in the unswerving loyalty of Liberal-Conservatives from one end of this country to the other.

'And I am sure the new leader, whoever he may be, will find his highest inspiration in that same loyalty, and for him, whoever he may be, this is my last word, let him have sympathetic success strewed before his feet, and on his brow be set the laurel of victory.'

April 6, 1934

JOHN MACGILLIVRAY – PORTRAIT PAINTER

Sir,

During the latter part of January I began sitting for my portrait to John MacGillivray, [now deceased] son of my old friend, Dugald MacGillivray of Halifax. The portrait is to be presented to Acadia University; and the donor, as I learn, is Senator W.H. Dennis of Halifax.

John MacGillivray has required a very great number of sittings; but he has made good progress and I am confident that the portrait will be a distinctive success. John is a young man of interesting personality, of highly nervous temperament, well-read in English literature, equipped with extremely strong opinions and confident views, and very casual in the everyday affairs of life. In addition, he has a fine sense of humour and thoroughly enjoys relating incidents which tell strongly against himself. While working in England last summer, he was painting a landscape in a pasture where cows congregated. Returning one day after luncheon, he found that they had swallowed all his paints and that one enterprising animal had licked all the paint off the canvas upon which he had been working for several days.

Then there was an account of locking himself out of his bedroom in an apartment house in New York, so that he was obliged to ascend to the next story and, descending by the fire-escape, enter his room through the window, which fortunately was open. While painting my portrait, he emerged from the Laurentian Club [in Ottawa] one night, in very scanty attire, for the purpose of making inquiry as to a fire alarm. At the time, the thermometer registered about 15 below zero; and he discovered that the door had locked itself behind him. Having made loud outcry, he eventually received a key lowered from a third-story window by a benevolent soul who seems to have made a practice of admitting belated revellers.

John lives for the most part in dreamland; but he seems thoroughly unconscious of this characteristic which, however, he observes in his sister, Mary, wife of David MacKeen. His description of Mary's preoccupation with art, and of David's helplessness in relation to household arrangements was very amusing.

After practically finishing my portrait he went to Toronto where he painted the portrait of Sir Robert Falconer for presentation to Pine Hill Theological College at Halifax. He expected to leave Ottawa on a Friday but various aberrations delayed his departure until about the following Wednesday.

Unfortunately, his physique is not very strong; and he does not know how to care for himself. I bestowed upon him much good advice which probably had as much effect as if delivered to empty air on the banks of the Rideau river. If his health improves, it is almost certain that he will make his mark as a portrait painter.

He is gifted with unusual power of graphic description. After returning from Toronto, he said, in response to inquiry as to his lodging, 'I am still at the ante-chamber of Death.' He thus designated the Laurentian Club where he had met several elderly residents who impressed him as of an extremely fossilized type.

I remain, Sir, Yours in sympathy,

April 19, 1934

VISIT TO ATLANTIC CITY – DINNER IN OTTAWA TO THE CHAIRMAN OF BARCLAYS BANK LIMITED

Sir,

Last winter we remained in Ottawa without going south. This year we left for Atlantic City on March 15, and returned April 4.

During March, Atlantic City greeted us with two snow-blizzards; and twice during our visit the snow-plough was required to clear the boardwalk.

Easter arrived April 1; and, as the weather had become somewhat milder, the crowds at Atlantic City exceeded anything I had ever known. The press reported five hundred thousand people on Easter Sunday; but this, I think, was a very great exaggeration. However, the boardwalk, on that day, was a mass of slowly moving humanity.

While in Atlantic City, I met Dr William Cavan of Toronto who, in the autumn of 1919, after I had broken down in health, came to Ottawa for the purpose of examining me in consultation with the late Dr J.F. Kidd. I reminded Dr Cavan that on that occasion he had said: 'If it were not for your splendid inheritance, you would have been dead before this. As it is, you have no organic disease, but that will come very soon if you keep on.'

On Saturday, April 14, I gave a dinner at my house, in honour of Frederick Crauford Goodenough, Chairman of the Board of Barclays Bank Limited, and W.O. Stevenson an important officer of that bank. The other guests included, the Prime Minister, Rhodes, Perley, G.P. Graham, Arthur Purvis, R.H. Coats, Sir William Clark, W.C. Clark (Deputy Minister of Finance), Colonel Eric MacKenzie, General MacLaren and Colonel G.P. Murphy.

It was an important evening, as I took opportunity to bring into touch with Mr Goodenough, the Prime Minister, Sir George Perley, Mr Rhodes, Senator Graham, the Deputy Minister of Finance and Coats, Dominion Statistician.

This dinner led to a rather intimate conversation between Mr Goodenough and Mr Bennett in which the former undertook to formulate plans for Bennett's consideration respecting conversion of Canada's debt at a lower rate of interest, as well as proposals that might assist in relieving the railway situation. These subjects I subsequently discussed in returning from Montreal with Mr Goodenough on April 18.

I remain, Sir, Yours in sympathy,

May 15, 1934

INTERVIEW WITH THE PRIME MINISTER

Sir,

Yesterday I had an extremely interesting interview with the Prime Minister in which our conversation ranged over a great diversity of questions. He seemed in excellent form and expressed himself with wonderful lucidity and vigour.

In the first place I spoke to him with regard to Mr Goodenough's desire to assist in a complete readjustment of Canada's financial affairs, as set forth to me during his recent visit. Mr Goodenough thought that the proposal might be made so broad as to offer some solution of our railway problems. Mr Bennett expressed great admiration for Mr Goodenough's character and ability and appreciation of that gentleman's desire to be of assistance. In this connection, I mentioned the hope of Mr Purvis[17] that Canada's monetary system might eventually be divorced from that of United States. Mr Bennett considers that this is not practicable at present.

We briefly discussed the Marketing Bill which the PM regards as a safeguard against possible dangers that may arise in the future.

I told him of the report brought by Arthur Purvis from New York; the bankers, pessimistic, even despondent; some of them declaring that US is on the brink of a precipice; on the other hand, the manufacturers rejoicing in excellent business conditions and clearly optimistic. The banks, according to Purvis, are converting their reserves into very short-term obligations or into cash, as they are desperately afraid of such inflation as may bring about a dangerous crisis. I told him Purvis had reported that the President is becoming petulant, as his alphabetical policies are not accomplishing anticipated results, and that his influence, although still very powerful, is declining and may be negligible within a year.

Bennett does not doubt that the President is considerably influenced by his desire for a second term. To this, he attributes Roosevelt's recession from his pronouncement last autumn when he declared that by reason of her token payment, Great Britain was not in default.

In Bennett's opinion, throughout the US in the great mass of the people there is a feeling of hostility to Great Britain. He cannot account for this but it may perhaps be due to Great Britain's greater success in overcoming the depression and in balancing her budget.

He cannot forecast the probable action of Great Britain with respect to the debt payment falling due in June.

The PM considers that a crisis will be reached in 1937. If US succeeds in carrying on without disaster during the presidential election in 1936, all may be well; on the other hand, disaster of so terrible a character may ensue that US will break up or disappear as a great power. 'The Presidential Election in the United States has

17 Then President, Canadian Industries Ltd.

an enormous influence upon this country', he observed: 'although', he added, 'I would not dare to say 'that in public.'

I spoke of Walter Carpenter's opinion that disaster in US might mean immense opportunity for Canada. Purvis did not explain upon what Carpenter based this view. Bennett agreed with Carpenter; but said that this opportunity was also attended with corresponding risk.

He told me, in very strict confidence, of his view as to selection of a governor for the Central Bank. He had not acquainted his colleagues with that view. The course he proposes was suggested to him by Mr Goodenough; and, after hearing his reasons, I quite agreed that the proposal would be wise and expedient.[18]

... I told him that Beatty [President, Canadian Pacific Railway] had expressed to me a very high opinion of Dunning's [former Minister of Railways and Canals and of Finance in Mackenzie King administration] ability and character. Bennett said he was sorry we had selected Dunning,[19] and that Beatty had given him an absolutely different opinion. Bennett thinks Dunning lacks courage and decision and that he is continually playing politics. I expressed dissent and told him that on Canadian Investment Fund Board we had found Dunning well-informed, capable and useful. He eventually admitted Dunning's ability; but he thinks that he would be of no use in difficulty or crisis and that he lacks courage, backbone and resourcefulness. Dunning, he said, had been dominated by Thornton [Sir Henry Thornton – former Chairman of Canadian National Railway] to an astonishing extent and had expressed great apprehension of disaster if Thornton should resign. The arrangement for the two-million dollar hotel at Vancouver was made by Thornton without Dunning's knowledge.

I mentioned Ballantyne and said that his accession to the Board [of Barclays Bank (Canada)] would have pleased me; and that he would have been useful. Bennett concurred.

18 This paragraph refers to the appointment of the first Governor of the about-to-be organized Bank of Canada. Mr Goodenough was Chairman of Barclays Bank Limited and presumably in his conversations with the Prime Minister (Bennett) had suggested that the first governor should be found in England. By the summer of 1934 the Canadian press was in full cry urging that a Canadian be selected. In the early fall of that year Mr Graham F. Towers, a Canadian, who was at that time a senior executive of the Royal Bank of Canada at its head office in Montreal, was appointed. Mr Towers and Mr Bennett agreed that some central bank experience should be supplied by a deputy-governor from England, at least for a few years. As a result it was arranged, later that fall, that the then Secretary of the Bank of England, Mr J.A.C. Osborne, would be appointed Deputy-Governor.

19 The reference is to selection as a director of Barclays Bank (Canada).

According to Bennett, Dunning's main purpose is 'to get a place on St James Street'.

I remain, Sir, Yours in sympathy,

June 11, 1934

MOSQUITO PEST – SLEEPING OUTDOORS; PARLIAMENTARY PRESS GALLERY ANNUAL DINNER

Sir,

The ice did not disappear from our south glen until about the middle of May. After a short interval the ice was succeeded by mosquitoes which have been an intolerable pest during the past three weeks. Appended hereto are copies of letters which I wrote to the Mayor of Ottawa on June 8, 1933, and on May 31, 1934.

Sleeping out of doors, I am continually thrilled with the extraordinary beauty of the sky in the early morning.

Again and again have I observed the beautiful bit of cloudland floating below the morning star and above the dawn. Then one notes frequently the breeze that just precedes the dawn.

My bed is so situated that I can observe the feathery, lace-like outline of the tops of the fir trees, and especially the early foliage of the Manitoba Maple (or Box Elder) which is then far more beautiful than in its later development. It is an exquisite mixture of gold and green which gradually changes into the usual green of its foliage as the leaves develop.

Very often in the evenings we sit on the upper verandah, just above the sun-room, and watch with much interest the occasional games of very crude baseball played by boys and girls of from twelve to sixteen in Macdonald Park. Their remarkable grace and fleetness make it a delight to watch them. Ottawa is indeed most fortunate in its many playgrounds.

For the first time in many years, I attended the Annual Dinner of the Parliamentary Press Gallery on Saturday evening (June 9). There was a great gathering; and the arrangements were excellent. Mr Emile Benoist presided and acquitted himself admirably. On the right of the president was the Governor-General who made a very happy speech; and I sat at his right. On the left of the president was the Prime Minister who had to speak, not only for himself but for Mr Mackenzie King who unfortunately was unable to be present. Mr Bennett, after speaking for himself, suddenly changed into the role of Mackenzie King and described that gentleman's reactions after he had joined the staff of the *Toronto Globe* soon after leaving the university.

There were many toasts and several excellent speeches. R.S. White, MP, proposed the toast to the press in general and gave a delightful and instructive address.

When the toast-list was nearing completion, the president requested me to say a few words which I emphatically declined to do. However, some messages were sent up to him; and I observed one member of the press gallery violently gesticulating at Mr Benoist who, without any further notice, called upon me to speak. They gave me a remarkably fine reception before and after my little address which concluded with my thanks for their invitation and for the privilege and pleasure of being present once more at their annual dinner: 'You have brought me a breath of the fragrance of years long since gone by.' I received many congratulations; and I especially value those from R.S. White and Grattan O'Leary.

I remain, Sir, Yours in sympathy,

June 8, 1933

To His Worship
The Mayor of Ottawa
Transportation Building
Ottawa

Dear Mr Mayor,

In common with very many other citizens of Ottawa, I am much concerned about the plague of mosquitoes which has rendered outdoor life exceedingly uncomfortable and at times practically impossible. The present condition is particularly severe upon elderly persons and very young children who are also debarred from open-air life during the inclemency of the winter season.

It is believed that in communities no more progressive than Ottawa the plague of mosquitoes has been abated by the adoption of efficient methods for the extermination of their larvae. It seems due to our citizens that the civic authorities should make a public statement of the reasons why such methods have not been adopted or have failed in our city.

The civic authorities cannot be insensible to the detriment which the present plague has occasioned. An eminent physician has informed me that such conditions prejudicially affect the health of many persons and especially of young children. One can hardly believe that a mosquito regime will increase the attractions of our city to summer visitors.

As to the intensity of the plague, there can be no question. Some ten days ago I was afflicted in the Laurentian Hills by the ferocious attacks of black flies. Upon my return to Ottawa, I found the mosquitoes quite as numerous and equally fierce.

In bringing these considerations to your attention, Mr Mayor, I do not forget or overlook the excellence of civic administration in almost every other aspect. But I also remember the very heavy burden of civic taxation.

Yours faithfully,

May 31, 1934

Private and Personal

My dear Mr Mayor,

I venture to commend to your consideration the representations set forth in a letter dated June 8, 1933, which was addressed to your predecessor, and copy of which I enclose.

In reply to this communication I had a letter from Mr Allan; and I enclose the relevant portion thereof.

Ottawa has been gaining an unhappy reputation as headquarters of the mosquito pest. Many persons believe that this reputation has had a detrimental effect in deterring tourists who otherwise would visit this city.

This year the mosquitoes seem worse than ever. Having just returned from a fishing camp in the Laurentian Hills, I find the mosquitoes as numerous and active here as there.

Pray do not trouble to acknowledge this letter. From time to time I shall venture to bring to your attention suggestions respecting the welfare and progress of the city that seem to me worthy of your consideration.

With kind regards, I remain, Yours faithfully,

COPY OF EXTRACT FROM ALLAN'S LETTER OF JUNE 10, 1933

I find on inquiry that a special Mosquito Control Committee had charge of operations for two or three years previous to 1930, at which time the Committee disbanded with a recommendation that the work be taken over by the Federal District Commission. This Committee had simply been operating as an experimental one on contributions received from the Federal District Commission, the City of Ottawa, Canadian International Paper Company, the Quebec Department of Health, the Department of National Defence, Rockcliffe Park Village, the town of Eastview and Gloucester Township, and it was apparently felt by the Committee that having demonstrated the effectiveness of the treatment some body with more permanency and more authority, such as the Federal District Commission, should assume the responsibility. I think that possibly this decision was partly due to the difficulty of securing contributions from the sources named in the year 1930.

I wish, however, to advise you that I took the question up with the Federal District Commission at the meeting yesterday and I feel satisfied that some action will be taken by this body. Nothing of course can be accomplished this year but I endeavoured to impress upon the Commission the necessity for making all preliminary arrangements before the year is out.

June 27, 1934

EIGHTIETH BIRTHDAY

Sir,

Yesterday (June 26) I completed my eightieth year; and my birthday anniversary was greeted with a flood of messages by cable, telegram, telephone and personal calls.

I received messages from Right Honourable J. Ramsay MacDonald, Prime Minister of Great Britain, on behalf of himself and his colleagues of the cabinet, from the Governor-General, from David Lloyd George, from Lord and Lady Willingdon, from the Prime Minister of Canada, from F.C. Goodenough and from scores of Canadians in all walks of life. The appreciation expressed in many of these messages touched me greatly. Appended are copies of some of the messages, as well as newspaper articles.

The weight of four-score years ought to seem more oppressive than it really does. As a boy of nine, I looked up with great reverence to a boy of thirteen in the same class who, in my opinion, had reached a very advanced age, as the other boys were eleven or twelve. At eighty years, I am profoundly thankful to have a reasonable measure of health and strength which has been gradually regained after a complete collapse of my health in the autumn of 1919.

Winston Churchill has discussed the question of living one's life over again if that were possible; and he concludes that he would not care to do so, unless he could begin the new life with the knowledge and experience acquired during the life already lived. Probably that would be the general verdict. One cannot help feeling that although there have been many errors and imperfections, yet even more serious ones have been avoided.

Some years ago, I read an article by Oliver Wendell Holmes in which he wrote of having read with great appreciation Cicero's *De Senectute*. I procured that book and perused some of its pages; but I did not derive the benefit therefrom that Oliver Wendell Holmes expressed.

In my own case, one peculiar experience, which I have not noted elsewhere, has greatly impressed me. In youth and middle age one feels not so much a fear as an intense shrinking from the thought of death. I believe that in the normal human being this feeling gradually disappears as one advances in years. Certainly that is my own experience. I quote from memory Oliver Wendell Holmes' beautiful lines:

Not bedtime yet; the night winds blow,
The stars are out, full well we know
The nurse is on the stair
With hand of ice and cheek of snow
And frozen lips that whisper low
Come children it is time to go
My narrow couch to share.

No years the waking heart can tire:
Not bedtime yet!
Come stir the fire and warm your dear old hands.
Kind Mother Earth we love so well
Has many a story yet to tell
Before we hear the curfew knell,
Still glow the burning brands.

And when, our pleasant evening past,
The nurse long waiting comes at last,
Ere on her lap we lie
In tired Nature's sweet repose,
At peace with all our waking foes,
Our lips shall murmur ere they close
Good-night and not Good-bye.

Probably the most beautiful and touching description of old age ever written is contained in Chapter 12, *Ecclesiastes*: (Verses 1–8)

1 Remember now thy Creator in the days of thy youth, while the evil days come not, nor the years draw nigh, when thou shalt say, I have no pleasure in them;
2 While the sun, or the light, or the moon, or the stars be not darkened, nor the clouds return after the rain:
3 In the day when the keepers of the house shall tremble, and the strong men shall bow themselves, and the grinders cease because they are few, and those that look out of the windows be darkened.
4 And the doors shall be shut in the streets, when the sound of the grinding is low, and he shall rise up at the voice of the bird, and all the daughters of musick shall be brought low;
5 Also when they shall be afraid of that which is high, and fears shall be in the way, and the almond tree shall flourish, and the grasshopper shall be a burden, and desire shall fail: because man goeth to his long home, and the mourners go about the streets:
6 Or ever the silver cord be loosed, or the golden bowl be broken, or the pitcher be broken at the fountain, or the wheel broken at the cistern.
7 Then shall the dust return to the earth as it was: and the spirit shall return unto God who gave it.
8 Vanity of vanities, saith the preacher; all is vanity.

And, so, after this rather sombre picture, I bid you, dear Limbo, to be of good cheer, remembering Browning's exhortation:

God's in His Heaven –
All's right with the world!

I remain, Yours in sympathy,

Right Honourable Ramsay MacDonald's Cable

Please accept heartfelt congratulations from myself and my colleagues in the Cabinet on the attainment of your eightieth birthday. Today brings back to us many and happy memories of your long record of distinguished service to Canada and to the Commonwealth both in war and in peace.

Right Honourable David Lloyd George's Cable
Felicitations on reaching the eightieth milestone of a career of distinguished service for your own country and the Empire.

Lord and Lady Willingdon's Cable
Many many happy returns from us both.

Sir William and Lady Clark's Message
Love and heartiest congratulations from us both and best wishes for many happy years.

Sir Frederick Williams-Taylor's Cable
Felicitation, Admiration, Continuation.

Right Honourable R.B. Bennett's note:
You have attained an age that few men reach. Today you celebrate the 80th anniversary of your birth, and will receive expressions of goodwill and appreciation from men and women in all parts of the world. May I be one of those who, in all sincerity, wish you many happy returns of a day that must bring to you memories, and, without feelings of egotism, a consciousness of having rendered great and useful service to your country and the world, during a long and distinguished public career.

It is my earnest hope that you may be spared to celebrate many more anniversaries and bring joy and happiness to a host of friends, amongst whom I should like to count myself.

Your faithfully,

June 26, 1934

Halifax Herald
GREAT SON OF NOVA SCOTIA

Rt. Hon. Sir Robert Laird Borden
Today Canada's most distinguished citizen, Sir Robert Borden, celebrates his 80th birthday. He was born at Grand Pré, Nova Scotia, June 26, 1854, and today at his Ottawa home will be receiving congratulations, not only from all parts of Canada, but from friends and admirers throughout the world.

When Sir Robert resigned the Canadian Premiership in July, 1920, he was then the only surviving Prime Minister who had served as such continuously throughout the war. Today, at the 80th milestone of life, he retains his mental alertness and vigor and continues to contribute to great and important affairs the value of his counsels and ripe experience.

Twenty years ago today Sir Robert Borden, at his office in the East Block on Parliament Hill, was receiving the congratulations of friends and supporters on the occasion of his 60th birthday.

It was a calm, peaceful day in June. No hint of impending disaster was in the air. Truly, as Churchill has written, 'the Old World in its sunset was fair to see.'

Two years before, as Prime Minister of Canada, Sir Robert Borden had warned Parliament and the Canadian people that war might burst upon the world 'with appalling suddenness.' Two days later that immense and solemn warning was fulfilled.

June 28, 1914 – a shot at Sarajevo – and mankind was plunged into a maelstrom of blood and terror!

Sir Robert Borden was Prime Minister of Canada when the World War came: he was Prime Minister at the Armistice. He bore the great burden of Canada's immense war effort, and stood forth as an Empire figure in the counsels of the Allies.

When peace came he gave to the League of Nations the strongest support of which he was capable.

> Amid the chaotic conditions, resulting from the world-wide conflict, he has declared, the war-scourged nations sought a new orientation, and so the League of Nations was born. It is a wonder that it ever survived; it is amazing that it accomplished the concrete results that have been achieved; it is a miracle that today it embraces 54 nations united in the solemn and supreme purpose of peaceful endeavor for international accord and justice.

Born at Grand Pré on June 26, 1854, Sir Robert Borden today celebrates his 80th birthday. He will be showered with congratulations and good wishes; and of all the messages he will receive at his Ottawa home, none will be quite so warm and hearty and spontaneous as those from his old friends, his own people, in Nova Scotia, who hold him in such affectionate esteem. He is Canada's first and most distinguished citizen – and Nova Scotia is proud of having given him to Dominion and Empire.

101 JUNE 27, 1934

June 26, 1934

Montreal Daily Star

A NATION'S HEALTH IS A NATION'S WEALTH

Sir Robert Borden

Canada's War Premier – Sir Robert Borden – today passes the Biblical milestone of four-score years amidst the congratulations and genuine good feeling of the entire Canadian people. Sir Robert's place in history is secure. It is not only that he stood at the helm through by far the most troublous and trying years that this young Dominion has ever known – or, possibly, may ever know – but that he had won before that period two great victories for the growing status of Canada, one that secured our fiscal independence on this Continent when it was menaced by the Reciprocity offer of 1911, and another when he made us an integral part of the naval defences of the Empire by his contribution of capital ships to the Admiralty.

After the War, he was able to compel complete recognition of our nationhood by achieving a position of equality for Canada at the Naval Conference in Washington. We did not go to either of them as subordinates but as full members, and this was due to the courage of Sir Robert Borden. A loyal Imperialist, he was always a good Canadian. He was never content to be a 'Colonial.' He carried forward during his Premiership the stout campaign for recognition in London as well as in the capitals of foreign nations of the essential national entity of this Dominion to which Sir Wilfrid Laurier had made such notable contributions.

It was a tragedy for Canada when his failing health no longer permitted him to keep the Premiership. He was one of the casualties of the War. Undoubtedly, his unceasing labours and his great anxieties through that terrible four years broke even his splendid health. Once the burden was removed, he became himself again and has for some fifteen years taken an active part in the financial and social life of his countrymen and has borne toward politics the impressive and beneficent attitude of a universally recognised Elder Statesman.

His years of leisure have been gracefully spent. Some few responsibilities, such as the presidency of Barclays Bank (Canada), have not unduly burdened him and he has had an abundance of time for literary enjoyments. Always a student, the absorbing career of a public man denied him for decades the pleasures of the library to which he has now returned with great relish. A willing counsellor of his successors, his advice has always been eagerly sought. Not infrequently, he has represented his country with dignity and honour. His countrymen will hope that he will long live to deserve their respect and enjoy their affection.

June 27, 1934

The Chronicle-Telegraph, Quebec

SIR ROBERT BORDEN AT EIGHTY

If old age brings death and consequent mourning with it, as in the case of Mr Drouin to whom we have paid our tribute in the foregoing article, it also has its 'Indian summer' when the men of action and patriotic service, still retaining a hale virility, can enjoy the honors paid to them by a whole population.

This is the happy situation of Sir Robert Borden, who has just been celebrating his eightieth birthday, an event that is being hailed with deserved eulogies, in all parts of Canada. Sir Robert, in fact, has long since reached that point of prestige when a public figure ceases to belong to a party or faction and becomes the property of the nation. If this country were to choose a native-born Governor tomorrow, no one would be more likely to meet with universal acclaim than he.

After many trials and unusual responsibilities as Prime Minister, Sir Robert, by reason of his devotion to duty and his faculty of rising to each emergent occasion, finally exercised a position of unquestioned national leadership before his voluntary retirement from office. Well may the writer of a special article in the Ottawa Journal observe:

'Sir Robert reached the apex of his career at Versailles. Practically on his own initiative he insisted that Canada must sign the peace treaty as a separate and distinct nation. In ringing tones he emphasized the magnitude of her contribution – 60,000 dead on foreign battlefields, more than 100,000 maimed and broken, a young country crippled with a colossal debt – surely she had paid the wages of nationhood and such a demand was but simple justice for valor and self-sacrifice. His eloquence overbore all opposition and amidst the gleaming mirrors of Versailles all the Dominions separately signed the great treaty and the British Commonwealth of Nations came into being.'

That is one of the major contributions that any of her sons have made so far to Canada's nationhood.

June 25, 1934

The Ottawa Journal

SIR ROBERT L. BORDEN GREAT CANADIAN AT 80

Written for The Journal by R.B.F.

To the cradle of every man destined to achieve greatness is born one crowning gift. Other gifts there are which will speed him on his way to the high places, but this is as the frankincense and myrrh – the gift of kings – which will be the major inspiration of his actions, the very marrow of his imaginings, the shining oriflamme listing him in the records of his time.

In the case of Sir Robert Borden, who today is receiving congratulations from far and near on the celebration of his 80th birthday, this fundamental quality is not far to seek. It has been with him always, from that morning hour when he went out from an Acadian hamlet to woo fortune in the capital of his province, through all the vicissitudes of a public career set in the long 'wilderness' of opposition, in the storm and travail of a great conflict, bearing his message even to the glittering forecourts of Versailles – ever and always his quiet, undemonstrative but intensely sincere Canadianism, his love of country, has been the mainspring of his endeavors.

For a leader to possess this quality is to hold the open sesame to public confidence. Mistakes in policy, errors in judgment, rancor against unpopular laws made necessary by the exigencies of the hour – all these can be forgotten, if he is recognized as the state's man, the people's man, the man who sets country above self, above party, above the insurgency of special interests.

To hold such a dowry is to leave the company of the successful, the splendidly gifted, and to enter the thin ranks of the great, of those with whom the historian must deal as major influences in national development.

Such a historian, we think, will give high place to the name of Borden, must rank it eventually with those of Macdonald and Laurier, a triumvirate of builders inspired by the same motive: Macdonald, dreamer devout by vision led beyond his time and place setting a colony of backwoods settlements on the road to nationhood; Laurier, polished unifier seeming to step from the entourage of an old world court and splendidly uniting its diversified elements in that lofty endeavor; Borden, sane and sound leader in its most momentous hour, manfully bearing the burden of Armageddon and the vast obligations of that nationhood which had come into being.

Sir Robert's entry into public life was almost an accident. When he unwillingly took over the leadership of the Conservative party he was already a man of middle age, had achieved eminence in the courts, accumulated a comfortable competence, was certain of high judicial preferment, had a constitutional distaste for the bitter partisanship of party strife. He assumed the leadership with misgiving, with doubts of his fitness for the task, actuated solely by the belief of his followers that he could be more useful to his country in the turmoil of public life than in the administration of its laws.

The story of the way he 'carried on' through dark days of disillusion and defeat to the spectacular triumph of 1911 provides splendid justification of those who never faltered in their allegiance, a tribute to the character of the man 'who contrived all things with modesty, to do well the appointed task, to be loyal to those things that were seemly and of good repute.'

In fact just that plain, old homespun word 'character,' combined with genuine love of country, afford the clearest index to the quality of his leadership.

Speaking of his forebears in Nova Scotia one writer says: 'The Bordens lived quietly, went to church regularly, attended to all their duties zealously, and were esteemed by all their neighbors as honest, upright, progressive people.'

Surely this goodly heritage bore fine fruit in their most distinguished offspring. Outstanding as his mental endowment, there have been leaders more brilliantly gifted, more spectacularly endowed with qualities that make immediate appeal to the imagination, but none has inspired a greater measure of confidence, a confidence based on proven soundness and high character tested in the fierce ordeal of victory and defeat.

Those who have had any contact with Sir Robert appreciate his point of view, know only too well that he would be the last to take credit to himself for his wartime leadership. And yet what a splendid contribution it was! The man and the hour were ideally mated. Stability, good judgment, glorified commonsense, tactful reliance on civil and military advisers, determination to do a big job in a big way with the minimum of discord and confusion, whole-hearted loyalty to a great cause, unremitting application to the myriad demands of duty, the clarion call for unity, the unfailing faith in justice and ultimate victory. If Sir Robert was not dowered with genius at birth he undoubtedly developed a genius for leadership in a time of national emergency.

Sir Robert reached the apex of his career at Versailles. Practically on his own initiative he insisted that Canada must sign the peace treaty as a separate and distinct nation. In ringing tones he emphasized the magnitude of her contribution – 60,000 dead on foreign battlefields, more than 100,000 maimed and broken, a young country crippled with a colossal debt – surely she had paid the wages of nationhood and such a demand was but simple justice for valor and self-sacrifice. His eloquence overbore all opposition and amidst the gleaming mirrors of Versailles all the Dominions separately signed the great treaty and the British Commonwealth of Nations came into being.

These things are for the whole of Canada, but we in Ottawa have a special interest in this birthday. Sir Robert and his gracious life partner, 'to whom,' he has said, 'goes all the credit for any success I have attained,' are our fellow citizens, have been so for nearly 40 years. We, too, take pride in his long record, in his splendid leadership in days of peril, but perhaps we like to think of him best as our most eminent citizen, particularly in the 15 years since his 'retirement.'

Truly his has been a very busy and joyous type of superannuation. In these 15 years we see him active, as a man 30 years his junior, about the affairs of the League of Nations, crossing to Europe to attend its deliberations, delivering lectures at Oxford and other great universities, attending directors' meetings, innumerable social and public functions, as the well-loved guest of honor at veterans' banquets, writing his memoirs, delving into the early history of Canada, cultivating prize roses in the garden of his beautiful home on Sandy Hill, doing his daily mile and half from there to the centre of the city, writing to the press, backing all worthwhile community enterprises, bringing to all his contacts an old world courtesy, kindliness and modesty, qualities which would have made him outstanding if he had made no other contribution to society.

For these and many other reasons he is being tendered congratulations today. For him 'the shadows of evening may be lengthening, but there is morning still in his heart,' and all must wish that he may be long spared to enjoy the goodwill he has created and the golden sunset of a great career.

June 28, 1934

The Mail and Empire – Toronto

CANADA'S ELDER STATESMAN IS CONGRATULATED

'The days of our years are three score years and ten; And if by reason of strength they be four score years.' These words of the Psalmist are called to mind by the fact that Sir Robert Borden has just celebrated his eightieth birthday. It is surely by reason of strength – strength of body and mind and character – that he has entered his 81st year while still in the possession of as much vigor as that ordinarily enjoyed by much younger men.

He was fifty-seven years of age when he defeated the Reciprocity Treaty at the polls and established the Conservative party once more in power; sixty years of age when the outbreak of the world war imposed upon him that long series of heavy obligations which came with the conflict and the post-war period; in his 65th year when the war ended and he still retained adequate vigor to take a prominent part in the negotiations at Versailles and to uphold the cause of the Empire and of the Dominions in the peace treaty.

It is doubtful, moreover, if any other available man could have so effectively led Canada throughout the war. His greatest achievement was perhaps the formation of the Union Government, composed of Conservatives and Liberals, which unified the nation in support of the hard-pressed Canadian army at the front. His victory at the polls in the wartime election of 1917 proved an inspiration to our fighting men, and they played a major role during the last hundred days of battle, which broke the German lines and resulted in the Armistice and peace.

Since his retirement from the premiership in 1920, he has continued to be active in public affairs. He has taken a leading part in the work of the League of Nations at home and abroad; he has constantly lent the prestige of his name and personality to many good causes; on many occasions his experienced advice has been sought and obtained by his successors in office; and he is today universally respected as Canada's Elder Statesman *par excellence.*

As president of Barclays Bank in Canada and of the Crown Life Insurance Company, he is still a real factor in the financial affairs of the country. That he plays golf and daily walks a mile and a half to his office, where he is writing his memoirs, affords ample proof of his continued vigor. A lover of books, he spends much of his time in his fine private library, and he is ever welcome at dinners, where he shines as an accomplished raconteur. His old age is crowned by the love of innumerable friends and by the admiration of a nation.

June 26, 1934

The Montreal Gazette

SIR ROBERT BORDEN

The eightieth birthday of Sir Robert Borden is an event upon which the Dominion may congratulate itself and him. In the tranquility of retirement, occupied with his books and with his garden, Sir Robert looks from a position of serene detachment upon the crowding and fast-moving events, national and international, in which he was for so many years a dominant figure. Bearing lightly the honors which have been heaped upon him, the greatest of the elder statesmen and the first of Canada's citizens is physically strong at four score years and is intellectually no less alert than when, a quarter of a century ago, he was fighting the battles of Conservatism against a government holding what seemed to be an impregnable place, or when later, as Prime Minister, he guided the destinies of the Dominion through the critical and anxious years of the Great War and rose to eminence in the councils of the Empire. His name is to be found upon treaties and conventions involving the most momentous issues in world history, and it is honored everywhere.

In the imposing list of distinguished sons whom Nova Scotia has given to the public life of the Dominion, Sir Robert Borden stands easily first. Born at Grand Pré, in a region steeped in the traditions of the Acadians, Sir Robert has retained through his long career a profound and abiding love for the gentler things of life; but in the building up of a successful legal practice and afterward in the labor and stress of political warfare and in directing the energies of the nation in war and in peace, there was little leisure to indulge such inclinations as now lead him down the paths of his beautiful garden at Glensmere. Always an omnivorous reader, his books have been to him his closest friends and his fine library is today his favorite retreat, while, as president of Barclays Bank (Canada) Limited, and of the Crown Life Insurance Company, his business interests and activities are sufficient to maintain his contact with non-political affairs. But from politics, in which for twenty-five years he was a central figure, he keeps aloof, having richly earned the leisure which he enjoys. No man stands higher in the esteem and affection of his fellow-citizens, every one of whom will join today in the wish that he may be spared for many more years as one with whom time has dealt kindly and from whom age has exacted its minimum of tribute.

June 26, 1934

La Presse – Montreal

SIR ROBERT BORDEN

Le tres honorable sir Robert Borden célèbre aujourd'hui son quatre-vingtième anniversaire de naissance. L'ancien premier ministre du Canada aura reçu à cette occasion des félicitations et des souhaits auxquels nous désirons joindre les nôtres, formant surtout le vœu qu'il jouisse d'un état de santé qui lui permettra de poursuivre ses chers travaux personnels en même temps que de vaquer à ses affaires et de s'intéresser aux questions publiques.

Car, bien qu'il soit sorti de la politique depuis 1920, sir Robert n'a jamais cessé d'étudier nos problèmes nationaux et même, à maintes et maintes reprises, il s'est fait propagandiste de l'union canadienne, imitant l'exemple de sir Wilfrid Laurier, son adversaire au temps des luttes parlementaires d'autrefois, qu'il estimait profondément et avec qui il conserva toujours de cordiales relations, même lorsqu'il ne put partager ses idées.

S'il s'emploie ainsi à resserrer les liens qui unissent les provinces et les populations du Dominion, c'est que l'expérience qu'il a recueillie au cours de sa vie politique, dans la pratique des affaires et dans les milieux éducationnels où il eut souvent à paraître et à parler, a montré à sir Robert que notre jeune pays ne commencera réellement à progresser que du moment où les représentants des différentes nationalités chez nous auront décidé véritablement de travailler de concert. Et, pour notre part, nous ne voyons pas de plus belle mission pour un citoyen qui a occupé des postes éminents et exercé des fonctions importantes.

D'ailleurs, l'ancien premier ministre du Dominion paraît trouver dans les activités diverses auxquelles il se livre l'équilibre nécessaire à la conservation d'une bonne santé. Président de la Banque Barclay (Canada) et de la compagnie d'assurance 'Crown Life', toujours épris de littérature et d'histoire, ayant constamment un travail intellectuel sur le métier, il n'a pas le temps de s'occuper du passage des ans, ce qui est la meilleure condition où une personne arrivée à un âge avancé puisse désirer parvenir.

Remercions sir Robert de mettre au service de son pays et de ses concitoyens ses études et son expérience; il donne certes un bel exemple de patriotisme pratique. C'est, à n'en pas douter, grâce, pour une large part, à l'influence d'hommes publics ou l'ayant été, comme lui, que la population canadienne est restée calme et généreuse au sein de la crise économique qui s'achève. Avec tous ses amis et ses admirateurs, nous disons à sir Robert: santé et prospérité !

June 29, 1934

ONTARIO ELECTIONS – 1934

Sir,

Doubtless with great surprise you have observed the results of the Ontario elections, held on June 19.

All the conditions tended to the overthrow of the Henry government; yet it was thought that 'Old Man Ontario' would still prefer decency and security to froth and lack of policy. However, Mr Henry and his colleagues were not very skillful in their defence; and the notorious Mitchell Hepburn literally 'bellowed' himself into power.

Canadians, whether Liberals or Conservatives, have been justly proud of two great Ontario Liberal leaders, Edward Blake and Oliver Mowat. From these to Mitchell Hepburn is a terrible descent.

'Oh what a fall was there my countrymen.'

Hepburn's lack of dignity, and even common decency, might have been pardoned during his campaign but they persist ever since his success at the polls. His coarseness, his clownishness, his maladroit approach towards subjects which he obviously does not understand, stamp him as a man whose future career will be no credit either to himself or to the province.

Although he has sixty-five seats and the Conservatives only 17 in a house of 90, his immense following was elected by a minority of the total vote.

It seems singular that a man of Mr Mackenzie King's qualities should be inclined to associate himself so intimately with Mr Hepburn. Even those who disagree vehemently with Mr King's policies and who are most thankful that during these years of depression he was not invested with the reins of power, even these must admit that on practically every occasion he has borne himself with dignity. Why he should wish to associate himself with a clown like

Hepburn is a mystery, unless it is explainable by his intense desire to have the assistance of Hepburn at the federal elections.

It is possible that Hepburn may develop steadiness and sanity beyond all present expectation.

Herewith is a copy of a letter which I addressed recently to the proprietor of your valued contemporary the *Ottawa Journal.*

I remain, Sir, Yours in sympathy,

June 22, 1934

To P.D. Ross, Esquire
17, Blackburn Avenue
Ottawa

Personal

My dear Ross,

Having read with great interest the political editorials in the *Journal* both before and after the recent election in Ontario, may I be permitted to express my warm appreciation. In each case the utterances were cogent and admirable.

I greatly enjoyed your blast at Hepburn when you presided at a political meeting shortly before the election. It remains to be seen how far that gentleman is capable of reasonable and healthy development. His rather fantastic and somewhat clumsy utterances since the election do not seem to invest his future career with any great promise. If I were still in public life and had the duty of directing an attack against him, I should be inclined to advise the weapon of ridicule, not in the least malicious, but light-hearted and flavoured with a provoking humour. Hepburn will probably have poor defence against that form of attack.

His promises of reducing expenditure were of course absurd and could only be fulfilled if he were as economical of the public revenues as he was of truth during the campaign.

I greatly deplore the defeat of Charles McCrea to whom I have expressed my keen regret. In your comment upon such incidents you have laid your finger upon a vital weakness in democratic institutions.

But not infrequently, Demos is quick to take cognizance of its errors. About the best government that Nova Scotia ever had was defeated last year by 22–8 in a house of 30. The result was attributable to business depression, unemployment and the wild promises of men now in power. From many reliable quarters I am assured that if the Nova Scotia government went to the country tomorrow it would sustain an even more overwhelming defeat than was administered to its predecessor.

Pray do not trouble to acknowledge this letter,

With kindest regards, I remain, Yours faithfully,

Sir Robert had also attached to this Limbo letter the following editorial published in the newspaper *Jack Canuck* in Toronto on June 28, 1934.

THE PEOPLE'S VERDICT

In no undecided manner, the electors of the Province of Ontario have followed the slogan of Mitchell Hepburn, 'We need a change.' But, it is our earnest hope that the old adage will not be true in this case, that 'Changes are Lightsome, and Fools Like Them.'

Jack Canuck bows to the electors' verdict. The position taken by *Jack Canuck* in an open letter to readers two weeks ago was not based on any biased opinion for any political party, but was given, as a closely studied opinion that this was NOT "The Time for a Change." The next four or five years will answer this statement.

The will of the people has placed Mitchell F. Hepburn in the Premier's seat for the Province of Ontario. Whether Mitchell F. Hepburn will be able to measure up to the high standard set by his predecessors, rests with Mitchell F. Hepburn and the future.

His is a colossal task. Under any circumstances, the guiding of this province in a time such as this was colossal, but the Premier-elect has made it a much harder task for himself and his party by the many, varied, and extraordinary promises he made from the platform in the Province during his campaign.

Mitchell Hepburn has capabilities. No one can deny that after seriously studying the type of campaign he conducted. But, whether these capabilities could be construed as generally associated with statesmanship, solidity, or sincerity of purpose, we leave to the people of the Province to determine.

The Premier-elect has youth; that to some people is in his

favour. But, the advantage of youth may, or may not, offset the lack of political experience; the lack of big business executive experience; and certainly will not offset the extravagance of unweighed language, or the voicing of meaningless phrases, interspersed with catch-words, and Americanized slang. Maturity, however, may come with the seriousness of the problems which will daily beset the new Director of the Province's Destiny, and we sincerely trust that calm, sober reflection, after the jubilation has subsided, will formulate in the mind of this youthful aspirant to fill the shoes of a Mowat, or even a Laurier, with the colossal task which confronts him.

Jack Canuck will watch, with a great deal of interest, for such a metamorphosis, and will also watch closely, and check closely to see how near Mr. Hepburn will come to implement the extravagant promises he made from the hustings of Ontario.

Jack Canuck also asks its readers to check up Mr. Hepburn on these promises, and herewith appends only a few of what this paper considers the most extravagant of them all, and suggests that this may prove a very interesting competition by marking them up, as they are fulfilled.

Keep this list and check it for yourself:

Cut the administration costs by 50 per cent
Clean up the hydro
Clean out the surplus big men drawing large salaries in government departments
Dismissal of the minimum wage board
Clean out the commissions, such as the Workmen's Compensation Board, and 22 others
Give all Tory appointees, particularly the recently appointed employees, their walking ticket from Queen's Park
Clean out the Lands and Forests Departments
Dismiss the fire marshal and all his assistants, and make the Provincial police do the job
No member of the cabinet to hold directors' positions in any companies
Construction of the Trans-Canada Highway on a pay-as-you-go policy
Dismiss the Lieutenant-Governor
Cancellation of timber dues
Fumigation and auction sale of cabinet ministers' automobiles in front of the parliament buildings
Will ride to parliament buildings on a bicycle
Immediate employment of the unemployed, the money to be provided from the abolition of boards and commissions

Revenue from gasoline tax to be used only on maintenance of roads and highways
Reduction of taxation and debt by governmental economy
The providing of relief for the needy from Ontario government sources only
A better system of relief grants
Proclaim the new liquor law as brought in by the conservative party
Investigation into long hours, low wages, farmers' marketing problems, and child labour
Investigation of the alleged liquor toll gate, by Arthur Slaght at no cost to the tax-payers
That the liquor commission will be operated at a cost to the tax-payers not to exceed an outlay of $6,000 in salaries
No dismissals from the civil service
Elimination of the $1.50 fee for school children's examination papers
All highways' construction on a pay-as-you-go policy
Elimination of laboratory research departments, leaving this work to the federal government
Meeting the requests of catholic deputations for a share of municipal taxes for separate schools

At the outset of this article, we said this was a colossal programme. Now, we say it is stupendously colossal! Mitchell Hepburn, we wish you joy with this programme! And, to the people of Ontario we say, 'Wait and See!'

Sir Robert was a voracious reader and a great lover of poetry. The following Limbo letter was written after he had read a small volume of poems *A Dryad in Nanaimo* by Audrey Alexandra Brown.

He had an extraordinary memory and I have included as if it were a part of this letter (which it was not) a letter written by him to his secretary, Miss Kathleen Kearns, in the fall of 1936 together with a letter written to Mrs Hugh (Marie) Bullock in New York on November 13, 1936 and the *olla podrida* referred to in that letter.

Mrs Bullock is the wife of Mr Hugh Bullock KBE, head of the financial house of Calvin Bullock, Inc in New York and President of Canadian Investment Fund, Ltd, Canada's first mutual investment fund, of which Sir Robert was chairman from its inception in 1932 until his death in June, 1937. Mrs Bullock was the founder of the Academy of American Poets in 1934, the outstanding poetry organization in the United States, and has been its president for many years.

July 11, 1934

A DRYAD IN NANAIMO – OLLA PODRIDA

Sir,

Recently my attention has been directed to a volume of poems *A Dryad in Nanaimo,* by Audrey Alexandra Brown. I took the volume with me while journeying to Montreal two days ago and was delighted with all that I read, especially the poem that bears the name of the volume, and above all the poem, *Laodamia.*

I read *Laodamia* again that night; and once more on the following day; and I am still under the spell of its sheer beauty of thought and expression.

Attached hereto is an appreciation of the poems by my good friend and former colleague, Martin Burrell.

That this helpless crippled girl, who has not walked for five years, who has not stood on her feet for three years, who never was at school after she had attained the age of twelve, who was brought up under difficult conditions, sometimes verging on abject poverty, that this child should have written *Laodamia* is almost a miracle.

The theme is old but she has robed it anew in exquisite beauty. The alchemists of old sought unsuccessfully to transmute metals. This alchemist of Nanaimo transmutes words into jewels that glow through her pages.

The reluctance of resistless time most often, but not always, overbears fame that seems enduring. Over twenty centuries ago, the boast of a Roman poet, *Non omnis moriar,* was prophetic. Fifteen centuries later, a greater than Horace truly foretold his own eternal fame.

If the maturer years of this wonderful girl should fulfill the promise of *Laodamia,* her fame may also escape the oblivion which surely awaits names that today are household words. *Non omnis moriatur.*

I remain, Sir, Yours in sympathy,

OTTAWA JOURNAL

December 15, 1934

LITERATURE AND LIFE, A BOOKLOVER'S CORNER

Five months have passed since I wrote in this column an appreciation of Audrey Alexandra Brown's poetic work and spoke at some length of her character and circumstances. I was particularly glad when, some two months later, it was decided to republish her slender volume of poems, entitled *A Dryad in Nanaimo*, which saw the light three years ago, and to add to the new volume many poems written since that time.

The new book is before me. Macmillans have published it and the book in respect to binding and paper and type is one which reflects credit on Canadian enterprise. The gold-leaf 'jacket' is artistic and attractive and gives the little volume a most Christmassy look. Professor Pelham Edgar again writes the Introduction. Very aptly he remarks, in regard to the new poems, that 'here is wine from the same vineyard.' He observes that poetical historians of the future will be puzzled to account for the unusual qualities of Miss Brown's imagination. But can we account at any time, or under any circumstances, for the divine afflatus, that inspiration which, like the wind, bloweth where it listeth, nor can we tell whence it cometh?

Imagination, said Napoleon, rules the human race. It is the great quality assigned 'to elevate the more than reasoning mind, and colour life's dark cloud with orient rays.' For the poet it is the supreme gift. And upon this young, and physically afflicted, poetess of Nanaimo it has been conferred by the gods without stint. Keats, Spenser, Coleridge, Francis Thompson, and many other of our noblest singers were endowed in high measure with this great quality. And we must add Wordsworth to the list, though one is bound to say it sadly forsook him in some of his work.

That a wide knowledge of life in its multitudinous aspects is a good equipment for poets, as well as for other mortals, goes without saying. But knowledge without imagination is a poverty-stricken and dull thing. One may cite the case of that well-known Canadian poet, Duncan Campbell Scott. It will be remembered that his poem, 'The Piper of Arll,' so impressed John Masefield, the present Poet Laureate, that it was the means of turning his own mind to poetry as a vehicle of expression, and without his contributions to English verse that branch of English literature would be distinctly poorer.

And yet in the case of Scott's poem it was clearly imagination which was responsible. For this song of a ship of mystery, a tale filled with romance, redolent of the sea, was the creative work of one who had had little or no experience of ships or the sea. And so it is with Audrey Brown. True, she has lived by the sea and knows much of its beauty, its mystery, its power. But her somewhat cramped circumstances, her physical disabilities, and her lack of this world's goods, have prohibited contacts with many sides of life and nature. But books she has had, though none too many, and her reading has been reinforced by a powerful imagination and a poetic gift which has enabled her to transcribe in lovely verse everything that has floated through her mind. I was greatly impressed by this when reading her first volume, especially that noble poem, 'Laodamia,' which everybody will rejoice in seeing reprinted here.

The imaginative quality displayed in 'Laodamia' is shown by the fact that Audrey Brown wrote the last six stanzas first, and then gradually built up the whole story from such scant reading as she had done in the Greek classics, with the result that we have a poem of exceptional beauty and showing an absolute continuity of thought and narrative. The same genius is shown in 'The Wood of Circe,' which she sent to me in manuscript form. On reading it in this volume, I feel exactly as I did when I spoke of it so highly in my article last July. And here again imagination plays its powerful part, for she told me that a single line of that poem had rather haunted her mind, and it was in brooding on that line that she evolved the whole picture of the Sorceress, given to us here in such flawless beauty.

Imagination also is shown in the longest of her new poems, 'Nadya Cyrilovna in Paradise.' As she entered so finely into the Greek scene and atmosphere with 'The Wood of Circe,' and 'Laodamia,' so she here enters into that of the Russian. Something she must obviously have read of the history, of the tragedies, of the savage cruelties, of the nobilities, the profound pathos, in the character of those peoples in the North, but to picture these things in so moving and beautiful a form is to show gifts rare indeed. How tragically is here portrayed the wild grief of Nadya, as the mob, filled with blood-lust, murder those who are dearest to her. Her dazed brain senses the horrors:

Pulsings and drummings: the thick beat
Of eternal and unresting feet,
With a thunder of hooves that followed after,
And wild crying and crazed laughter.
Such sounds, such sounds, that when the street
Ached to a tread of soldiers' feet,
And I heard thin voices call
Out of a dream, below the wall, –
I woke, as from delirium wakes
A dying man when day breaks,
So spent, it is peace to yield his breath
And lay his head on the arm of Death.

And at last death meets Nadya, too, and with it come vision, and peace.

... I am laid to be healed
In the fair peace of field
And hill and pool and star.
I am laid where lilies are,
Laid to wait for Him
Here at Bethesda's rim.

When his foot passes,
I shall rise from the flowered grasses.
He will so shine on me
That my blind heart shall see:
He will speak, so clear
That my deaf heart shall hear.
– O break of immortal Spring!
He will speak, and answering,
My dumb heart shall sing!

I have sometimes wondered why Audrey Brown has not expressed herself in that time-honoured form of verse, the sonnet. Perhaps she yet will. Nor do I think she will fail in that comparatively small but greatly-ennobled corner of the poetic field. An arbitrary fixation of fourteen lines, with one dominant theme, to some singers might prove cramping. Yet the sonnet, so defined and limited, has proved to be for some writers 'not bonds, but wings.' Our own Archibald Lampman gave us some of his best work in that form. 'With this key Shakespeare unlocked his heart.' Wordsworth gave us many of his best poems in the sonnet. Indeed, it was Wordsworth who gave the sonnet so much of its popularity and acclaim.

Elizabeth Barrett Browning, who does not seem to be read much now, wrote, in her Portuguese sonnets, some of the best love-songs in the language. Nor let us forget that in Milton's hands the sonnet 'became a trumpet whence he blew soul-animating strains.' Of the moderns, Edna St. Vincent Millay chose this poetic form with fine effect, and unequal though her work may be, her best sonnets will never die. So I rather hope that the author of *A Dryad in Nanaimo* some day will turn to the sonnet and there achieve the distinction that she has attained in other poetic forms.

Through the fine offices of some friends, Audrey Brown is now in a Solarium for crippled children in far-off British Columbia. For a year she will undergo special treatment which will mean absolute rest. But she minds not, for there is before her the shining hope that she will be enabled eventually to walk once more. Through the kindness of those same friends she has had lately a complete change of environment, new contacts, fresh experiences, and I can well believe that all these things will find a flowering in her future work, and that even a greater enfranchisement of spirit will come in the after years.

What one is again and again struck with in her verse is its spontaneity. I am not unaware that concentrated thought often goes to the selection of the absolutely fit word or phrase. Indeed, we have an illustration in the case of Keats himself, who, in the famous 'Ode to the Nightingale,' changed his first rendering of certain lines to something more hauntingly beautiful. Yet much of his loveliest verse came as the inspiration of the moment, and some of it written with extraordinary rapidity. Similarly with this young poetess of the West. Some of the finest poems in her new volume were begun, she told me, in the afternoon and finished next morning. There may have been an alteration of a phrase or word here or there. But in the main the poem stood as first written. And as we consider the rhythmic beauty of the lines one is constrained to say, 'this is Genius.'

To accomplish such things means, of course, not only that the mind is saturated with beautiful thoughts and imagery, but that in long and continuous mental handling of that flexible and noble instrument, the English language, the word becomes the fit vehicle of the imagination. We have quite high authority for the truth that

> Many are the poets that are sown
> By Nature! men endowed with highest gifts –
> The vision, and the faculty divine –
> Yet wanting the accomplishment of verse.

And, conversely, there are those who have a certain facility in verse-making, but no vision, no faculty divine at the back of it. Alas, of such, real poets are not made. The desire to poetize is inherent in mankind, and doubtless there is a satisfaction in self-expression. Have we not all been bards at one time of our life or another? Some of my readers will recall the gentle irony of that delightful and whimsical parson, the Rev. Homer Wilbur, in connection with the poetic efforts of a young friend.

> When I was of your age, I also for a time mistook my desire to write verses for an authentic call of my nature in that direction. But one day as I was going forth for a walk, with my head full of an 'Elegy on the Death of Flirtilla,' and vainly groping after

> a rhyme for 'lily' that should not be 'silly' or 'chilly,' I saw my eldest boy busy over the rainwater hogshead, in that childish experiment at parthenogenesis, the changing a horse-hair into a water-snake. An immersion of six weeks showed no change in the obstinate filament. Here was a stroke of unintended sarcasm. Had I not been doing in my study precisely what my boy was doing out of doors? Had my thoughts any more chance of coming to life by being submerged in rhyme than his hair by soaking in water? I burned my elegy and took a course of 'Edwards on the Will.' People do not make poetry; it is made out of 'them' by a process for which I do not find myself fitted.

Some people are, as we know, congenitally incapable of writing poetry, some incapable even of reading it with any enjoyment. To the latter unfortunates we extend our compassion and must refrain from arguing the point. But, even though we are not possessed of a highly critical faculty, we are nearly all endowed with a mysterious quality which somehow enables us to sense the difference between great poetry and quite excellent versification. And there is a vital difference. 'Oh, the little more and how much it is! And the little less, and what worlds away!'

There are people who look for neither rhyme nor reason in poetry. There are, indeed, those who regard rhythm as a negligible quantity in poems, forgetting that rhythmic song and dance are linked up with the very evolution of poetry as we now understand the term. I would go farther and suggest that, even for the best prose, rhythm is an essential quality. That the modern followers of the Symbolists are making an impression on their generation which is likely to be permanent I greatly doubt. Nor can I believe that the vagaries of a Gertrude Stein, or of James Joyce in his latest manifestations, will influence more than a minute fraction of those whose conception of poetry is something vastly different to these windy and meaningless outpourings.

Most of us will turn with happy relief to the work of a new singer like Audrey Alexandra Brown, who believes that poetry is none the worse for having some intellectual basis, and whose fine imagination and loveliness of phrasing will delight those of us who still believe that Keats and Wordsworth, Milton and Spenser, were great exponents of this noblest of the arts. The temptation to quote at length from the poems in her recently-published book is strong. It seems impossible for her to write a single stanza without some touch of beauty in the phrase or thought.

I open the book at random. Here is a stanza descriptive of the bitter grief at the palace when Laodamia is brought the news of her husband's death on the sands before Troy.

And they lamented, and the hollow wall
Answered their weeping, and the palace heard;
The shadowy silence of the air was stirred
By fragile voices, like the dead who call
To unregarding ears beyond their grave –
Like the low wind, and like the long withdrawing wave.

She is no slave to traditional forms, and the occasional irregularities of the metre give an additional charm to her verse, as when at the close of that beautiful imaginative poem, 'The Mermaid,' we are told that the fisherman will never return 'to the glowing lamp and the hearth a-burn,'

He has forgotten human breath;
He has forgotten fear
And faith,
And joy
And sorrow,
And life
And death.

Each reader will doubtless have preferences for special poems in this little volume. I have found a deep pleasure in them all. I can well believe that, if her health is restored, this young Canadian poet of the distant West will climb even greater heights, and the music of her voice be listened to with delight by those as yet unborn. In closing, I find no words so appropriate as her own concluding lines in the last poem in the book, 'The Poet to His Verse.'

Flutter and fly, little song – flutter and fly!
They will bless me, folk who never have heard my name,
When they hear the trill of your music, sweet and high
    Out of a windless sky:
    Flutter and fly!

I have also attached to this Limbo letter an appreciation of Miss Brown by Sir Robert and by Thomas B. Roberton which appeared in the *Winnipeg Free Press* in January, 1935. ED.

121 JULY 11, 1934

AUDREY ALEXANDRA BROWN
AN APPRECIATION

By Sir Robert Borden

Audrey Alexandra Brown, daughter of an immigrant from the British Islands, was born early in the present century at Nanaimo, British Columbia. She was brought up in very straitened circumstances, left school at twelve, and had little opportunity for reading or education. She is a helpless cripple; she has not walked for seven years, nor stood for five years. Her brother, to whom she was devotedly attached, went overseas and was killed in France or Flanders.

Audrey is a rare spirit, brave, patient, tender, in whom there glows a spark of the divine fire. Three years ago she published a slender volume, *A Dryad in Nanaimo*. In the principal poem 'Laodamia,' she has invested an ancient theme with exquisite beauty of thought and expression. Her letters are as wonderful as her poems. A competent judge said to me: 'This girl has revived the lost art of letter-writing.'

A new edition of *A Dryad in Nanaimo* has just been published by Macmillans (Toronto). It contains additional poems and includes everything published in the first edition.

THE DRYAD OF NANAIMO

By T.B.R.

Tomorrow being the anniversary of Robert Burns, when devotees of the poet will gather together in numerous places to do honor to his immortal memory, and thereby celebrate the importance of that strange and rare human manifestation which is known as Poetry, we propose this year to give our piece about The Bard a somewhat different turn.

We will leave the unfortunate concocters of the "Toasts" severely alone, beyond wishing them good luck in their truly awful task. And we will leave Robbie alone, too, poor lad, not in any sense to neglect him, but in order to do something which he himself would have most heartily approved.

We will use up our space on this great poetic anniversary to draw public attention again to a poet who is living in the little town of Nanaimo, in Vancouver Island, British Columbia. A Canadian girl who ranks so high as a maker of poetry that if she had the recognition she deserves her fellow-countrymen would discover that they have in her a national figure, and one of the very finest things which Canada has produced since the country became a Confederation. This girl is Audrey Alexandra Brown, the second and enlarged edition of whose book of poems was issued about last Christmas, and seems to be thoroughly unknown to most of the booksellers in Winnipeg.

Audrey Brown is a genius. In a world which contains more writers than at any time in history, and many of them exceedingly good writers, too, she has something which not one in a million possesses. And, what is worse for them, never, no matter how hard they work and write, can possess. She has the gift which enables her to take ten words and put them together so that they make beauty. That is what Keats could do, and William Morris. Audrey Brown can do it, too. Out there in Nanaimo by the sea, unknown to most of the general population of Canada, and hardly a name to the harassed merchants who wrestle daily with the tons of books which fall – (such a good term) – from the presses of the publishers.

There is among those whom we have heard speak about Audrey Brown a tendency to hesitate about her. The impression is conveyed that she is a young person with a facility in rhyming and that this facility is a two-edged gift. Pelham Edgar, in the preface to the second edition of Audrey's poems, speaks of her poetic 'precocity and masterly but dangerous ease of utterance,' and while one knows what he means his appraisal is a little cautious.

Miss Brown has such an innate passion for colored words that she allows them sometimes to escape and flit about in her lines to the embarrassment occasionally of the reader who may feel a touch of impatience at being disturbed by the flutter of an intrusive wing however golden it may be. Audrey's pen is full of magic, and she loves it. Consequently there is an opulence of allusion in her lines that more penurious and pedestrian natures may find trying. But to say that her masterly ease of utterance is 'dangerous,' when this mastery of poetic form is her special gift, is as sensible as it would be to say that the ease with which Mr Weissmuller did the crawl stroke was dangerous to his progress as a swimmer. What we mean is, that Audrey Brown knows so much more about poetry than anybody else in Canada that it is dangerous – let us use the word properly, this time – to criticize her. She produces poems. And poems are things you take as you get them. We do not know of any poet whose lines seem always right; and we know plenty of poetic masterpieces which in some of their words or lines seem to stumble. But what does that matter? It may not be the poet, but we, who slip. And if the flaws really are flaws, there is nothing one can do about them. That, apparently, is how poetry comes.

Audrey Brown is not a simple girl who makes pretty rhymes that please her friends. She is of the choir celestial and she knows all about the literary technique of getting her poems into their appropriate metrical shapes. She is a literary virtuoso with a wide range of form, and an almost impeccable control of all the forms she uses.

She can write alternating rhymes which weave the verse on a warp-and-woof pattern; very difficult to do; becoming stiff and dead in journeyman hands, but in hers so spontaneous and telling that you forget to note the workmanship. She can write perfect two-line and three-line rhymed verses, and she can swing the powerful multi-syllable line with ringing fervor on patriotic themes.

All this implies study as well as natural ability, and suggests that her 'dangerous ease of utterance' has been acquired by good hard work at the craft of writing, and that her 'ease of expression,' consequently, is no mere loose verbal fluency, but is controlled writing directed to preconceived effects in which the poetic thought is given in carefully premeditated words.

Miss Brown's words, instinct with music, and glowing with color, may have diverted attention from the fact that she is, like Keats himself, a profound thinker about the environment and circumstances – called life and nature – in which she moves and of which she is part. The poems are all expressions of a supersensitive mind on phases of human emotion and feeling. Her models, perhaps, are not original. A Greek legend: the mermaid who lures the fisher-lad to the world under the sea; the hunter who falls in love with the dead swan; – the limitations in such themes are obvious; but not to Audrey Brown. Once again the ancient sorrows inspire the authentic music of immortality; the heart is touched and the pang of resignation induced by the poet's words is the deepest and purest experience which the mind can feel.

'And in that twilight world, whose floodless sea
Washes the margin of a silent land,
We shall not walk alone, but hand in hand,
And Love shall warm our immortality
With an eternal spring; since even death
Cannot dispart our souls, nor chill our mingled breath.'

Audrey Alexandra Brown is a great poet. Tomorrow the world is celebrating a rhymster who is one of the gods of song. An appropriate date surely, to direct attention to the Canadian girl who, unnoticed almost, is making her beautiful melodies in far-away Nanaimo, and who should be warmed and heartened by timely appreciation from her own people.

There will be monuments to her some day, that is certain. But in the meantime the thing to do is to buy her book of poems, and put the laurels on her now, while they may do her some good.

November 13, 1936

My dear Marie,

Your delightful letter reached me a few days ago in the midst of many engagements and preoccupations. By an early post I shall send you the *olla podrida*[20] for which I beg your forgiveness. My Secretary, Miss Kearns, took it with her to New York but under strict injunction that it should not be delivered except with an explanation which she was unable to give on account of your absence. She was to tell you that I was (and am) guiltily conscious that it was not at all what you desired; and that you were to be perfectly frank as to whether you desired to have this medley.

Since dictating it, further memories from time to time have crowded upon me but not all have been added.

I do indeed hope you will send what you call 'some dreadful thing of mine.'

Fleur is at a most interesting age; and I am delighted to know that she is making such rapid progress in speech and in locomotion. It will be a great pleasure to see her when next we have the opportunity of passing through New York.

My wife has had a most tiresome, but not serious, illness from which she has now definitely emerged, although she has not fully regained her accustomed health and strength.

Audrey Alexandra Brown has become almost, if not quite, self-sustaining through her contributions (chiefly prose) to the press. She has the entrée to several of our leading newspapers and is making a brave, and I think, successful attempt to support herself. But she has friends in the East who, from time to time, give assistance as it is required for her needs. Recently I had from her a most delightful

20 A Spanish phrase meaning a dish composed of different sorts of meat and vegetables boiled together.

letter, copy of which I enclose, as well as copy of a recent poem published in Toronto *Saturday Night*.

Laura joins me in love and all good wishes and in kindest regards to Hugh; and I remain, my dear Marie,

Yours affectionately,

Miss Kathleen Kearns
c/o Mrs G.V. Kearns
1973 Batchelder Street
Brooklyn, NY, USA

Dear Miss Kearns,

Doubtless you recall my reminiscent efforts when I was anxious to assist Mrs Hugh Bullock in any available way by suggesting material for her proposed anthology. I am guiltily conscious that this is not in the least what she desired; but, having strayed forth on this by-path, I found myself unable to stop. You may remember the story of the member of the Legislature of Quebec who, during the last hour of a very lengthy speech, became quite incoherent. When asked by his colleagues why he had made such a fool of himself and why he had not stopped earlier, he replied: 'I tried a great many times to stop, but I couldn't.'

In practically every case, as you know, the passages enumerated had lingered either fully, or in part, in my memory; and from time to time as fresh recollections arose, the list and the references were extended.

As to setting forth my favourite quotation, I should not like to undertake it, because I am sure that I should repent of any selection that I might put forward.

If Mrs Bullock should return to New York during your stay, please communicate with her and tell her what sort of medley has been prepared and typewritten. It may be that she will be curious to see it, even if fully aware that for her purpose it is entirely useless and futile. Please do not deliver it to her, unless you are quite satisfied that she really desires to have it. And, in presenting it (in case you should do so) pray present also my humble apologies.

I remain, Yours faithfully,

OLLA PODRIDA

EXTRACTS FROM SHAKESPEARE'S SONNETS

His belief in the immortality of his poems

Sonnet LV
Not marble, nor the gilded monuments
Of princes, shall outlive this powerful rime;
...
Nor Mar's his sword nor war's quick fire shall burn
The living record of your memory.

Sonnet LXIII
...
For such a time do I now fortify
Against confounding age's cruel knife,
That he shall never cut from memory
My sweet love's beauty, though my lover's life:
His beauty shall in these black lines be seen,
And they shall live, and he in them still green.

Sonnet LXXXI
...
From hence your memory death cannot take,
...
Your name from hence immortal life shall have,
Though I, once gone, to all the world must die;
The earth can yield me but a common grave,
When you entombed in men's eyes shall lie.
Your monument shall be my gentle verse,
Which eyes not yet created shall o'er read;
And tongues to be your being shall rehearse,
When all the breathers of this world are dead;
You still shall live – such virtue hath my pen –
Where breath most breathes, even in the mouths of men.

Sonnet CI
O truant Muse, what shall be thy amends
...
Excuse not silence so: for't lies in thee
To make him much outlive a gilded tomb,
And to be praised of ages yet to be.
Then do thy office, Muse; I teach thee how
To make him seem long hence as he shows now.

Sonnet CVII

...

Now with the drops of this most balmy time
My love looks fresh, and Death to me subscribes,
Since, spite of him, I'll live in this poor rime,
While he insults o'er dull and speechless tribes:
And thou in this shalt find thy monument,
When tyrants' crests and tombs of brass are spent.

Sonnet CXXIII

No, Time, thou shalt not boast that I do change:

...

Thy registers and thee I both defy,
Not wondering at the present nor the past,
For thy records and what we see doth lie,
Made more or less by thy continual haste.
This I do vow, and this shall ever be,
I will be true, despite thy scythe and thee.

CASUAL REMINISCENCES OF POESY

English Bible and Shakespeare

Psalms

19:1–14	The heavens declare the glory of God
23:1–6	The Lord is my Shepherd

Ecclesiastes

12:1–8	Remember now thy Creator

Paul, First Epistle to the Corinthians

15:51–8	(In form prose; in truth a poem)

Hamlet

3.1.56–89	To be, or not to be
1.3.55–80	Yet here, Laertes!
3.1.158–69	O, what a noble mind

King Lear

5.3.270–3	I might have saved her
5.3.305–11	And my poor fool
5.3 BEGIN	Vex not his ghost
END	Stretch him out longer

Macbeth	
5.5 BEGIN	Tomorrow, and tomorrow and tomorrow
END	Full of sound and fury, signifying nothing.
2.2 BEGIN	Sleep that knits up the ravell'd sleave of care
END	Chief nourisher in life's feast.
Othello	
1.3.76–128	Othello's speech
5.2 BEGIN	I pray you, in your letters
END	And smote him, thus.
The Tempest	
4.1 BEGIN	The cloud-capped towers
END	And our little lives are rounded with a sleep.
Merchant of Venice	
4.1 BEGIN	The quality of mercy
END	When mercy seasons justice.
5.1 BEGIN	How sweet the moonlight sleeps upon this bank
END	Doth grossly close us in we cannot hear it.
Romeo and Juliet	
4.5 BEGIN	It was the lark, the herald of the morn
END	I must be gone and live, or stay and die.
Midsummer Night's Dream	
5.1 BEGIN	The poet's eye in a fine frenzy rolling
END	A local habitation and a name.
Julius Caesar	
3.2 BEGIN	I come to bury Caesar
4.3 BEGIN	There is a tide in the affairs of men
END	Is bound in shallows and in miseries.

Scores of other exquisite passages come to one's mind, such as:

Under the Greenwood Tree
Blow, Blow, thou Wintry Wind
I know a bank

Also: See list of quotations attached.

Foreign Poetry

Horace: *Carmen 30. Liber 3*
Exegi monumentum aere perennius,

Regalique situ pyramidum altius;
Quod non imber edax, non Aquilo impotens
Possit diruere, aut innumerabilis
Annorum series et fuga temporum.
Non omnis moriar multaque pars mei
Vitabit Libitinam usque ego postera
Crescam laude recens, dum Capitolium
Scandet cum tacita Virgine pontifex.

Carmen 2, Liber 1
Integer vitae scelerisque purus

Liber 1, Satire 9
Liber 2, Satire 8

Homer: A beautiful line from Homer:
'Aigle pamphanoosa di'aitheros curanon ike'

Translation by Oliver Wendell Holmes:
'Splendour far shining through ether to heaven ascended.'

Goethe: 1 *Wilhelm Meister*, Book 2, Chap. 13
Wer nie sein Brot mit Thränen ass
Wer nie die kummervollen Nächte
Auf seinem Bette weinend sass,
Der kennt euch nicht, ihr himmlischen Mächte.

Translation by Sir Robert Borden:
Who never ate with tears his bread,
Who never through night's care-racked hours
Has wept in sadness by his bed,
He knows you not, ye Heavenly Powers.

2 Kennst du das Land
3 Der König in Thule

Schiller: *Der Taucher*
Die Erwartung
Des Mädchens Klage (NOTE: See Bulwer Lytton's translations)

Arnault: *La Feuille*

Beranger:	*Le Roi D'Yvetot*
L'Attaignant:	*J'Ai Du Bon Tabac Dans Ma Tabatière*
Berenger:	*Combien j'ai douce souvenance ?*
A. Monod:	*Le Bonheur Du Chretien.*
Maeterlinck:	Et si'il revenait un jour que faut-il lui dire ?
	Beautifully translated into English: And if he should yet return what shall I then say? A translation (quoted by Lord Morley in his *Recollections*) from one of the minor Greek poets. I hold him happiest Who, before going quickly whence he came, Hath looked ungrieving on these majesties, The world-wide Sun, the stars, water and clouds And fire. Live, Parmeno, a hundred years, Or a few weeks, these thou wilt always see, And never, never any greater things.
(Hymnus in Nativitate Christi)	*Adeste, fideles.*
(By Jacobi Tudertis)	*Stabat mater*
(Magnentii Hrabani Mauri)	*Veni, Creator Spiritus*
(Regis Roberti (?))	*Veni Sancte Spiritus*
(Thomae De Celano)	*Dies Irae*

Miscellaneous

Aldrich, Thomas Bailey	Palabras Carinosas BEGIN: Good-Night! I have to say good-night To such a host of peerless things!
Anon.	Helen of Kirconnell
Arnold, Matthew	The Better Part

Arkwright	O Valiant Hearts
Brooke, Rupert	The Soldier The Dead
Burns, Robert	Highland Mary For A'That and A'That The Cottar's Saturday Night Ae Fond Kiss Auld Lang Syne
Brown, Audrey Alexandra	Laodamia (Extracts to be selected) The Browns The Halcyon To Bethlehem
Browning, Robert	Pippa Passes Home Thoughts from Abroad
Brown, T.E.	My Garden
Byron, Lord	Waterloo Isles of Greece She Walks in Beauty
Bunyan, John	The Shepherd Boy Sings in the Valley of Humiliation
Bryant, William Cullen	Thanatopsis
Buchanan, Robert	Selene the Moon
Buchan, John	Fisher Jamie
Blake, William	Reeds of Innocence
Bridges, Robert	Difficult to make a selection; but 2 stanzas (lines 39–51) on page 133, 'The Testament of Beauty' (Clarendon Press 1929) are very beautiful.
Carman, Bliss	Low Tide at Grand Pré November Twilight Marian Drury End of the Trail Before the Snow Wild Geese Prayer of the Archangel

Coleridge, Samuel	The Rime of the Ancient Mariner Page 638 (Oxford Book of English Verse) Part V, first 4 lines: Page 641, lines 7–10; Page 635: 'Till clomb above the eastern bar 'The hornéd Moon, with one bright star 'Within the nether tip.' Hymn to Sunrise at Chaumoni
Craik, Diana Mulock	Too Late Philip My King
Carey, Henry	Sally in Our Alley
Cunningham, Allan	Hame, Hame, Hame
Collins, William	How Sleep the Brave
Campbell, Thomas	Ye Mariners of England Hohenlinden
Cornwall, Barry	The Oak
Cowper, William	John Gilpin
Pickthall, Marjorie	A Wood-Carver's Wife, Selections from a very beautiful poem
Miller, Joaquin	Columbus
Housman, A.E.	The Shropshire Lad (Selections) Last Poems (Selections) 31, 33, 38

The following is a poem that I cannot locate at the moment. The first stanza is probably incorrect; it is set down from memory.

There's a breathless hush in the close to-night –
Ten to make and the game to win!
A bumping pitch and a blinding light,
An hour to play and the last man in.
And it's not for the sake of a braided coat,
Or the selfish thought of a season's fame,
But the captain's hand on his shoulder smote –
Play up, play up, play up the game.

The sand of the desert is sodden red,
Red with the wreck of a square that broke;
The gatling's jammed, the Colonel's dead;
And the regiment's blind with dust and smoke.

The river of death has brimmed its banks;
England is far; and honour a name;
But the voice of a school-boy rallies the ranks,
Play up, play up, play up the game.

This is the word that year by year,
While in her place the school is set,
Everyone of her sons must hear,
And none that hears it dare forget.
This they all with a joyous (quiet?) mind
Bear through life, like a torch in flame;
And, falling, fling to the ranks behind,
Play up, play up, play up the game.

This poem which is quoted by Sir Robert from memory with only one or two minor errors is by Sir Henry Newbolt and entitled 'Vitai Lampada.' ED.

De Vere, Aubrey	Sorrow
Emerson, Ralph Waldo	Brahma
English, Thomas Dunn	Ben Bolt
Field, Eugene	Little Boy Blue
Finch, Francis Miles	The Blue and The Gray
Foster, Stephen C.	My Old Kentucky Home Old Folks at Home
Gray, Thomas	Elegy Written in a Country Churchyard
Goldsmith, Oliver	Selections from Deserted Village
Harte, Bret	Dickens in Camp Plain Language from Truthful James Jim The Society upon the Stanislaus
Hay, John	Jim Bludsoe
Henley, W.E.	Unconquerable
Howe, Joseph	The Indian Names of Acadia
Hood, Thomas	The Bridge of Sighs

Holmes, Oliver Wendell	The Deacon's Masterpiece Dorothy Q The Chambered Nautilus Not bedtime yet
Howe, Julia Ward	Battle Hymn of the Republic
Hemans, Mrs	Lady of Provence
Herrick, Robert	To Julia
Herbert, George	Virtue
Johnson, Ben	To Celia
Kilmer, Joyce	Rouge Bouquet
Keats, John	Ode to a Nightingale Ode on a Grecian Urn St Agnes' Eve
Kipling, Rudyard	Recessional L'Envoie Gunga Din The Ballad of East and West The English Flag We have fed our sea for a thousand years
Lindsay, Lady Anne	Auld Robin Gray
Longfellow, Henry W.	Selections from Evangeline The Old Clock on the Stairs Hymn to the Night
Lowell, James Russell	The Courtin Blessing is She
Lampman, Archibald	Alcyone A Vision of Twilight A Spanish Taunt
Lytton, Bulwer	The Wife of Miletus
Lorne, Marquis of	Unto the Hills
Massey, Gerald	Babe Christobel
Menzies, G.K.	Poaching in England
MacDonald, George	Song (from Wilfrid Cumbermede) I dreamed that I woke from a dream.

McCrae, Col. John	In Flanders Fields
Mahony, Francis	The Bells of Shandon
Moore, Thomas	The Light of Other Days
Magnan, J.C.	Dark Rosaleen
Mickle, Wm. J.	There's nae luck about the house
Macaulay, Thomas	Lays of Ancient Rome
Babington	Invincible Armada Naseby Ivry
Masefield, John	West Wind Vision
Milton, John	On Shakespeare On His Blindness Hymn on the Nativity Lap me in soft Lydian airs, Married to immortal verse Such as the meeting soul may pierce In notes, with many a winding bout Of linked sweetness long drawn out.
Newbolt, Sir Henry	Drake's Drum.
Newman, John Henry	Lead Kindly Light.
O'Neill, Moira	A Grace for Light Corrymeela
Pagan, Isobel	Ca' The Yowes to the Knowes
Pope, Alexander	The Dying Christian to his Soul.
Phillips, Stephen	Herod Marpessa
Poe, Edgar Allan	The Raven The Balls
Proctor, Adelaide	Hush A Woman's question.
Rosetti, Dante Gabriel	The Blessed Damozel
Rosetti, Christina	When I am Dead

Rogers, Samuel	Genevra
Robinson, Edw. Arlington	Flammonde
Roberts, Charles G.D.	Blomidon O Solitary of the Austere Sky The Tide on Tantramar Street Song at Night (New York Nocturnes) Canada Brooklyn Bridge
Stevenson, Robert Louis	The Descending Star Not Yet, My Soul, These Friendly Fields Desert.
Scott, Duncan Campbell	Blackbird Rhapsody Autumn Evening Evening at Ravelle
Shelley, Percy Bysshe	To a Skylark Hymn to Pan Rarely, Rarely comest thou To Night
Swinburne, Algernon Charles	Chorus from Atalanta
Stephens, James	In the Poppy Field
Taylor, Bayard	Bedoin Song
Trowbridge, John Townsend	The Vagabonds
Thackeray, Wm. Makepeace	White Squall The Ballad of Bouillabaisse
Thompson, Francis	Hound of Heaven In No Strange Land (Extract from In No Strange Land) The Angels keep their ancient places; – Turn but a stone, and start a wing ! Tis ye, Tis your estranged faces, That miss the many-splendoured thing. But (when so sad thou canst not sadder)

	Cry; – and upon thy so sore loss Shall shine the traffic of Jacob's ladder Pitched betwixt Heaven and Charing Cross.
Tennyson, Lord	Lady of Shalott Tears, idle tears Crossing the Bar Break, Break, Break Selections from In Memoriam
Twain, Mark	Epitaph
Vaughan, Henry	The World
Wither, Henry	The Hardy Lover
Wordsworth, William	Ode on Intimations of Immortality from Recollections of Early Childhood She was a Phantom of Delight Milton The world is Too Much With Us. We Must be Free or Die.
Whittier, John Greenleaf	Maud Muller Barbara Frietchie
Yeats, W.B.	The Song of Wandering Aengus
Omar Khayyam	The Rubaiyat: Verses 7, 12, 15–17, 19, 20, 21, 24, 27, 28, 31–36, 40–41, 71, 100, 101

Extract from 'Herod', by Stephen Phillips

HEROD
And he shall charm and soothe, and breathe and bless,
The roaring of war shall cease upon the air,
Falling of tears and all the voices of sorrow,
And he shall take the terror from the grave.

GADIA
The malady is too old and too long rooted,
The earth ailed from the first; war, pestilence,
Madness and death are not as ills that she
Contracted, but are in her bones and blood.

HEROD
And he shall still that old sob of the sea,
And heal the unhappy fancies of the wind,
And turn the moon from all that hopeless quest
Trees without care shall blossom, and all the fields
Shall without labour unto harvest come.

Extract from 'Marpessa', by Stephen Phillips

And though the first sweet sting of love be past,
The sweet that almost venom is; though youth,
With tender and extravagant delight,
The first and secret kiss by twilight hedge,
The insane farewell repeated o'er and o'er,
Pass off; there shall succeed a faithful peace;
Beautiful friendship tried by sun and wind,
Durable from the daily dust of life.
And though with sadder, still with kinder eyes,
We shall behold all frailties, we shall haste
To pardon, and with mellowing minds to bless,
Then though we must grow old, we shall grow old
Together ...

Extracts from Tennyson's 'In Memoriam'

BEGIN
...
And shall he
Man, her last work, who seem'd so fair,
Such splendid purpose in his eyes,
Who roll'd the psalm to wintry skies,
Who built him fanes of fruitless prayer,

END
O life as futile then, as frail!
O for thy voice to soothe and bless!
What hope of answer or redress?
Behind the veil, behind the veil.

BEGIN
And suck'd from out the distant gloom
A breeze began to tremble o'er
The large leaves of the sycamore,
And fluctuate all the still perfume,

And gathering freshlier overhead,
Rock'd the full-foliaged elms, and swung
The heavy-folded rose, and flung
The lilies to and fro, and said

END
'The dawn, the Dawn', and died away
And East and West, without a breath,
Mixt their dim lights like life and death,
To broaden into boundless day.

Epitaph

By Mark Twain (Quoted from memory)

Glad summer sun, shine kindly here;
Soft southern breeze, blow gently here;
Green sod above, lie light, lie light,
Good-night dear heart, good-night, good-night

Further Quotations from Shakespeare

This royal throne of kings, this scepter'd isle,
This earth of majesty, this seat of Mars,
This other Eden, demi-paradise,
This fortress built by nature for herself
Against infection and the hand of war;
This happy breed of men, this little world,
This precious stone set in the silver sea.
Richard III, 2.1

O England! model to thy inward greatness,
Like little body with a mighty heart,
What might'st thou do, that honour would thee do,
Were all thy children kind and natural!
Henry V, 2

Let never day nor night unhallow'd pass,
But still remember what the Lord hath done.
Henry VI, Part 2, 2.1

Love all, trust a few,
Do wrong to none; be able for thine enemy
Rather in power than use.
All's Well that End's Well, 1.1

Good name in man and woman, dear my lord,
Is the immediate jewel of their souls;
Who steals my purse steals trash; 'tis something, nothing;
Twas mine, 'tis his, and has been slave to thousands;
But he that filches from me my good name
Robs me of that which not enriches him
And makes me poor indeed.
Othello, 3.3

To Thee I do commend my watchful soul
Ere I let fall the windows of my eyes;
Sleeping and waking, O, defend me still.
Richard III, 5.3

The man that hath not music in himself
Nor is not moved by concord of sweet sounds
Is fit for treasons, stratagems and spoils
The motions of his spirit are dull as night
And his affections dark as Erebus.
Let no such man be trusted; Mark the music!
How many things by season season'd are
To their right praise and true perfection.
Merchant of Venice, 5.1

Wilt thou have music? Hark! Apollo plays
And twenty caged nightingales do sing.
Taming of the Shrew, 1.2

Our indiscretion sometimes serves us well
When our deep plots do quail.
Hamlet, 5.2

Ingratitude, more strong than traitor's arms,
Quite vanquished him; then burst his mighty heart;
Julius Caesar, 3.2

Oftimes excusing of a fault
Doth make the fault the worse by the excuse.
King John, 4.2

When love speaks, the voice of all the gods
Makes heaven drowsy with the harmony.
Love's Labour Lost, 4.3

If our virtues did not forth of us t'were all alike
As if we had them not.
Measure for Measure, 1.1

True hope is swift and flies with swallow's wings:
Kings it makes gods and meaner creatures kings.
King Richard III, 5.2

Ay me! for aught that I could ever read,
Could ever hear by tale or history,
The course of true love never did run smooth.
Midsummer Night's Dream, 1.1

O, how full of briars is this working-day world!
As You Like It, 1.3

Man, proud Man,
Drest in a little brief authority,
...
Plays such fantastic tricks before high heaven
As make the angels weep.
Measure for Measure, 2.2

And this our life, exempt from public haunt,
Finds tongues in trees, books in the running brooks,
Sermons in stones, and good in everything.
As You Like It, 2.1

Sweet are the uses of adversity;
Which, like the toad, ugly and venomous,
Wears yet a precious jewel in his head.
As You Like It, 2.1

Thrice is he armed that hath his quarrel just,
And he but naked, though lock'd up in steel
Whose conscience with injustice is corrupted.
Henry VI, 2

Now God be praised that to believing souls
Gives light in darkness, comfort in despair.
Henry VI, 2

Men at some time are master of their fates.
Julius Caesar

If it be a sin to covet honour,
I am the most offending soul alive
Henry v, 4.3

The best wishes that can be forged in your thoughts
be servants to you
All's Well That Ends Well

Truth is truth to the end of reckoning
Measure for Measure, 5.1

Take the instant way;
For honour travels in a strait so narrow
Where one but goes abreast.
Troilus and Cressida, 3.3

Wise men never sit and wail their woes
But presently prevent the ways to wail
King Richard II

Use every man ... after your own comfort
and dignity; the less they deserve the more
merit is in your bounty.
Hamlet

O, while you live, tell truth
and shame the devil.
King Henry IV

O Lord, that lends me life,
Lend me a heart replete with thankfulness.
King Henry VI, 2

Farewell, a long farewell to all my greatness
End: Never to hope again.
Henry VIII

Joseph Howe

The Indian Names of Acadia

The memory of the Red Man
How can it pass away,

While their names of music linger
On each mount, and stream, and bay?
While Musquodoboit's waters
Roll sparking to the main;
While falls the laughing sunbeam
On Chegogin's fields of grain.

While floats our country's banner
O'er Chebucto's glorious wave;
And the frowning cliffs of Scatarie
The trembling surges brave;
While breezy Aspotogon
Lifts high its summit blue,
And sparkles on its winding way
The gentle Sissibou.

While Escasoni's fountains
Pour down their crystal tide;
While Ingonish's mountains
Lift high their forms of pride;
Or while on Mabou's river
The boatman plies his oar,
Or the billows burst in thunder
On Chickaben's rock-girt shore.

The memory of the Red Man,
It lingers like a spell
On many a storm-swept headland,
On many a leafy dell;
Where Tusket's thousand islets
Like emeralds stud the deep;
Where Blomidon, a sentry grim,
His endless watch doth keep.

It dwells around Catalone's blue lake,
Mid leafy forests hid –
Round fair Discouse, and the rushing tides
of the turbid Pisiquid.
And it lends, Chebogue, a touching grace,
To thy softly flowing river,
As we sadly think of the gentle race
That has passed away forever.

De Mille, James

Sweet Maiden of Quoddy

Sweet Maiden of Passamaquoddy,
Shall we seek for communion of souls
Where the deep Mississippi meanders
Or the distant Saskatchewan rolls?
Ah, no in New Brunswick we'll find it –
A sweetly sequestrated nook –
Where the swift gliding Skoodoowabskooksis
Unites with the Skoodoowabskook.

Meduxnakik's waters are bluer;
Nepisquit's pools are more black;
More green is the bright Cromocto,
and browner the Petitcodiac;
But colors made radiant in autumn,
I see when I'm casting my hook
In the waves of the Skoodoowabskooksis
Or perhaps in the Skoodoowabskook.

Let others sing loudly of Saco
Of Passadumkeag or Miscouche,
Of Kennebeccasis or Quaco,
Or Miramichi or Buctouche;
Or boast of the Tobique or Mispec,
The Musquash or dark Memramcook;
There's none like the Skoodoowabskooksis
Excepting the Skoodoowabskook.

Think not, though the Ma-ga-gua-da-vic,
or Bocabec, pleases the eye;
Though Chi-put-nec-ti-cook is lovely
That to either of these we'll fly.
No! when in love's union we're plighted
We'll build our log house by a brook
Which flows to the Skoodoowabskooksis
Where it joins with the Skoodoowabskook.

Then never of Waweig or Chamcook
I'll think, having you in my arms;
We'll reck not of Digdeguash beauties,
We'll care not for Popelogan's charms;

But as emblems of union forever,
Upon two lovely rivers we'll look;
While you'll be the Skoodoowabskooksis
I'll be the Skoodoowabskook.

August 2, 1934

A MEMOIR – TOM BLACKLOCK

Sir,

Today, I heard the sad tidings that a dear friend whom I had known for many years had passed beyond the veil.

I first met Tom Blacklock in 1907, while engaged in a political tour of the prairie provinces. At Weyburn I asked him to give me his estimate of the outlook of immigrants from United States who had settled in large numbers around that district. 'Have they a Canadian spirit? Do they regard themselves as true Canadian citizens? Are they interested in our public affairs?' Tom Blacklock's reply was characteristic. 'Among these men who have been in Canada not more than two or three years, there are those who already are giving lessons in patriotism to native-born Canadians.' From many communities in southern Saskatchewan they came in large numbers to my meetings and I concurred in Blacklock's estimate.

Later, Tom Blacklock came east; and for many years before his death he lived in Ottawa. He was always most loyal and most sincerely attached to me during my leadership of the Liberal-Conservative party. From time to time, after my retirement, I discussed with him political conditions.

In one of the campaigns when Mr Meighen and Mr King were rival leaders, they engaged in long-range verbal hostilities that were rather ineffective on both sides. Blacklock became impatient and wrote to Meighen a letter which Tom afterwards showed to me. It was keenly critical of the course Meighen was pursuing; and I recall one phrase which ran somewhat like this: 'Please bear in mind that the people of Canada are not in the least interested in your opinion of Mr King or in Mr King's opinion of you.' Meighen took the letter in very good part; and showed it to several of his friends.

Tom's thorough loyalty to Meighen was indicated in a later campaign when the *Montreal Gazette* was quietly hostile to Meighen's leadership. As correspondent for the *Gazette*, Tom attended

Meighen's meetings and sent reports that, from the standpoint of the *Gazette*, were unduly favourable to Meighen. He was admonished but declined to adapt himself to the *Gazette's* standard, and was dismissed when he could ill afford the consequent loss of income.

In contrast to this, he was treated with fine consideration and generosity by Senator Dennis of *The Halifax Herald*.

... His was a rare spirit; and his memory will not pass from the hearts of those who knew him best.

I remain, Sir, Yours in sympathy,

August 13, 1934

INTERVIEW WITH PRIME MINISTER – BUSINESS CONDITIONS IN UNITED STATES

Sir,

Today I had an interesting interview of half an hour with the Prime Minister; and afterwards I lunched with him. He was in good spirits but rather shrank from his proposed visit to Geneva, as he believes that little or nothing will be accomplished. Evidently he is very weary and I am convinced of his strong desire to be rid of his political responsibilities. For this he might welcome defeat. But in that case, it might be difficult to retire with honour from a position of such transcendent importance.

During the past four years he has devoted himself with all his strength and energy to the affairs of our country in this terrible period of anxiety and difficulty. This was quite right, as no consideration of party interest should have interfered with his supreme task.

Yet, he is not only Prime Minister but leader of his party; and there are other considerations to be taken into account. A leader is the trustee of the policies and the welfare of his party. Persistent neglect of organization must lead to ultimate defeat and it is dereliction of duty to follow a course leading inevitably to disaster. In this respect Bennett incurs strong criticism and censure not only from his party but even from some of his most important colleagues.

Some of Bennett's colleagues impute to him lack of sense of proportion, vacillation, a tendency to waste time and to postpone decisions, failure to consult them on matters of utmost importance, extreme discourtesy on occasion, lack of self-control, temperamental outbursts tending to sap their loyalty.

On the other hand, they agree on his high courage, his remarkable ability, his amazing energy, his tireless industry. They acknowledge that on occasions of supreme moment he has shown himself skillful and masterful, dominating the situation to the undoubted and lasting advantage of our country's welfare. And they concede his kindliness of heart and his generous instincts. However, they believe that his neglect to direct or to authorize effective or indeed any organization is guiding the party to ultimate overwhelming defeat.

At our interview we discussed various aspects of business conditions. I told him that, from a reliable source, I had learned the following:

> On March 6, 1933, President Roosevelt, who had been only two days in office, was quite determined to pay off the national debt of the United States by a huge issue of greenbacks. Woodin[21] protested vehemently against it and finally persuaded the President by saying: 'For Heaven's sake, don't do it now: you can do it at any time.'

Bennett is not impressed with Roosevelt's ability or foresight and believes that, for the most part, his policies are mere experimentation, and sometimes of an unfortunate character. But he concedes that at the outset Roosevelt acted with high courage and controlled an extremely difficult situation arising from the absurd banking system of United States.

Yours sorrowfully,

September 17, 1934

OVERSEAS CHAPLAINS – REV. R.H. STEACY AND OTHERS

Sir,

Yesterday while attending service at All Saints' Church, Mr Hepburn [Canon Hepburn] announced that Rev R.H. Steacy (rector of one of the Anglican churches in this city) was to preach the sermon that evening. After looking over the new Parish Hall which has made

21 William H. Woodin – the President's first Secretary of the Treasury.

an important addition to the church and the construction of which has been carried out most efficiently, I had an opportunity of speaking for a moment to Mr Hepburn and I expressed to him in brief but cogent terms my estimate of Mr Steacy.

Steacy went overseas as chaplain, and eventually attained the rank of lieutenant-colonel. During my visit to Great Britain in 1917, I was pestered both by him and by Father Burke with regard to promotion and increased pay. To what extent Father Burke performed his duties, I do not remember; but I heard sufficient of Steacy to be convinced that he was absolutely useless. Colonel Almond gave me a graphic account of the indolence and self-seeking that characterized Steacy who proved himself to be a self-centred, useless, inefficient creature, heedless of his duty and bent solely on gaining higher rank and increased pay.

After his return to Canada some lewd Liberals of the baser sort brought from Winnipeg a creature by the name of Flynn who, at a public meeting of which Steacy was chairman, uttered most filthy falsehoods with regard to my personal character. I never could learn what the charges were except that they were filthy and unprintable. The *Ottawa Journal*, at the time, made a caustic comment in which it said that Flynn should be sent to jail.

Steacy was not only self-seeking and contemptible in many aspects but he was also vindictive. His presence at the meeting alluded to was doubtless due to his failure to obtain from me all that he desired.

Canada sent many splendid chaplains overseas, such as Father O'Leary, Colonel Almond, Channell Hepburn and others equally notable. But there were some even more useless and contemptible than Steacy. I was told of three, one an Anglican, one a Roman Catholic and one either a Methodist or Presbyterian who, collectively, furnished an astonishing example of vice and dishonesty.

I heard of an Anglican chaplain who, before proceeding overseas with his regiment, declined to administer Communion to those who were not of the Anglican Communion. Had I known of this at the time, I certainly would have dismissed him.

In marked contrast was Father O'Leary who, amidst the wounded and dying, gave spiritual consolation without ever for a moment considering the belief or adherence of those to whom he ministered. His was a very moving example; of such is the Kingdom of Heaven.

I remain, Sir, Yours in sympathy,

September 22, 1934

THE *OTTAWA CITIZEN* – EDITORIAL 'IN DEFENCE OF PARLIAMENT' – NEGOTIATIONS WITH SIR WILFRID LAURIER RE UNION GOVERNMENT

Sir,

On occasion there is in the *Ottawa Citizen* an excellent editorial. The proprietors, Wilson and Harry Southam, are splendid citizens and have been constant in their endeavour to serve the right as they see it. The chief editor, Charles A. Bowman, is an idealist, although somewhat wrong-headed in his idealism. Within the past year, he told me that he felt himself handicapped by a persistent urge to set things right in the world and to intervene for that purpose.

But the usefulness of this newspaper is marred by a constant tendency to relate its endeavour to three main considerations. First, it is wholly engrossed in what is known as the 'Douglas Social Credit System', although I doubt whether the proprietors or the editor, or even Douglas himself, understand that system. I have attempted to discuss it with economists of great ability; and they could make nothing of it. I listened to an address by Douglas at a Canadian Club luncheon, during the past year, and it seemed to me that he was pursuing an ideal without in the least knowing how to attain it.

Next, is the strong adherence of the proprietors to the cult of Christian Science, although that does not crop up so frequently as the Douglas cult.

And lastly, readers of the *Citizen* are not infrequently reminded of the editorial conviction that a remarkable wisdom and virtue appertain to that Journal and its editorial utterances.

In today's *Citizen* there is an editorial under the title of 'In Defence of Parliament', in which great praise is given to Mr Mackenzie King by reason of his stand for political democracy against dictatorship.

The following is quoted from the editorial:

> He refused to associate himself with union government to enforce conscription during the war – when Sir Wilfrid Laurier's instinctive reliance on elementary liberalism caused him similarly

> to withstand the pressure. He is likewise letting it be known that he will have nothing to do with current scheming to set up another union government.

The *Citizen* is prone to rely upon its impressions as if they were facts. The reference to Sir Wilfrid Laurier's refusal to enter Union Government is both maladroit and unfounded. That refusal was not based on 'instinctive reliance on elementary liberalism'. N.W. Rowell, Arthur Sifton, J.A. Calder were strong and ardent Liberals. Is it possible that they abandoned elementary liberalism when they agreed to enter the Union Government?

On May 25, 1917, Sir Robert Borden proposed to Sir Wilfrid Laurier that a Union Government should be formed with equal representation of the two political parties, outside the office of Prime Minister. At that time, the Liberal-Conservative party had a majority of more than forty in the House of Commons. Sir Wilfrid Laurier stated that he was opposed to compulsory military service unless it received the approval of the people by plebiscite or at a general election. Otherwise, he feared that it would be difficult to enforce such a law in the province of Quebec.

On May 28, Sir Wilfrid Laurier and Sir Robert Borden had another conference at which Sir Robert asked whether Sir Wilfrid had reached a conclusion. Sir Wilfrid replied that his supporters were divided in opinion and that he still adhered to his view that conscription should not be enforced until after a general election or a referendum. Then Sir Robert Borden said to him, 'Sir Wilfrid, you have already seen the draft of the Military Service Bill and you agree that, if the principle of conscription is accepted, the provisions of the bill are reasonable. I suggest, therefore, that we form a coalition government, pass the Military Service Bill with the proviso that it shall not come into force until proclaimed by the Governor in Council after a general election. Parliament would then be dissolved and the coalition would make its appeal to the electorate. If it should receive their mandate, the Military Service Act would be proclaimed and enforced. If, on the other hand, the coalition government should meet defeat, we shall have done our best and the responsibility will rest on others.'

Sir Wilfrid seemed much impressed with this proposal, took out his note book and asked Sir Robert Borden to repeat it while he set it down in writing.

Several other conferences took place; and on June 4, Sir Wilfrid Laurier called upon Sir Robert Borden and renewed the discussion which he opened by inquiring as to the personnel of the Conservative wing of the coalition cabinet. Sir Robert Borden immediately reminded him of his (Sir Robert's) view that in so supreme a crisis they should rise above all considerations of party interest or advantage. Much more was it necessary to disregard mere personal claims or considerations. Therefore, Sir Robert undertook to make the Conservative wing of the cabinet acceptable to Sir Wilfrid. This was going very far, as it practically entrusted to Sir Wilfrid the nomination of the Conservative members of the government. However, Sir Robert felt it his duty to go to that length; and he was determined that the negotiations should not be broken off on the minor issue of personnel.

On June 6, Sir Robert Borden arranged an interview with Sir Wilfrid to take place at nine o'clock. Sir Wilfrid announced his final conclusion that he could not become a member of the proposed coalition, as he was opposed to conscription. He feared the effects of Bourassa's influence and propaganda; and he felt that his own position would be stronger if he remained in opposition. At this and previous interviews he expressed his intention of enjoining, in every possible way, respect for and observance of the proposed Military Service Act, if it should be enacted by parliament.

It must be borne in mind that Sir Wilfrid Laurier was then in his seventy-sixth year. If he had been ten or fifteen years younger, I am confident that he would have entered the proposed coalition. He held an unrivalled position in the affection and reverence of the French Canadians and he was convinced that he would lose this pre-eminence if he should commit himself to a policy of compulsory military service. I am convinced that he under-rated his influence and that Quebec would have followed where he led.

But in addition to the personal motive, there was, I believe, a higher influence. The prestige of Mr Bourassa, not then perhaps at its highest point, was still sufficiently powerful to arouse in Sir Wilfrid's mind a grave apprehension as to the effect of violent propaganda led by his former follower. Not only on this but on previous occasions, in intimate conversation with Sir Wilfrid, I concluded that he regarded Mr Bourassa's teaching as inimical not only to the spirit of Canadian unity but to the best interests of the province of Quebec. Thus, an instinct of patriotism led Sir Wilfrid to believe that, in view of considerations which I have merely outlined, his duty was to stand apart from the proposed coalition.

The *Citizen* is equally wrong with regard to Mr Mackenzie King. That gentleman took an interest in the establishment of union government. His most intimate Ottawa friend, the late John Gilman

Foster,[22] approached Sir Robert Borden during the progress of negotiations and assured him that Mr King was quite prepared to enter Union government. Sir Robert had no doubt that this intimation came directly through Mr Foster from Mr King himself.[23] Sir Robert would have welcomed Mr King as a colleague; but the Liberals with whom he was negotiating had no thought of Mr King and had the right to select their own colleagues.

The *Citizen* is not alone in this tendency to inaccuracy which is especially observable in the news columns of many newspapers, particulars of which I have given, on occasion, in my letters to your journal which, fortunately, is altogether free from this vice.

I remain, Yours in verity,

The following is the editorial in the *Ottawa Citizen* of September 22, 1934, referred to in the foregoing Limbo letter. ED.

IN DEFENCE OF PARLIAMENT

Mr Mackenzie King's stand for political democracy against dictatorship is neither exaggerated nor trumped up for election purposes. He has always been most punctilious about observing the rights of parliament. He has favored reform steps toward strengthening the parliamentary instrument of government, such as proportional representation to make parliament more truly the mirror of the nation. But he has ever refused to countenance the undermining of parliamentary authority or the over-riding of the British principle of responsible government. He refused to associate himself with union government to enforce conscription during the war – when Sir Wilfrid Laurier's instinctive reliance on elementary liberalism caused him similarly to withstand the pressure. He is likewise letting it be known that he will have nothing to do with current scheming to set up another union government.

For a year or more behind the scenes, there has been an effort to bring the parties together – as Mr E.R. Peacock urged indiscreetly

22 United States Consul-General at Halifax (1897–1903) and then at Ottawa, 1903–1927. He resided at the Roxborough Apartments in Ottawa from 1912 to 1927.

23 Mr Mackenzie King, in the House of Commons in 1944 denied that anyone had approached Sir Robert with his (King's) permission. See further on this subject: Professor Dawson's biography (Vol. I) of Mr King, published by the University of Toronto Press in 1958 (pp. 265 and 266) and The Canadian Historical Review, Vol. XLIII, No. 3, of September, 1962 (page 275), which latter reproduces a letter written by me to the Editor of that Review on this subject. ED.

in public at the Dominion Day banquet in London, given by the Canadian High Commissioner, Hon. Howard Ferguson – to form a so-called national government. The main motive of merging the parties is to find a convenient substitute for political democracy. It is to eliminate the opposition party from parliament, so that government can be carried on like any dictatorship.

National government is disguised dictatorship – used to impose conditions of needless hardship upon the nation for the benefit of special interests. The British people were misled into accepting it in 1931 – in the belief that the United Kingdom would otherwise be forced off the gold standard, with consequences as disastrous as the inflation of the German mark ten years ago. When Philip Snowden discovered how he had been used as chancellor of the exchequer, under advice from the Bank of England and financial authorities in the City, he resigned. Several Liberals withdrew subsequently. The British electorate will probably make an end of the national government at the first opportunity. Whether they return Labor, Conservative, or some other party, they intend to return to the tried method of party responsibility.

The Liberal leader in Canada, William Lyon Mackenzie King, is staying true to tradition when he declines to have anything to do with camouflaged dictatorship.

October 17, 1934

VISIT OF MARQUIS OF LOTHIAN TO OTTAWA

Sir,

Today I had a long conversation with an old friend, Philip Kerr, (now Marquis of Lothian) whom I knew intimately during the War when he was *Fidus Achates* to Lloyd George both in the Imperial War Cabinet and at the Paris Peace Conference.

He told me that Lloyd George expects eventually to join the Union government. At present, he is in his seventy-second year and should have five years more of active participation in public affairs.

L.G. would have been taken into the Union government at its inception but for an operation which he had to undergo at that time. His expectation is to intervene for the purpose of compromise between the Union government and the Conservative die-hards in the controversy, or rather the struggle, with regard to India. In other words, he will, at a suitable emergency, 'crash the gate' of the Union government.

Lothian was the guest of honour at a luncheon of the Canadian Institute of International Affairs (Ottawa group) on the same day at the Rideau Club. Both in conversation during the morning and at the luncheon he gave a vivid presentation of world conditions, as he sees them. His conclusions may be stated concisely as follows.

Japan, having denounced the Washington Naval Agreement, will insist upon naval parity with Great Britain and United States. When that has been accomplished, Japan will practically dominate the Pacific, as neither Great Britain nor United States can concentrate in eastern [*sic*] waters any force capable of offering successful resistance.

If United States could come to an agreement or even a definite understanding with Great Britain, this situation could be met. But, under United States' singular system of governance, no such agreement or understanding seems possible. United States expects that Great Britain will build to meet Japan; but, as Lothian explained to President Roosevelt in a recent conversation, the British taxpayer is at the limit of his resources. Roosevelt, however, feels that Great Britain will build; and he asserts with emphasis that United States will build to meet Japan.

In the British Cabinet there is strong division of opinion as to whether, in the absence of agreement or understanding with United States, Great Britain should come to an understanding with Japan. There is strong support for this view which, however, might definitely and dangerously antagonize public opinion in United States.

The situation is not unlike that which arose in 1921, when the attitude of the Canadian government prevented renewal of the Anglo-Japanese Treaty which was desired by Australia and New Zealand but which would have aroused a dangerous antagonism in United States.

Japan's increased naval strength would imperil British interests in the Far East and might enable Japan to dictate her own terms in the event of differences involving British interests.

It may be necessary to accept for a time such a situation in the expectation that United States, with immense interests in the Pacific, will not fail to meet Japan's challenge.

All this is mere conjecture, as the situation is too complex for any forecast of value.

I remain, Sir, Yours, etc.,

October 18, 1934

ROSS–HEPBURN (HYDRO COMMISSION)

Sir,

In conditions of extreme public unrest, singular creatures come to the surface. Mitchell Hepburn became Premier of Ontario a few months ago after a long tenure of office by the Conservative party. He has exposed and remedied some deficiencies of that government; but his antics are arousing both astonishment and concern throughout Ontario.

His latest demonstration is an attack upon P.D. Ross, one of Ottawa's most highly respected citizens, who, for eighteen years has given faithful and efficient service to the Ottawa Hydro Electric Commission. Ross gave also most useful service to the province of Ontario in a lengthy and highly important investigation respecting certain aspects of public welfare. Not only did he decline remuneration, but paid his own expenses. ...

In the same press that published Hepburn's contemptible sneer that Ross was concerned to draw $1,000. from the Ontario government, there appeared the announcement that Mr and Mrs Ross had contributed $1,200. to the Federated Charities of Ottawa.

It is a long and shameful descent from Edward Blake and Oliver Mowat to Mitchell Hepburn.

Facilis descencus Averno;
...
Sed revocare gradum superasque evadere ad auras,
Hoc opus, hic labor est.

But Ontario may be trusted to regain its sanity; and to consign Hepburn to the limbo of things shameful but forgotten.

It is said that Hepburn is doing more for the Liberal-Conservative party in Ontario than that party is doing for itself. Possibly that is not saying very much.

The feeling in Ontario regarding Hepburn will eventually be that of John Gilpin's horse toward his rider:

His horse, who never in that sort
Had handled been before
What thing upon his back had got
Did wonder more and more.

I was told recently, on excellent authority, that before sending for Chief Engineer Gaby and two other officers of the Ontario Hydro Commission for the purpose of dismissing them, Hepburn called into his office newspaper reporters. Upon the arrival of Gaby and the two others, Hepburn, in the presence of the reporters, said, 'Pack your bags and get out.'

He is wholly lacking in a sense of the dignity of his office. In manners he is a boor, in vindictiveness a savage, and in veracity an Ananias. He boasts of economies, but his chief economy is of the truth. If all tales be true, he leads a dissolute life of which I have had reports from persons professing intimate knowledge of his habits.

I remain, Sir, Yours, etc.,

November 28, 1934

EDITORIAL IN THE *ST. THOMAS TIMES-JOURNAL*; RECIPROCITY AGREEMENT OF 1911

Sir,

I have been favoured with an issue of the *St. Thomas Times-Journal* of November 22nd, in which reference is made to my recent address at the Annual General Meeting of Barclays Bank (Canada).

While some portions of the editorial are passable, it is painfully apparent that the writer is profoundly ignorant of my attitude regarding protection and of the considerations upon which I opposed the Reciprocity agreement of 1911.

In 1911, it was proposed that Canada should enter into an arrangement with United States to be consummated by legislation passed in each country. The result of that arrangement would have altered vitally currents of trade as they then existed. You may recall President Taft's famous declaration that 'the amount of Canadian products we would take would produce a current of business between western Canada and the United States that would *make Canada only an adjunct of the United States*.' The objection I urged was the possibility that, without a moment's notice legislation by Congress might leave Canada, under the new development, in a difficult if not hopeless situation. Doubtless you appreciate the extent to which Congress, under such circumstances, would give consideration to difficulties inevitably arising in our country.

My view was set forth in a message to the Canadian people issued at Halifax on September 18, 1911. Until Canada led the democracies of the American Continent in the world war, nothing ever gained for her more sincere respect in United States than her rejection of the reciprocity arrangement.

So far as protection of our industries is concerned, it must be remembered that we adjoin a nation of immense wealth and resources which maintains a high protective tariff against us. To export our raw materials to United States, followed by the influx of our unemployed labouring population into that country to be employed in producing commodities that would have given work to our people if produced in Canada, and finally to send our good Canadian money abroad for the purchase of such commodities – such a policy to be rejected needed only to be named.

Leading industrialists in United States had publicly announced that their surplus of commodities would be sold abroad at a profit, if possible; but in any case they would be sold. If our industries were crushed by such methods, I did not believe that the United States' trusts would have been more considerate of our people than of the consumers whom they oppressed at home.

The question of our political autonomy had also to be considered, as we were then (and we still are) under the shadow of developments in United States.

I entirely approve of such reduction or elimination of tariffs as will permit freer trade, but under arrangements invested with the elements of stability and fairness.

I remain, Sir, Yours faithfully,

NOTE: The following is the editorial in the *St Thomas Times-Journal* of November 22, 1934, referred to in the foregoing Limbo letter.

BORDEN'S PLEA FOR TRADE

The passing of the years fortunately tends to broaden and to mellow. In days gone by Sir Robert Borden, Canada's wartime Premier, was a high protectionist and a firm believer in fiscal nationalism. In the 1911 campaign, when he led the Conservative forces to victory against the Laurierites whose battlecry was 'Reciprocity with the United States,' Sir Robert was keen on preserving the Canadian market for Canadians. Now, in 1934, he evidently realizes that this can be carried too far.

Addressing the general meeting of Barclay's Bank (Canada) in Montreal, he deplored the fact that 'economic nationalism still holds many nations in thrall,' and urged the resumption of international trade. In sinister contrast to modern means whereby co-operation and mutual understanding may be effected are, he said, the abnormally high tariff barriers, continually and systematically strengthened. They tend to keep people apart, and while they will not endure, the situation resulting is dangerous and may be destructive. If anybody had predicted in 1911 that Sir Robert, then plain 'R.L.', would talk as he has just done, the prophet would have been laughed at.

But Sir Robert Borden deserves credit for developing with the years. And he seems to have had plenty of company, even within the ranks of the once protectionist Conservative party. Many of the leading members of this party have come to realize the fallacy of 'economic nationalism.' In 1911 they vigorously waved the old flag and declared vehemently against reciprocity with the United States which, they claimed, would mean the economic and political ruin of Canada. Now they are willing to discuss reciprocity, apparently having no fear of the once fearsome bugbear of annexation. Very little is heard nowadays of the National Policy, or NP, as it was better known in the days of its originator, Sir John A. Macdonald. This policy, which carried many Conservative armies to victory, was designed to protect Canada's infant industries (many of them were pretty husky babies) from the competition of foreign manufacturers, even to the point of soaking the consumer most unmercifully.

The fact that the NP has now passed into the discard is a hopeful sign as it indicates that Canada is losing its nationalism and broadening out. The nation has begun to realize that it cannot live unto itself, and that economic nationalism means economic stagnation. A nation such as Canada, with its great natural resources, must have outside markets for its products if it is to enjoy its fullest economic development. But it cannot have these markets unless it opens its markets to the products of other countries. One way not to promote international trade is by erecting high tariffs. There is no doubt that these fiscal banners have impeded world trade, without the resumption of which on an intensive scale there can be no general and lasting recovery from the depression. In reduced tariffs and reciprocal trade lies the economic hope of the nations. This does not necessarily mean that reasonable protection will be denied a nation's industries. It means rather that the nations will facilitate trade in those products which can be exchanged to mutual advantage.

December 17, 1934

ADDRESS OF HON. W.D. HERRIDGE AT CANADIAN CLUB LUNCHEON

Sir,

The day before yesterday I attended a luncheon of the Canadian Club at which Major W.D. Herridge, Canadian minister at Washington, was the guest of honour.

Evidently he had given much thought to the preparation of his speech; and he expected to make a profound impression.

The speech did impress me – but rather disagreeably. It was unnecessarily prolix; the speaker did not know how to use his voice and was sometimes almost inaudible (which occasionally was fortunate); there was too much rhetorical exhortation; there were too many high-flown phrases devised for effect; there was too much demagogic gesture; too much appeal for 'clear' and 'national' thinking; and, withal, I greatly doubted the sincerity of the speaker, as he has inherited some of his father's histrionic aptitude. [His father was Rev W.T. Herridge, Moderator of the Presbyterian Church in Canada.]

The speech was designed as a destructive attack upon the existing social order which, beyond doubt, must be modified in some of its aspects, as I have frequently declared. But, before destruction there must come fullest consideration of what can be substituted. Herridge declared that he would, without hesitation, sacrifice the capitalistic system if he believed that such sacrifice was necessary. This rather fatuous and futile declaration he evidently regarded as the high note of his address.

A few days afterwards, I met a man of Herridge's age who was absolutely certain of Herridge's insincerity; and further he told me that the Prime Minister [Bennett – Herridge's brother-in-law] had severely castigated Herridge after the lecture.

In my addresses at the annual meetings of Barclays Bank (Canada) last year and this year as well, I have pointed out deficiencies in the existing social order and I have emphasized the need of wider conception. But, I prefer advance by reasonable and gradual methods of the British type, rather than by rash experimentation presently prevailing to some extent in United States.

At the conclusion of Herridge's speech, the Prime Minister, by whom I sat, turned to me and said: 'That speech arouses in me distinctive antagonism.' 'In me, also,' I replied.

In due course the address brought forth vapid editorial comment, especially in the *Ottawa Citizen* which is always conspicuous in this regard.

I remain, Sir, Yours in sympathy,

PS. Later, I received from an indignant lady in Hartford, Conn., the accompanying letter.

December the sixteenth

Sir Robert Borden,

Sir:

In the New York Times this morning, I notice the enclosed article.

May I express to you, as an American, the chagrin I feel that any person from our country should 'hint' to Canada that it 'needs a new deal'?

To my mind Canada at the present moment is in the most enviable position of any country in the world.

To begin to tell you what the New Deal has done to my country would be impossible. All that our forbears have worked to build in the way of stability and honor has gone, gone too far to be retrieved.

From the extensive propaganda broadcast by the present leader and his followers one would assume that the United States was recovering. Just the contrary is true. Billions of money is being spent to help loafers, bums, bootleggers and the absolutely lower type of politician. Whereas the back bone of the nation is being wiped completely out. The suffering amongst the old families, families whose forbears came here three hundred years ago are being forced by taxes to support all kinds of wild projects and graft. Their families are now almost penniless, selling their homes or having them taken away, paying for the barest necessities on the instalment plan, being unable to give their children only the most common school educations. One hears little of this because they are people of pride and breeding who are meeting the situation with the lack of whining that their background demands.

Why do they not rise up and try to adjust things? They are in the minority, their honest efforts are over ridden and they are over ridden and are being obliterated. The suffering amongst them is acute, while the criminal class constantly increases.

The 'New Deal' is not for Canada, or for any of the British Colonies. It would mean their ruin. Canada has much more to lose if she adopts the methods of the present United States.

Believe me, very sincerely,
(Sgd) Cordelia H. Gardner

December 15, 1934

New York Times

HERRIDGE HINTS CANADA NEEDS A NEW DEAL; ASSAILS SYSTEM GIVING PROSPERITY TO FEW

W.D. Herridge, new Canadian Minister to Washington, gave indication in a speech at the Canadian Club today that he believed the time had come for a New Deal in Canada.

The radical phrasing of his speech, delivered with his brother-in-law, Prime Minister Bennett, at his elbow, caused surprise.

Sir Robert Borden and Mackenzie King, former Prime Ministers, and W.B. Robbins, Minister from the United States, were also at the head table.

'Had I the power I would throw over our economic system in a flash if I thought there was a better one available,' he declared, adding:

'High finance cannot expect that we should subscribe unequivocally to the view that it has a monopoly of intelligence.'

Classical economists, he said, had declared that the present depression was only a phase in the trade cycle.

'They tell us just to grin and bear it and to remember that all our fuss and struggle are only calculated to prolong the agony,' he went on. 'Doubtless their talk is very fortifying unless you happen to be hungry. The system goes triumphantly on and the people perish.

'If increased consumption demands increased production and if increased production requires concentration of business and if concentration of business interfere with the old competitive system and the open market place and produce disequilibrium in the operation of the system, does it follow that certain classes of the community must inevitably suffer and that other classes must as inevitably prosper unless or until the system is changed?

'Are those who are profiting like sweepstake winners to be congratulated as the group arbitrarily chosen by Providence to be the beneficiaries of a system which just wont work in any other way?

'Let us search through this system from top to bottom and see what is wrong with it and what we can do to right it.

'It is not improbable that I shall be censured for such talk as this. Some of the system's myrmidons will say it is *lese majeste*. But there is nothing sacred about the economic system but the welfare of the people.'

January 18, 1935

RADIO ADDRESSES OF RT. HON. R.B. BENNETT

Sir,

On January second, the Prime Minister, (Right Honourable R.B. Bennett) began a series of radio addresses. The tone of his speech that evening was unexpectedly socialistic. As in his campaign of 1930, he promised more than he can perform; e.g., to end unemployment. Neither he nor another can achieve that result. Unemployment has been with us from time immemorial and it will continue with us to the end.

The series was continued by four further addresses before the opening of parliament and by a speech in Montreal to the Board of Trade.

The speeches were couched in quite general terms and professed to set forth a policy for ridding the capitalistic system of certain features which have been successfully exploited by cunning financiers to their enormous advantage and to the equal detriment of the general public. In this reform the Prime Minister is assuredly on the right track. He stressed the importance, indeed the necessity, of such interference by government in business activities as would prevent recurrence of disastrous and dishonest methods. But the socialistic tinge of his addresses was rather disconcerting at first to leaders in business, industry and finance.

It is said, upon most reliable authority, that the propaganda thus put forth by Mr Bennett, and the policies thus enunciated, were undertaken and carried out without previous consultation with any of his colleagues, several of whom were extremely disturbed by his course.

On Tuesday, January 8, I visited Montreal and had contact and discussion with several important persons. The memorandum which I attach, as a curiosity, records my impressions.

1 *Pater conscriptus* – refers to Honourable C.C. Ballantyne [prominent Montreal businessman and former colleague of Sir Robert in Union government] to whom I thus accord the Roman designation. He was most enthusiastic, ready to bet that Bennett would win; he thought that the opposition of the *Gazette* would be helpful, except locally; and he told me that the interest in the PM's broadcasts was so intense that people consulted his programme before accepting invitations to dinner.

2 *Scriptor et Fidus Achates* – Lord Atholstan [publisher of the Montreal Daily Star] and his editor, A.R. Carman, with whom I conferred during the morning of my visit. Their attitude was most friendly; but they were doubtful as to the effect of the proposed policies. 'Will they (the people) believe him (Bennett)?' However, they admitted that the PM had begun his reforms last session; further, they agreed that Bennett, even with a socialistic and radical tinge is preferable to King in borrowed Conservative garb. All would depend, in their opinion, on the concrete proposals submitted to Parliament by the PM.

3 I lunched that day with Arthur Blaikie Purvis [then president of Canadian Industries Limited] whom I have designated *Aurelius*. He is a man of remarkable ability and of excellent ideals. He told me that businessmen in United States fear that Roosevelt, by inspiration of fierce antagonism and distrust among the common people against all men who have been successful in business, industry or finance, has raised a ghost he cannot lay. Leading men in that country believe that the President is intellectually incompetent for his task. Purvis regretted (as I do) that Bennett should have used expressions implying that all Canadian industrialists are tyrannical, unjust and oppressive. Subject to this, he approves.

During his recent visit to London, Purvis was in touch with people of the first rank in both politics and business. There is a most efficient and useful 'brain trust' in Great Britain, but without executive power.

4 That same afternoon, I called upon E.W. Beatty [then president of the Canadian Pacific Railway] whom I have designated as *Mer-*

curius. His attitude is set forth in the accompanying memorandum which also

5 records views communicated to me, respecting the Prime Minister, by persons already mentioned and by others.

After my return to Ottawa, I gave to Mr Bennett (January 9) a copy of this memorandum with appropriate comments and explanations.

Since the government's policies have been announced in the speech from the throne the situation has somewhat developed.

The leader of the opposition (Mr Mackenzie King) took a rather shrewd course in first making a lively attack upon the government's record and in following this with an offer to cut short the debate and to cooperate in bringing into immediate effect Bennett's policies which King claims to have held and put forward many years ago. As to this, there is the natural retort: 'Why did you not put them into force during your nine years of premiership?'

Undoubtedly, the Prime Minister has entirely changed the current of political thought in Canada by his enunciation of these policies. It is a remarkable achievement and illustrates his high courage.

He will receive the support of the Co-operative Commonwealth Federation (CCF) who criticize his proposals as weak and inadequate, although valuable so far as they go. It is idle to speculate upon the outcome. The Liberal-Conservative party is animated with new-born hope of success at the general election which must take place during the present year. Before the PM's broadcasts, the result was a foregone conclusion, as the Liberals would have won by at least two, perhaps three, to one.

The opposition will challenge Bennett's policies as 'deathbed repentance'; they will challenge his sincerity and characterize his proposals as an 'election trick', instigated by Herridge. Whispers of this are already abroad; and it is unfortunate that the Prime Minister's broadcasts should have been preceded by Herridge's socialistic speech on December 15. Herridge is by no means a popular figure. There is more confidence in his histrionic capacity than in his sincerity.

It is absurd but, at the same time, amusing to predict the result of the next election. Presently I should say – 40 per cent Conservative, 40 per cent Liberal and 20 per cent CCF. This conjecture is a thousand times absurd, as no opinion at this stage could be of much value, even if it proceeded from a close student of existing affiliations and tendencies. My estimate is based merely upon my profound ignorance.

I remain, Sir, Yours, etc.,

January 9, 1935

MEMORANDUM

Plancus Narrator

1 Pater Conscriptus
In 'high g'; betting; afraid to visit in morning but starting in afternoon; thinks *Gazette* very helpful, except locally; hopes PM will write Fred Southam; interest intense in broadcasts.

2 Scriptor et Fidus Achates
Friendly; dubitantibus; will they (hoi polloi) believe him (Bennett)? Admit PM began last session; admit B. with socialistic and radical tinge better than K. in borrowed Conservative garb; all depends on concrete proposals; no election until results therefrom; what about Senate? Whispers that business has nothing to fear dangerous if they spread to masses. On the other hand, there is a converse danger.

3 Aurelius
He is the noblest Roman of them all. Roosevelt has raised ghosts that he cannot lay; much concern in US for this reason; intellectually incompetent for task. PM tars all industrialists with same stick; should correct this. Aurelius had interesting contacts in Great Britain. There, there is 'Brain Trust', but with no executive power, purely advisory. Plancus urges PM to send for Aurelius whom Plancus regards as ablest businessman in Canada – a man who combines splendid ability with fine ideals. He disputes some of PM's premises.

4 Mercurius
Somewhat critical but entirely loyal. He read to Plancus highly critical opinion of undisclosed economist; confirms Aurelius as to danger in US, especially urges that PM should explain with great distinctness that he is following G.B. not Roosevelt. Thinks latest speech best.

5 Fama Vacua et Vana Jactat
PM an incalculable asset to country during past four years; admirable PM; much less efficient as head of Cabinet; still less as party-leader; temperamental, variable, inconsistent; ignores colleagues; influenced by Herridge under allurement of Washington 'Brain Trust' pipe-dreams.

January 20, 1935

BESTOWAL OF HONOURS IN CANADA

Sir,

In 1917, there was great outcry respecting the bestowal of honours in Canada; and, not only in that year but, in the following year the question was raised in the House of Commons. The character of the debate and my attitude thereon are set forth in my memoirs. [Vol. 2, pp. 792–7]. At that time, I prepared a memorandum on the subject; but in the meantime my views have undergone a change. At present, I should be inclined to vote for the abolition of all titles in Canada. My friend, Perley, is strongly opposed to this; and in his attitude I see evidence of a tendency always manifest among persons who have been resident for a few years in London. Breathing the atmosphere of feudalism, there still prevailing, they cannot divest themselves of its effect.

In June 1914, in compliance with a telegram from the King, I accepted the honour of GCMG, which I had previously declined. Today, I should be perfectly content to give it up; and in many parts of the country I am much better known as R.L. Borden than as Sir Robert Borden.

In my opinion the practice of accepting minor British honours cannot tend to increase the self-respect of Canadians. The higher honours have been, and they always must be, reserved to persons residing in the British Isles, and especially to the old historic families, the governing families of Great Britain who, on occasion, have given to their country splendid leadership but who long monopolized its wealth and its honours. I do not question this reservation of the higher honours, for indeed it could not be otherwise; but I do maintain that Canada, as a self-governing nation of equal status with Great Britain, should establish her own system of honours, if such a system is desirable, and not be content with crumbs that drop from the table of Great Britain.

It is said that titles serve to strengthen the tie that unites the oversea nations and Great Britain; but this is by no means evident to me. The Imperial Privy Council may be, and doubtless it is, of some assistance in this respect. For I regard admission to the Imperial Privy Council as an honour second to none within the bestowal of HM, so far as the Dominions are concerned.

The Imperial Privy Councillorship is associated with the wearing of what is known as a 'Windsor' uniform of the first-class, although my friend, Martin Burrell, stoutly denies the accuracy of this designation. Probably it is the most uncomfortable raiment ever devised by the diabolical ingenuity of military or court tailors.

When first I became a Privy Councillor, I was rather enamoured of such vestments and I expended pretty liberal amounts in procuring all the garments that were pressed upon my attention by my London tailors. Some of these I have worn only once or twice and others not at all. *Requiescant in pace.* After all, they are but the absurd trappings of a defunct feudal system.

And that reminds me that in the Imperial War Cabinet during the War, on an occasion when I was sitting by Curzon [Lord Curzon of Kedleston], he put to me the following inquiry: 'What is Canadian opinion with respect to the social order prevailing in this country?' I replied: 'If you wish me to speak frankly, we regard your social order as little more than a glorified feudal system.' The conversation ended abruptly.

On another occasion (after dinner at Buckingham Palace, I think) Lord Chaplin[24] told me rather boastfully that he had initiated the embargo which, for many years, had prevented the importation of Canadian cattle. It was really a measure of fiscal protection under the hypocritical pretence of safeguarding British cattle against disease. That afternoon, in a certain committee, there had come to my attention conditions which I regarded as outrageous and which had resulted from heartless failure to enact or enforce regulations necessary for the protection of Canadian soldiers against certain temptations.[25] I had told the committee that never again, under such conditions, would a Canadian force be landed upon British soil. So, turning upon Chaplin, I said with all the sternness I could command: 'If you British had had as much regard for the welfare of our soldiers as for the health of your cattle, we should be much better satisfied

24 Sometime Minister of Agriculture in the United Kingdom.
25 Sir Robert is referring to the incidence of venereal disease.

than we are today in Canada.' Once more the conversation ended quite abruptly.

I remain, Sir, Yours, etc.,

NOTE: In 1966 I received the following memorandum from the late Mr Harold Daly QC of Ottawa. ED.

Have just read about Roy Thomson having to give up his Canadian citizenship in order to get a Peerage, and am reminded of the House of Commons resolution passed in 1919 prohibiting the conferring of titles on Canadians. The resolution was introduced by Nickle the MP for Kingston Ontario who was sore because the heads of McGill and Toronto Universities had been knighted and his father-in-law, the head of Queen's University, had not. Sir Robert Borden, the Prime Minister, was not averse to titles, he had used them skillfully to get rid of people who wanted to be in the Cabinet or some other job where he did not care to use them. He had even allowed two peerages (Shaughnessy and Atholstan) to be conferred on distinguished Canadians but he had given his consent before any of these titles were conferred. But recently Sir Joseph Flavelle had been made a baronet and Sir Robert had not been consulted beforehand, whether this was an accident or not I can't say. Sir Robert was a stickler for Canadian sovereignty and was not prepared for the giving of titles without the previous consent of the Canadian government; so he let the resolution go through and no more titles were conferred on Canadian citizens until the 1930s when Bennett came to power. I remember Bennett telling me to look up and let him know how many Canadians were knights and try to find out what the greatest number of knights in Canada had been, I forget the figure but there were many fewer knights than there had been. Bennett began with caution, he first had Perley elevated from KCMG to GCMG, when that caused no outcry he got an opinion from the Justice Department that the 1919 resolution only applied to that parliament and then went ahead and had several knighthoods conferred on Canadians.[26] After Bennett ceased to be Prime Minister in 1935 there have been no more titles conferred on Canadian citizens.

26 Dr Frederick G. Banting, co-discoverer of insulin; Edward W. Beatty, chairman, Canadian Pacific Railway; Lyman P. Duff, Chief Justice, Supreme Court of Canada; E. Wyly Grier, artist and portrait painter; Ernest C. MacMillan, musician, composer, conductor; Charles E. Saunders, distinguished entomologist and public servant.

February 6, 1935

COMMENTS ON MEMORANDA SENT TO THE PRIME MINISTER

Sir,

From time to time I have sent memoranda to the Prime Minister containing information that might be useful to him in connection with policies announced in his broadcast addresses, as well as in the throne speech at the opening of parliament.

On the latest occasion Mr Bennett seemed surprised at the extent and variety of my reading; and he asked me how I managed to find time therefor. I observed that I had much fewer pre-occupations than those which daily thronged upon him.

Herewith are copies of the memoranda which on that occasion I handed to the Prime Minister and which include:

1 Extract from John Buchan's *Oliver Cromwell*;
2 Extract from William Stearns Davis' *Influence of Wealth in Imperial Rome*;
3 A reference to *The Common People of Ancient Rome* by Frank Frost Abbott.

The last two mentioned volumes, as well as *Society and Politics In Ancient Rome* (also by Frank Frost Abbott) came to my attention more than twenty years ago and made a vivid impression upon me.

The opening chapter of *The Influence of Wealth In Imperial Rome* contains a graphic account of the business panic of 33 AD. Apparently my reference thereto led to its perusal by Mr Bennett who, in his recent address before the Montreal Board of Trade (January 26, 1935) quoted quite freely from Professor Davis' description of that panic which, in several of its incidents strikingly resembles the panic or collapse that began in the autumn of 1929. Mr Bennett's speech is attached.[27]

On January 29, I received from my friend, John A. Stevenson, representative at Ottawa of the London *Times*, the attached letter.

27 Mr Bennett's speech was not attached to the original of this Limbo letter nor have I been able to secure a copy from among either Sir Robert's or Mr Bennett's papers in the Public Archives of Canada. In view of this I have attached the account of the speech which appeared in the *Montreal Gazette* of January 28, 1935.

Subsequently I called him on the telephone and told him I could give him interesting information into the 'incursion into Roman history.'

Mr Bennett's reference to *Via Sacra* was taken from Professor Davis' description of that street (also known by another name) which was apparently the principal business street of Rome.

The incident afforded me a little amusement; but there is more than amusement to be derived therefrom.

So far as we can retrace the history of mankind, we observe that, except in certain aspects, there is nothing new in the most recent and startling of human events.

In attempting to gain even the feeblest comprehension of a universe, a thousand times greater than was dreamed of a century ago, we realize the pettiness of human achievement, of all our systems, empires, material greatness, and especially of all controversies, jealousies, ambitions, whether individual or national. And we are told that a relatively trifling variation in temperature would sweep from our earth every vestige of existence. All animate creation would disappear; mother earth would become a dead world.

But mankind has never ceased his endeavour to penetrate the mystery of existence of the universe. Amazing discoveries, by no means completed, have crowned his endeavour. He reaches out to the very limits of the universe and brings within our ken the structure and character of stars in the outermost nebula.

There has been amazing progress, also, within half a century, in knowledge of the nature and processes of the material world, in fuller insight into the mystery of animate things, in the control and use of the terrible destructive forces of nature, in the development of inventions hitherto undreamed of and in many other aspects of mankind's environment.

In the higher domain, in the world of the spirit, man's effort has been crowned with splendour. The illustrious of the centuries have bequeathed to us a transcendant heritage of the ideal and the spiritual. Must all this disappear because of vagaries in the path of some heavenly body? A poet [Tennyson] has voiced the question:

> ... And he, shall he,
>
> Man, her last work who seemed so fair,
> Such splendid purpose in his eyes,
> Who roll'd the psalm to wintry skies,
> Who built him fanes of fruitless prayer,

Who trusted God was love indeed
And love Creation's final law –
Tho Nature, red in tooth and claw
With ravin shriek'd against his creed –

Who loved, who suffered countless ills,
Who battled for the True, the Just,
Be blown about the desert dust,
Or seal'd within the iron hills?

No more? A monster then, a dream,
A discord, Dragons of the prime,
That tare each other in their slime,
Were mellow music match'd with him.

O life as futile, then, as frail!
O for thy voice to soothe and bless!
What hope of answer, or redress?
Behind the veil, behind the veil.

I remain, Sir, Yours, etc.,

1 Extract from John Buchan's *Oliver Cromwell* pages 405–6
He (Cromwell) had written thus after Dunbar (1650):

'Disown yourselves, but own your authority and improve it to curb the proud and the insolent, such as would disturb the tranquillity of England, though under what specious pretence soever; relieve the oppressed, hear the groans of poor prisoners in England; be pleased to reform the abuses of all professions; and if there be any one who makes many poor to make a few rich, that suits not a Commonwealth.'

2 Extract from *The Influence of Wealth in Imperial Rome* by William Stearns Davis (page 335) (Published by Macmillan Company, New York)

'No state ever excluded the ideal from its national and social life so strictly as did Rome. It taught its prosaic commercialism to all its provinces. It died a slow, lingering, painful death, after achieving the greatest seeming success in history. Its citizens served Mammon in the place of God with more than usual consistency. The power they worshipped carried them a certain way – then delivered them over to their own rottenness, and to the resistless enemy. Their fall was great – for their Empire with its social structure still looms as the greatest fabric ever reared by human ingenuity; while the lesson of their fall lies patent to the twentieth century.'

3 At pages 1 to 5 of *The Influence of Wealth in Imperial Rome* there is a graphic description of the business panic of 33 AD. See also Diocletian's Edict on the regulation of prices in *The Common People of Ancient Rome* (page 145) by Frank Frost Abbott. (Published by Charles Scribner's Sons, New York.)

House of Commons
The Press Gallery

Jan 28–35

My dear Sir Robert,

In case you have not noticed the enclosed in the *Winnipeg Free Press* I venture to send it. [See appendage to Limbo letter re Audrey Alexandra Brown.] I hope also you did not miss Bennett's amazing deliverance at the Board of Trade banquet in Montreal on Saturday as recorded in today's *Gazette*. It must almost have frozen the blood of some of his audience to hear his account of his conversion to state intervention through conversations with Litvinoff and Sir Stafford Cripps. The last straw must have been when he described John Strachey who was a Labour MP but is now an avowed Communist as 'one of the profound thinkers of these times.' Then there was his strange backward incursion into Roman history and the comparison of St James St to the Via Sacra. I have been talking to Senator Murphy about it and we agreed that never in history had such a speech been delivered by a Conservative premier. Be sure to see it. I am looking forward to Christie's comments. I hope Lady Borden and yourself are both well and I am,

yours very sincerely,
John Stevenson

PS T.B.R is a friend of mine, a Scot called Thomas Roberton who transformed himself from a working printer into a firstclass writer. J.A.S.

January 30, 1935

John Stevenson, Esquire
Press Gallery
House of Commons
Ottawa

Personal

My dear John,

I shall certainly read not only with interest but probably with surprise the speech mentioned in your note of Monday.

John Dafoe sent me the *Winnipeg Free Press*; and I rejoiced that Audrey had received so fine an appreciation. I expressed my thanks to Dafoe as well as to Roberton saying that I felt personally grateful.

With kind regards, I remain, yours faithfully,

Montreal Gazette

January 28, 1935

SOCIAL CONCEPT TO REPLACE
OLD ORDER: BENNETT

RUGGED INDIVIDUALISM MUST GO,
PRIME MINISTER DECLARES

GOVERNMENT HEAD ALSO INTERESTED IN
VIEWS OF CRIPPS AND JOHN STRACHEY

A social concept of living must replace the old rugged individualism, Rt. Hon. R.B. Bennett, Prime Minister of Canada, told a distinguished gathering in the Mount Royal Hotel Saturday night on the occasion of the annual dinner of the Montreal Board of Trade.

The Prime Minister implied that his talks with Soviet Foreign Minister Litvinoff at Geneva, and his study of the views of Sir Stafford Cripps and John Strachey, British radicals, had influenced him to a great extent, while he also pointed out the lessons that could be learned from the French and Russian revolutions.

Mr Bennett argued that science and invention had brought about entirely new conditions to those met in former years and 'we must now have the social ideal as distinguished from what we formerly conceived to be the individual right. The social trend must be the determining factor of the future, as the individualistic ideal was of the times gone by.'

Translating this view into the field of government, the Prime Minister, who declared that he had no intention of making a political speech on that occasion, said: 'If you think that over I think you will realize that more and more the obligation of the State, as representing the sum total of the forces of the country, must be apparent.' He frequently appealed to his hearers to study such questions and he believed that they, like him, would acknowledge that down through the nineteen centuries during which the capitalistic system had been developing it had gathered an accumulation of debris, 'as well as good.' It was the evils that must be remedied 'if we wish to maintain the system which has stood us so well in the past.'

Some of the most prominent leaders in the business, industrial and financial fields in Canada heard the Prime Minister express views that appeared at times startling but which were all underlined with his declaration that 'I stand by my Conservative principles.'

Congratulating the Board of Trade on its great accomplishments in the upbuilding of Canada, the Prime Minister reviewed the growth of the British Empire and paid tribute to those great figures who had left home to go out to the various fields across the seas to help in its development. It was about the time when the Montreal Board of Trade was first established that Britain fixed the gold standard which had played such a great part in developing trade throughout the world.

But the present times, Mr Bennett continued, were somewhat analagous to a time 1900 years ago when the credit of Rome was violently shaken. It was true that a riot had occurred in Palestine following a certain crucifixion but the main factors were the loss of ships bringing to the Imperial city their precious freight cargoes, and to a strike down in Phoenicia, and to a prominent man who had embezzled the monies entrusted to him. Rumors spread along the Via Sacra, what we would now call St James Street. There was a large firm that did a sort of overriding business. People saw their securities were frozen. In northern Gaul a moratorium was declared. A great firm went into bankruptcy and the *Journal* – analogous to the morning *Gazette* – of that day, announced that the firm had closed its doors. It was a very serious time.

And similar to what took place today, people looked to the government and 100 millions were given by the Imperial Treasury and the situation was saved. Rome continued for another 400 years, the Prime Minister proceeded.

'Now, the system they employed was not materially different to the system we have employed. It was a capitalist system, and during the intervening years it has flourished and it is the rock upon which has developed modern business. You and I have known no other, seen no other.

'But recently there have arisen eminent men, able men who have said the capitalist system cannot be saved. Those of you who read what Mr. John Strachey has said will know his views. He is one of the profound thinkers of our times and also a prolific writer on this theme.

'The system under which we have lived has been challenged as never before. It has been said it will no longer endure, that it cannot endure and must fall. Now I do not believe this system must fall. I believe this system can and may continue. But I believe there must be great modifications in the system if it is to continue to give us good service.

'But when the system is challenged in high places, when men of great thought and ability challenge the system then it is the duty of every one of you, the younger men in particular, to carefully consider what is at the base of the system and whether it is the thing it appears and whether it can revivify itself. That is the duty of the members of the Board of Trade. We must not be content to drift along and say in time all will be well.'

The Prime Minister recalled that communications for one thing had immeasurably outstripped those of the days of Imperial Rome and with such changed conditions they must reckon. 'Changed conditions,' he continued, 'mean changed results, and the conditions are very much changed from those with which we grew up to manhood from the days when we were boys.'

Mr Bennett said that the conditions of the 17th century were one thing and those of the 19th century were another. 'The law of supply and demand can be modified and changed by human action, as it has been.

'When you hear people say there is no such thing as change, I would remind you that there is change because the premises on which we build are so vastly different from those on which men first built their laws and made their regulations during the last century.

'The basic idea behind the capitalist system is the profit motive. The socialist does not approve of that idea. Shall we then substitute for the profit motive something else? It has been the governing motive since the beginning of the Christian era. Now if this motive is left unrestricted, uncontrolled or unregulated it will bring about a condition that is disheartening to mankind and ruinous to our civilization. But where shall regulation end? That is the question.

'The profit motive secured production, the basis of our life. It ensured the farmer produced grain and crops and the transportation companies supplied us with a mediocre service. The motive secured production, that has been its guiding principle.'

Mr Bennett went on to discuss the factor of the 'open market place' which recent conditions due to economic nationalization had ruled out. Then there was the 'flexibility' of the system with its checks and balances. 'Where are these checks and balances today?' he asked. He proceeded to outline steps taken in various countries to curtail production and destroy commodities.

'The essential thing to remember,' Mr Bennett commented, 'is that international trade as we know it no longer exists. Only one-third of the world's trade is left.' He enumerated the chief causes as the war, debts which the United States insisted should be paid in gold instead of goods, and, owing to the abandonment of the gold standard, the inability to have a yardstick to measure the value of currencies.

The Prime Minister pointed out the difficulties of governments faced with such perplexing conditions. It had to choose between imposing tariffs to protect its industrial workers and the welfare of the consumer.

'But I say with great frankness there are one or two industries I would never have allowed in this country' he added. 'The question is to balance the advantages and the disadvantages.'

Pointing out that there were certain changed conditions that were here to stay, Mr Bennett said, in his judgment, it was his conviction that they would never return to former conditions. 'Some of you might differ. I respect your views. You might be right, but I don't think so. We have those new conditions and we must deal with them.'

His conception was they could no longer view such matters in the light of the individual. Science and invention had brought about such conditions that the individual could no longer be regarded as the dominant factor. 'We must now think of the social ideal as distinguished from what we conceived formerly to be the individual right. Without such an ideal the struggle is not worth while. The social ideal must be the determining factor in the future as the individualistic ideal was in the past.

'There must be less and less opportunity for the exploitation of resources or people. I say that to you with great frankness, that must be so. How can it be otherwise? You may dismiss these thoughts or on the other hand say this is bunk, but I put it to you, what is the alternative? Human nature is very patient but it has occasionally asserted itself. It asserted itself in France, in Russia. It asserted itself in Germany and it is apparent in other countries of the world as well. The wise man is the one who foresees disaster and foreseeing it prevents it. Do you mean to tell me conditions can continue as they have been for very much longer?'

After referring to his conversations at Geneva with Litvinoff and expressing his admiration for the abilities of Sir Stafford Cripps, the Prime Minister went on to say that in his judgment they could save the system 'but only by having a social concept instead of individual rights.'

Declaring that the principle 'Who is my neighbour' was as old as time, Mr Bennett agreed that human initiative should have ample opportunity to expand. But 'we are so bound by shibboleths and so concerned about old things,' he remarked. He was a lover of old things, too, and a Conservative in the best sense of the word. But when conditions had created a state that was no longer beneficial it was their job to lop off the evils and see to it that it regained its health.

In a final appeal to business, he said that no government was so foolish as to suggest it would run business for the business people. But at the same time no government should fail to regulate conditions so as to secure the fullest opportunity to all concerned in the welfare of this Dominion.

Shortly after the Ontario legislature opened in early 1935 the Attorney General in Premier Hepburn's government, Hon. A.W. Roebuck, in a nine-hour speech spread over three days, attacked the legality of power contracts which had been entered into several years before with certain Quebec power companies by the Ontario Hydro-Electric Power Commission.

The word 'repudiation' came into common usage – the credit of the province and of the country was called in question and the bond market was adversely affected.

On April 1, 1935, the Premier introduced his power legislation which not only provided that the contracts for the purchase of power by Ontario from the Quebec Beauharnois, Maclaren and Ottawa

Valley companies would be cancelled but also purported to bar any recourse to the courts by any parties affected. The bill was finally passed on April 11.

The following Limbo letter was written by Sir Robert upon his return from holiday in the south. The reference to Thomas Ahearn is to the late T.F. Ahearn, a prominent Ottawa businessman and Liberal member for Ottawa West in the House of Commons; Taschereau is the late Hon. L.A. Taschereau, then Prime Minister of Quebec; McQuesten is the late Hon T.B. McQuesten, then Minister of Public Works and Highways in the Hepburn government and a member of the Ontario Hydro-Electric Power Commission. Stewart Lyon was at that time Chairman of Ontario Hydro.

In the fifth paragraph of this letter Sir Robert refers to an 'appended paper' submitted to him on the power contract situation by Loring C. Christie and in the last paragraph refers to 'information derived from Christie and from others' and 'an attached memorandum.' The author of the attached 'Notes on the Hydro-Quebec Power Contracts' dated March 12, 1935 was Christie.

The 'attached Memorandum' dated 4.5.35 was prepared by Christie, presumably for consideration by the Prime Minister (Mr Bennett).

The attached 'Notes on the National Emergency' dated April 11, 1935, the suggested draft press release of the power companies and the 'Footnote' dated April 16, 1935 were also prepared by Christie.

Sir Robert was, of course, the author of the memo dated April 23, 1935, and headed 'Items gathered by Autolycus – Snapper up of unconsidered trifles.' His reference to Nixon is to the late Hon. Harry C. Nixon, then Provincial Secretary in Hepburn's government. The reference to Slaght is to the late A.G. Slaght, QC, prominent Liberal and at that time Counsel for the Ontario Hydro-Electric Power Commission. ED

April 24, 1935

REPUDIATION BY ONTARIO GOVERNMENT OF QUEBEC POWER CONTRACTS

Sir,

During our absence in United States, the Ontario government, under the premiership of Mitchell Hepburn, repudiated by legislative enactment binding contracts of Ontario which the preceding government had entered into with four Quebec power companies. This action was based on the assumption that the contracts required Ontario to receive and pay for more power than could be used under present conditions. This consideration would have justified negotiation with the companies; but the stark repudiation which ensued was malevolent, stupid, maladroit, wholly indefensible and highly detrimental to the credit of Ontario and of Canada. In Great Britain and United States it has dried up investments in Canadian securities. Further, it has almost destroyed the abounding confidence of US investors in the stability of our institutions. Great statesmen of the Liberal party have invariably proclaimed the duty of a new administration to keep faith with the contractual engagements of its predecessor. Foremost among those who set forth this wholesome doctrine was William Ewart Gladstone.

Since returning to Canada, I have heard with amazement that businessmen of repute, such as Thomas Ahearn of Ottawa and men of the like type in Toronto, not only condone but support Hepburn's action. This is cogent evidence that political partisanship is closely allied with absolute stupidity.

Under our political system, a single instrument of governance can bring about confusion, even chaos, by exercising irresponsibly its powers to their full limit. Ontario has done this; and Quebec could retaliate by prohibiting the export of power to Ontario, in which case many communities in the latter province would be subjected to intense inconvenience and serious loss.

It is improbable that Taschereau will take any such course. Probably he is greatly disturbed by Ontario's repudiation but he must look to his political fences which are not very strong at the moment. He may refrain from any step that would injure Hepburn's influence in the approaching federal election.

Loring C. Christie, who for several years was legal adviser to the Department of External Affairs and confidential secretary to me as minister of that department, has submitted to me the appended paper in which he has, ably and impressively, set forth the situation as he views it.

In his opinion, Hepburn's hand was forced by Roebuck with whom Hepburn does not dare to quarrel, as Roebuck has knowledge of some extremely damaging circumstances in Hepburn's career. Roebuck and McQuesten who control Hydro (with poor Stewart Lyon in a farcical condition of helplessness) are 'red', unscrupulous Communists, ambitious and determined.

The development of such a situation is not inspiring to those who believe, as I do, that democracy is, on the whole, the fairest method of governance hitherto devised by the wit of mankind.

Based on information derived from Christie and from others I transmitted by mail to Mr Bennett (on April 23) at his temporary London address a copy of the attached memorandum.

I remain, Sir, Yours faithfully,

March 12, 1935

NOTES ON THE HYDRO–QUEBEC POWER CONTRACTS

Mr Roebuck's case is that these contracts were dishonestly made, the result of a sinister conspiracy between the Ontario Government (with the Hydro Commission as a willing tool) on the one hand and the several power companies on the other. At the tail-end of his charges he does bring in certain fancy legal points; but it seems plain that in his capacity of statesman he does not think these are enough by themselves. They are devised rather as a convenient even if doubtful pathway by which his hearers may, if they like, ease their consciences and crash through to freedom from the burdensome consequences of an iniquitous conspiracy.

To this main charge of dishonesty and conspiracy he brings no evidence. The essence of his case is that the quantity of contracted power is now so greatly in excess of Ontario needs that the judgment which authorized these contracts must necessarily be regarded as a dishonest judgment.

This is a conclusion. The essential facts of the power surplus, both in Ontario and elsewhere, have been in plain public view now for a long time. No one else in a responsible position, with any experience of the power industry or in affairs generally, has ever ventured to draw such a conclusion.

The conclusion may be tested by various yardsticks. One would be to consider the circumstances existing and known at the time of the contracts; another, to consider the judgment exercised by businessmen, administrators and financiers as regards power supplies for other regions of the continent and as regards other businesses involving the provision of great capital plant for long periods ahead.

What were the circumstances in which these contracts were made? Everyone in the power business knows that Hydro faced a shortage. The progressive needs could be estimated over a ten year period or longer by analytical methods which were well accepted by engineers and economists in the industry, and these methods were in fact used. Hydro was responsible for the industrial, commercial and domestic electrical needs of all the settled regions of Ontario – an unusually comprehensive responsibility which meant that the program must be especially large and that it must be especially secure and varied, since there was no competitor to meet these needs in the event either of new industrial expansion in the Province or of accident.

To meet these needs Hydro could consider three alternatives: (1) development of Ontario waters; (2) steam; or (3) Quebec power.

As regards the first – development of Ontario waters – there were only three sources that really counted. (a) As to Niagara, Hydro procured through Ottawa the signature of a treaty with Washington to permit further diversions of water and power development, but while this was ratified at Ottawa it was rejected by the American Senate. (b) As for the International Section of the St Lawrence the efforts initiated by Beck were continued; but it was plain they had no real chance, while even today no one can guess how many years more must go by before these waters – as well as Niagara – can be developed. (c) Nor was the development of Ontario's half of the Ottawa River sites within her power alone. The co-operation of the Quebec government as to boundary changes and jurisdiction was needed, and for some sites the co-operation of Ottawa as well; while there are special complications about the problem of a development jointly owned by a private company on the one hand and a public ownership enterprise on the other. In the event, these difficulties were solved in only one case – that of Chats Falls. It was common knowledge among all who followed public affairs in those days that urgent efforts were made to get into Ontario's half of these three waterways. The efforts were made during the period of negotiation of the contracts. Certainly no one could maintain a case that they were dishonest and insincere efforts.

As regards the second alternative – steam – no one ever seriously considered or would consider it as a real policy for primary power needs in Central Canada with its great water power sites and its total lack of coal. It would have meant a great capital investment, to be scrapped when Ontario waters were eventually developed, as they would certainly be some day after a change in the international and interprovincial situation; as well as great importations of coal from United States and transfers of Canadian funds in return. It would have put Ontario at the mercy of events in the American coalfields and of American prices and exchange fluctations. If any one pretends to use the steam idea today as a means of attack upon these primary power contracts, he ought to produce an analysis estimating what would have been the cost – capital plus operation plus coal – of the same kind of power from 1926 to date, and then compare the result with the so-called deficit of today, and he ought to take account of the disadvantages just mentioned. The real use of the steam estimates and propositions made during the period of the contracts was to bring down the price of Quebec power from $18 and $19 to the very favourable price of $15.

As for the third, and the only real, alternative to which the Hydro might turn – i.e. Quebec power – the case as put at the time was at least fourfold. It provided for Ontario's needs at a cost that was regarded as being as low as Ontario would have to face had she been able to develop her own waters. It did not involve an increase of Ontario's capital debt structure. It was regarded as gaining for Ontario an advantage over Quebec in accelerating Ontario's superior industrial development (a circumstance which gave rise to natural criticism in Quebec at the time). It kept money circulating in Canada that would otherwise go to the United States for coal.

Whether or not people now accept all these considerations they were certainly present at the time in the minds of those who were dealing with or seriously studying the subject. No one can say they were fanciful. Some will say they still hold substantially good and that eventually Ontario will rediscover that she made a good bargain. But certainly they cannot be distorted into the elements of a dishonest judgment.

It is said, however, that the parties kept on making these contracts in 1929 and 1930 when good administrators ought to have known that the present depression was coming. Doubtless some people at that time did anticipate a depression. But what they anticipated was the ordinary cyclical depression of relatively brief duration to which our economy had become accustomed. To the power industry such a depression would not be a matter of great gravity. That industry, by its nature, has to plan and take great capital commitments for long periods of years. The actual construction of water power plants is in itself a matter of four or five years and longer before the stage of full capacity is reached. The ordinary depression would be taken by the industry in its stride, and adequate plant had to be ready for the expansion to be expected once the country had started climbing the other side of the valley.

But not even Sherlock Holmes could find the man on this continent – particularly the businessman or financier or politician – who in 1929 or 1930 imagined *this* depression with its world scope and unprecedented depth. No one but a few of the then despised economists even hinted at it, and none of them saw its real character. There is nothing along these lines that can be twisted into dishonest judgment.

The case is, further, that there was not only dishonest judgment at the Hydro but that there was a conspiracy, which means that the power companies were bent upon unloading on the Hydro great quantities of power which they knew to be superfluous. But of course they employed the same kind of estimates and were moved by the same outlook regarding the economic future as the Hydro was.

This brings up the second yardstick mentioned above. As regards future power supplies for other regions than Ontario and as regards other industries or services involving the provision of capital commitments for long periods ahead, how did business men generally exercise their judgment during the time these contracts were made? If it were of interest figures could be produced to show that other regions on this continent are faced with the same position that faces Ontario today. Quebec herself has to face a similar surplus of power. Of the total capacity of the four companies contracting with the Hydro from 1926 onward, less than half was provided for Ontario; indeed they were forbidden by the Quebec government to sell more than half to Ontario, and their power cannot be sold in Quebec at greater prices than the Ontario price. The balance of their capacity was provided for Quebec uses; it represents today a burdensome surplus for Quebec. But it is due simply to the unprecedented world depression. It must be remembered that actually the power industry in Canada is 50% an export industry – that is to say, 50% of its output is consumed in making goods for export. It was on the basis of Canada's export trade that the magnitude of her power industry was planned and built.

Other industries and services involving large capital are in precisely the same boat today – all because of the depression. It has been estimated that the vacant space in the great business and residential buildings of New York city today equals the equipment of a city as large as Pittsburgh. Numerous other examples will occur to anyone – railways, and so on.

By hind-sight these may be regarded by some people as examples of unsound business judgment, but no one in such a connection ever suggests that the case is one of dishonest or corrupt judgment or conspiracy. In view of the Hydro Chairman's recent estimates, mentioned below, it may even turn out that Hydro's judgment was on the whole at least as good as that of any great enterprise on the continent.

To the extent to which they exceeded Quebec's then estimated requirements, the building of these Quebec power plants, the creation of these bond issues, were carried through to ensure electrical service *and stand-by* for the Hydro and Ontario. Ontario got the private companies to take on the capital risk, knowing that the power contracts would either be subjected to bond mortgages or would be advertised in connection with the sale of bonds. Because Toronto and the Niagara system use only 25-cycle power, the companies had to buy and install 25-cycle generators and other equipment, all built to Hydro specifications and at higher prices – equipment which is useless for anyone else, as Quebec and other regions can use only 60-cycle current. The Quebec government had to be asked to permit the power to go into Ontario; and it was this request and the prospect of contracts which induced the Quebec government to authorize the building of the several power developments at their present magnitude. In the face of criticism about power going out of Quebec the Quebec government recognized the claims of interprovincial comity.

The price was not regarded as extortionate; it was regarded as reasonable. The Beauharnois reorganization of 1933 shows that so far as that company's development is concerned, there is no bonanza in $15 power.

So far as Ontario's burden is concerned, it appears that as yet no deficit has really arisen. No burden has yet been cast upon the people, for the electrical rates have not had to be increased. Even if a real deficit should arise under the Hydro's 'power at cost' statutory accounting method, it could be overcome by a small increase in rates. In this connection it is well to recall the advertisements published in the Toronto papers some years ago (in 1928) by the Toronto Hydro to the effect that certain users of electricity (in the upper brackets of consumption) were getting their power at less than cost. This was part of a campaign to increase rates, which in the event the Commission failed to carry through.

However, it appears that the power contracts can be carried even without an increase in rates to the consumer. In the January and February 1935 issues of 'The Bulletin' published by the Hydro Commission and in a speech to the Toronto Electric Club on February 27, 1935, the new Chairman of the Commission reviews the financial and operating position. He indicates that the surplus is only a temporary surplus; he says that 'a year or two may elapse before the demand for power overtakes the obligations to accept supply under contract'. He refers to the contingency and other reserves, which were instituted a good while ago to meet the stress of difficult times. He indicates that the reserves have succeeded so far in taking up all the slack due to the Quebec contracts and other contingencies and that these reserves will continue to accumulate out of existing rates to such an extent that, in his words, 'it is my firm conviction that the fund will be sufficient to see us through the lean years.' He says further: 'I think we may safely say now that there will be no need to increase Hydro rates in any general way to provide the funds for the payment of power the Commission is forced to accept from the Quebec contractors.'

In the face of these circumstances, where is there any conceivable case for revision of the terms of these contracts? Under our economy there is only one thing which justifies a government or public body in asking its creditors to revise or ameliorate in any way the terms of its obligation – and that is a public declaration of inability to pay accompanied by definite evidence establishing that inability in the minds of reasonable men. Not only has Ontario not made such a declaration, but it appears from the public testimony of the chief administrator of her electrical utility that it will be able to pay for these contracts even out of the existing rates, which are regarded as among the lowest on the continent.

4·5·35

MEMORANDUM

Start with this: that, as will be seen, it is the clear duty of the Federal government to disallow Ontario's act of repudiation.

Let it be granted that this is an extraordinary power, to be exercised perhaps only in an emergency and for national purposes. But the emergency and the national purpose plainly exist. This action by the richest, the most powerful province in the Confederation, coming on top of like manifestations elsewhere in the Dominion, has profoundly shaken people's confidence inside and outside Canada. Ignore it officially, and you have in effect invited the provinces and municipalities across Canada to do likewise.

This is the sole instrument of state by which you can take official note of it – by which you can unmistakably exert Canada's will that her emergency shall be solved by orderly means within the framework of our accepted economic system and that her credit shall be preserved intact. There is no other instrument for the purpose: the courts are barred: the Canadian confederators in 1867, rejected the precedent of the American Constitution. But they created this power, and if ever an occasion could be conceived demanding its exercise, this is it. They were created a federal state, and if ever a case could arise going to the root of such an institution's effectiveness, this is it. Section 90 is there for a plain purpose, and its existence undoubtedly imposes a responsibility. The Ontario Act has been or will be certified and submitted to Ottawa.

You cannot evade the responsibility by any resort to calculations of party advantage. There is only one question you can ask yourself – a question of fact. Does a national necessity exist? You dare not assert that it does not. If the Federal government fails to disallow this Act and the general election proceeds on existing lines, you dare not assert to anyone, inside or outside Canada, that the present administration or anyone else can govern efficiently or can guarantee an orderly solution of our problem and the preservation of our credit. You can no more postpone your decision upon disallowance till after the election than a court could postpone its decision upon such a calculation. Section 90 cannot be read by the Governor-in-Council in any such sense.

The underlying conclusion, then, is that disallowance is an unavoidable and immediate duty: that is the starting point.

But if you must not attempt to *avoid* it upon grounds of party advantage, equally you must not attempt to *use* it for party purposes. In the end you may be driven to exercise the power alone, but before doing that you must exhaust every effort to secure the widest and strongest base upon which it can be exercised – that is, to bring in the other national parties to the greatest possible extent. The whole national financial position and the necessity of disallowance must be put to them. They too must be given the opportunity to sink party considerations, to act as national men, to share in the orderly solution of the whole emergency, of which this is but one manifestation.

That means a coalition – a National Government – as comprehensive as possible and as soon as possible before the election.

The issue: Are we to solve our national debt and credit emergency by orderly means and at Ottawa where it belongs, or, are we to allow it to be immeasurably compromised by the provinces and municipalities, where it does not belong? Is Canada a nation or an anarchy?

The platform: Broadly speaking, ask for a free hand, a 'doctor's mandate'. Promise treatment as drastic as diagnosis may show to be necessary. A Royal Commission on the whole debt and financial problem – federal, provincial, municipal – or some other form of thorough diagnosis – immediately. Bring in outside expert advisers, like Sir Otto Niemeyer or Sir George May. The reform program now in progress to be examined together on the widest basis that can be agreed upon as desirable and workable.

The personnel: This factor becomes relatively not so vital once agreement has been reached among steady men to cooperate with each other and with all orderly elements of the country. That in itself is the keystone of confidence.

On such a basis you can practically guarantee an orderly solution of our problems and the preservation of our credit, and you can guarantee it in the quickest time. You base yourself upon sure ground – upon the realities of federalism – upon the letter and spirit of the constitution. On any other basis you can guarantee nothing: you are in an incalculable realm both as to results and as to time; you will not have government at Ottawa, you will have abdication.

If Canada goes into the general election on existing lines, what will you have? You now have steady, capable men on both and indeed on all three sides, with essentially the same outlook on most of our problems and certainly on our present emergency. You will see them divided – arrayed against each other in an unreal fight – driven to press party advantage to the limit – wasting powder on each other over non-essentials – vying with gangsters, demagogues and crackpots, in all ranks – insensibly giving ground here and there to subversive or unworkable proposals. You will see a House of Commons of a temper and character from which you can guarantee nothing, from which good can be extracted only by chance and at an expenditure of time and confusion that will drain still lower our reservoirs of confidence. The whole spectacle will be an exhibition of unreality, fantastic to the point of insanity, that can only set the country back to some incalculable extent. It will be an assault upon the finest values of our community life, values that today, if ever, ought to be enlisted and mobilized by every resource of leadership; for if this is not somehow done, we shall have given away most of the battle, and we need not be surprised if other forces win large gains, if values bred of misery and despair and disillusionment are for a time seized and molded to subversive ends in Canada as elsewhere in the world of today. On what ground can Canada alone imagine herself able to carry on through this crisis under banners of 'politics as usual,' 'business as usual.' Practically every other community in the western world has been driven to drop such luxuries and turn to serious political thinking and means of government.

And a consideration of the gravest moment is this: that the chaotic political conditions that are likely to follow a general election fought on existing lines will be calculated to discredit democratic institutions themselves in this country.

The people of Canada are essentially a steady, cool-minded people when given a chance; they are today predisposed toward unity; many of them – no one knows how many, but it is a great number in all sections, certainly among the middle-aged and younger – being increasingly uncertain about their party moorings and political allegiances. They do not really wish to take part in such a spectacle as now seems about to be offered to them. The people will support any agreed effort on the part of their leaders that promises to lead them out of such a predicament.

April 11, 1935

NOTES ON THE NATIONAL EMERGENCY

Private

I

It has been clear enough for months that Canada really faces a national emergency. The Ontario repudiation of power contracts is only one part of it. Roebuck's three-day speech in the Ontario legislature began on February 27th. The gradual unfolding of this particular situation during the past six weeks has been extremely illuminating. The experience of the power companies and their security holders provides a concrete illustration which, better than any theorizing, shows the realities of the national emergency and shows what may be expected if existing methods are allowed to continue.

For illustrative purposes it is worth analyzing that experience at some length. It will be seen that a fundamental issue has been definitely and inescapably raised; that it can only be treated in fundamental terms; that it means that Canada now faces the kind of crisis that many other countries since the war have been able to solve only by fundamental means; that – to be more specific – it can only be met by a realignment of political forces and a National Government; that every one having any responsibility towards any particular aspect of the crisis, such as the Ontario issue, must think in such terms and cannot usefully think in any other terms at this moment.

II

First, then, consider the experience of the power companies and their security holders. As for the security holders, it is enough to recall that from the outset every bondholder and every representative of the savings of the people of Canada who attempted to make orderly representations to Hepburn Roebuck & Co were thrown out the door. As for the company administrations, as soon as the issue broke out it instantly became apparent that it was extraordinary, that ordinary means of redress had been barred, and that we had to resort to political channels. This was inescapable. It was clear that the first step must be to explore whether the federal Liberal leaders and the Quebec provincial Liberals were able and willing to solve the problem privately within the framework of their existing party organization. It was seen that this should be done before discussing with Federal Conservatives the idea of disallowance within the framework of their party alone – an idea which, it was further realized, might well be illusory and prove to be a boomerang so far as any practical settlement of the issue was concerned.

At this stage therefore we are waiting to see whether the solution can be found within the existing party frameworks. As we are facing a general election we must expect to meet from the politicians various sorts of compromise formulas. The real implications of this course are therefore worth pursuing in some detail.

On ordinary occasions compromise is a useful device both in business and politics. But can it be entertained in this case under the guns of this legislation?

By compromise I mean anything short of full reinstatement of the power contracts – any sort of revision that means less favourable financial terms – any reduction of price or any reduction or postponement of deliveries – unless the discussion is preceded by an orderly impartial procedure under which there can be established in the minds of reasonable men the real merits as to (a) the validity of the contracts and (b) the question of Ontario's capacity to pay, coupled with an understanding that the new legislative pistol shall not be proclaimed in any circumstances.

Consider how the idea of compromise would work itself out upon the power companies. Assume that it takes the form of a new so-called 'contract' after the Hepburn Act has been proclaimed – or assume that the Act is not proclaimed and that the existing contracts are revised either by a re-writing or by supplementary documents with the weapon of the proclamation in the background – it is immaterial which assumption you use. In any case, taking Beauharnois as an example, a vital part of the security – i.e. of the 'specifically mortgaged premises' – would have been altered. Eventually a bondholders' meeting would have to be called to authorize a new supplementary trust deed accepting the new so-called power 'contract' as part of the security instead of the old contract. To make the bonds exchangeable and marketable you would have to advertise opinion of legal counsel. What could counsel say? They could say 'The Company has signed what purports to be a contract with the Ontario Commission for so many horsepower, subject always to be altered to meet the convenience of the Commission according to the discretion of the Ontario legislature,' or words to that effect. In short, it is a one-sided option exercisable probably at the next depression. Possibly lawyers might find some less realistic form of words that would sound reassuring; but the company administration – directors and officers – would without legal help understand the realities of such a so-called 'contract' stretching over a long term of years. How could they possibly offer or support before the public of this country or any other such a bond? In short, the financing of a compromise made at the point of this legislative pistol becomes literally impossible.

This spelling out of the Beauharnois position is only one way of illustrating concretely that any compromise under the guns of this legislation is equivalent to repudiation. The only distinction is that revision under the threat of this statute is a more cowardly form of repudiation than outright cancellation; for it represents a design to have the power companies and security holders join the government of Ontario and become accessories and accomplices to the act of repudiation. (It may be noted that the case would have been essentially the same without the legislation – that is to say, if Roebuck & Co. had carried out what is said to have been their original design of simply declaring the contracts unenforceable, refusing to pay and denying the companies a fiat to sue in the courts. By means of their legislation however they have succeeded in forcing all the Liberal members of the legislature to share the job of loading the revolver. They have brought the whole party representation into a definite, public acceptance of responsibility for the act of repudiation.)

For the sake of further illustration it is well to remember that

Beauharnois has at least five other major contracts with governments which are vital to its whole existence and operation. With Quebec there are two: the 40,000 c.f.s. and the 30,000 c.f.s. emphyteutic water power leases. With the dominion there are three: the Montreal Cotton water power leases, the contract incorporating the main Order-in-Council, and the conveyance to the crown which created the 'easements, servitudes and other rights' to take water to the power house through the government's canal. If you accept any compromise in the case of the power contracts you have simply notified the gangsters of the political world that these other contracts are open to a similar operation. That world would even eventually, in the case of the dominion, refer to the Beauharnois legislation of 1931 as a precedent and, in making their case to the public, they would know how to obscure the circumstances which differentiate that case from repudiation.

III

Let us carry a little further the question whether this fundamental issue of repudiation – this national credit emergency – can be solved within the existing party frameworks. Let us still keep to the case of the power contracts as an illustration. First, assume that we rely on representations and negotiations carried on through the channels of the Liberal party – the federal and provincial organizations.

On that basis Mr Taschereau is in no position to avoid what by definition and realistic analysis represents repudiation. This is so because (a) he must exert every effort to avoid a serious conflict between his government and the Ontario government in the face of the approaching federal and Quebec elections, and (b) he wants to get Hepburn's co-operation in the newsprint situation, as shown by the Bill introduced at Quebec yesterday, and in other situations.

Consider Hepburn. It is now crystal clear that he is not his own master in this situation. That fact began to emerge at the end of February when, after his return from a visit to North Bay, he found in Toronto that Roebuck in his opening attack had gone beyond Hepburn's understanding. At that moment he had his chance to disavow and retrieve the situation by the exercise of instant firmness. If he ever wanted to, the fact is that he did not exert his will in that sense. Eventually he began to get on the Roebuck band wagon. Since then it has become clear it was a McQuesten wagon also, and McQuesten is understood to be a stronger though more silent man than Roebuck. Roebuck and McQuesten are the majority of the Ontario Commission and they are undoubtedly running it. They are in the Hydro conductor's box; they have called the tune; Hepburn has had to dance to it. Recent evidence makes it clear that even if he was not an original party to the design, he now knows that he must keep on with it. He knows that it is too late to disavow his colleagues. He dare not split with them.

Roebuck and McQuesten are the Hydro Commission. They are legally in control of the Commission. Any contract with the Commission has to be made by them in the first instance. In short, any so-called new power 'contract' will be dictated by them, and the influence that can be exerted upon them through the channels of the existing party framework by Mr Taschereau, through any go-between or otherwise would not be very substantial.

Consider the federal Liberals. There is no evidence to date that they can really do anything decisive to avoid what would amount to repudiation. Given the existing lines of battle for the coming elections there is little that they can do.

Consider the Conservatives. They may be driven to disallowance of the Hepburn Act in an effort to help the national credit. This would not in itself immediately help the power situation, for Hepburn would refuse to pay; though it would keep the contracts alive and leave open the chance for a later enforcement if in the long run political developments turned out to be favourable. But disallowance by the Conservatives alone, without the support of the Federal Liberals raises the grave dangers of a fight on issues of provincial rights. Such issues might be successfully raised in such a way as to obscure the national credit issue and if the Conservatives were beaten, Hepburn & Co. would take the election as an endorsement of his position. In the upshot the national credit emergency would get out of control for an indefinite time.

The possibility that the Lieutenant-Governor of Ontario might refuse to sign the Hepburn Bill also raises the danger that an election in Ontario might be precipitated and that the issue might be fought on other lines than that of the credit emergency and thus likewise put that emergency out of control.

It is thus clear that the effort to solve this question within the existing party frameworks can only mean at best a compromise which would be equivalent to repudiation, and it possibly means letting the national emergency get out of control indefinitely.

IV

We have thus seen that the best we can look for within the existing party frameworks is an act which is indistinguishable in principle from repudiation and which the world will so regard.

The case of the power contracts, here analyzed for purposes of illustration, constitutes only one part of the real national issue and emergency. There are many other similar examples that are crowding up for settlement by one means or another, orderly or otherwise – the railway debt contracted, like the power contracts, during the pre-depression period, the various provincial and municipal debts and so on. The Dominion Government and the Bank of Canada must be at a standstill in considering their refunding and other financial plans. The banks and others know how many situations there are.

They are all contributing parts to one dominating issue that has hit practically all countries since the war, that none has been able to avoid, that none has been able to solve except by extraordinary political means. In essence it is the problem of how our political system is to deal with the debt structure of the country, the credit structure, the rate of interest question – call it what you will.

There are two ways of dealing with that issue. One is the method of widespread arbitrary repudiations. The other is the orderly method – refundings, conversions, every orderly financial device that can be employed, including a Royal Commission on the debt structure if you like.

The case of the power contracts and bonds upon analysis shows clearly that within existing party frameworks we can only expect the disorderly method of repudiation. On existing party lines we can expect that the McGeers, Hepburns, Roebucks, Bouchards and Aberharts will either dominate one of the existing parties or will be so strong a force within it as to render it helpless to attempt any orderly solution. Some of these men will prove to be ruthless gangsters – there need be no mistake about that.

The conclusion is inescapable that we have definitely reached a point when all responsible men must empty their minds of party prejudice and bias and join together to form a coalition and a National Government.

It would of course be vastly preferable to have it done immediately. Let them do it now before the lines get drawn tighter. Let them ask for a free hand – simply for a 'doctor's mandate' to deal with the national credit emergency – that is to say, along the lines upon which the National Government in England was returned to power in 1931.

It would have to be recognized that such a coalition would have to promise to deal with the emergency drastically and that the substantial elements of the country would have to agree to accept sacrifice. This would be a necessary price to pay in order to insure that our difficulties may be worked out by orderly methods. It need not be argued that the alternative – the disorderly method – would inflict far greater injuries and that these would take far longer to retrieve.

A National Government formed after the approaching elections would of course be a much more difficult and doubtful affair. The gangsters by that time would have a big position.

V

It happens that the power companies and security holders have had the lead thrust upon them in meeting the initial manifestation of the real national emergency – that is to say, the initial manifestation of the first magnitude. The issue is now clearly established and they cannot escape the leadership at this stage. What can they do about it?

What they can do about it at this stage is simply negative. They can take the attitude that they must resolutely oppose the idea of compromise at the point of the Ontario legislature's pistol. By maintaining that attitude as long as possible they will give time for the issue to become more and more clarified in the minds of reasonable and resolute men generally throughout the country and therefore time for the orderly method to assert its claims for attention. In the gradual development of that method the power companies and security holders cannot take the leadership. They can only join the other stable forces in the country.

The power companies and security holders must play their part by discussion as long as they can upon the plane of fundamental principle. They must take pains to see that their case – which has never yet been fairly considered – is put forward upon correct lines of procedure. They might start by means of a public statement which would indicate a readiness to discuss their particular issue, but upon the understanding that the question of the validity of their contracts should be referred to the courts or settled by some other impartial means and that the question of Ontario's capacity to pay should also be settled by some impartial process of investigation, it being understood also that the new Act would not be proclaimed in any circumstances – a statement along the lines of the attached draft.

This would represent a wholly justifiable appeal to the kind of procedure which is universally recognized throughout the English speaking world.

While the power companies are developing their case along such correct and orderly lines it is for the responsible political and other leaders of the community to get together and start the necessary re-alignment of forces in the country.

It seems clear enough that this sort of approach is the only one that offers any real hope alike for the power companies and their security holders and for a solution of the national emergency, of which their case has now become a dramatic and unmistakable sign-post.

To leave such fundamental issues to be solved within the existing party frameworks is, in the first place, to surrender to party convenience, and that simply means that you become the prisoner of the gangsters. To surrender to party convenience without even a whimper, without making even the elementary demand for a fair trial, would be the last folly.

Of course the thesis of these notes offers nothing but a long and arduous task. The experience of the power companies gives a good illustration of how difficult it will be to create and maintain a united front. Many people will say to themselves, 'Well, I don't want to face fundamental issues; they are unpleasant; I am clever enough to play ball with the gangsters and protect my own particular position.' They are profoundly mistaken, as world-wide modern history has shown.

The national emergency is on top of us, not tomorrow but today. It requires an instant, supreme, sustained exertion of will. It will not wait. The gangsters will not wait. They have pulled out their pistols and started shooting. The time to start fighting back is at the sound of the first shot. L.C.C.

DRAFT REFERRED TO IN THE FOREGOING NOTES

The Quebec power companies have hitherto refrained from making any statement concerning their contracts with the Hydro-Electric Power Commission of Ontario, since they were advised by responsible quarters in Ontario and they themselves felt that such a course might only do harm while the question was still *sub judice* in the Ontario legislature. Now that the special legislation has been enacted, they believe, in view of the many inquiries received, that they should make a statement for the information of their security holders.

The contracts with the Ontario Commission and the securities issued on the faith of those contracts were made as the result of prolonged negotiations conducted on both sides by engineers, accountants and legal advisers of repute. Their validity was publicly attested on both sides by eminent legal counsel, as both the companies and the Commission were most anxious that no legal doubt could be cast upon transactions of such magnitude and duration.

These are not mere contracts for the delivery of certain quantities of articles or commodities and it only obscures realities to consider the matter as if they were. They are contracts under which the companies undertook to build and did build vast permanent plants and equipment for the purpose of guaranteeing electrical power service to the Commission and the Province of Ontario for forty years – to furnish power and energy up to the full limit of the quantities whenever demanded by the Commission – to act as stand-by at all times up to that limit – the companies being barred throughout the whole period from giving any commitments in respect of the greatest part of such quantities to any other customer. This is the customary and necessary basis on which the electrical power industry rests everywhere. The Quebec government had to be asked to permit the power to enter Ontario and the Ontario government made this request. The request induced the Quebec government to authorize the building of the several power developments at their present magnitude. It is well remembered that the idea of power going out of Quebec was strongly criticized at the time, but Quebec in the end recognized the claims of inter-provincial neighbourliness. It was fully contemplated on both sides that the contracts would be subjected to bond mortgages and that bonds would be issued and advertised thereon. In fact special provisions of some of the contracts contemplated such mortgages.

To the extent therefore to which they exceeded Quebec's then estimated requirements these great power plants were built for Ontario – to guarantee electrical stand-by and service for her industry and people – and upon the inducement of her duly constituted authorities. Upon the same inducement and to avoid increasing Ontario's capital debt structure the capital was provided by the companies and their security holders.

Naturally the companies are always willing to discuss any matter of mutual interest with a customer. The companies have never directly received any complaint from the Ontario Commission. Certain complaints however have recently been made on its behalf in the Ontario legislature. As indicated above, it now seems justifiable that the companies should make some comment.

One of the complaints questions the validity of the contracts. The second suggests that as a result of intervening events it is now beyond the capacity of Ontario or the electricity users of Ontario to pay the amounts specified in the contracts to be paid monthly and yearly in consideration of the companies having built these plants to secure electrical stand-by and service for Ontario.

There is a well established procedure for dealing with cases where governments or public bodies raise questions of this nature and ask their creditors to ameliorate the terms of their obligations. It is a procedure well known and frequently used throughout the English speaking world. It is universally recognized as the only kind of procedure which is calculated to maintain intact the essential element of confidence in our economic system.

As to the first complaint, this kind of procedure would refer the question of the validity of the contracts to the courts or would provide some other impartial means of settling the question beyond a doubt.

As to the second complaint, the procedure would be to refer the question of capacity to pay to some impartial process of investigation, so that it might be fully considered on its merits by engineers, accountants and economists.

The company administrators feel that their security holders would expect them to take the attitude that it is to be understood that any discussion with the Commission must be based upon an acceptance of a procedure of this nature and upon an understanding that the new legislation will not be proclaimed and brought into force.

April 16, 1935

FOOTNOTE

Since the general thesis of these notes revolves around the conception of 'credit' – particularly that of national credit – and since in discussion one sometimes becomes aware of a hesitancy as to the realities of that conception, a word may be added for the sake of clarity – the case of the power contracts and bonds again being used for purposes of illustration.

The realities of credit of course drive you to consider the simplicities of trust, confidence, belief. You get into the realm of calculation of intention and firmness of intention. In estimating a man's credit you have to ask what are the expectations, what are the probabilities, of his acting or behaving firmly in a certain way as regards the particular relationship which is to be entered into between you, either on his proposal or on yours.

The conception of national credit brings up similar calculations, but they are necessarily more complex than in the case of the individual. The nation is a complex. It is not merely the government, or the legislatures, or the politicians, or the corporations, or their managers, or the universities, or their heads, or the churches, or their heads. It is the thing that arises as a resultant from the interplay of the various behaviours of all these elements and others. To estimate the national credit you have to calculate what are the expectations, the probabilities, that out of this interplay there will always emerge a firm intent to keep to the given word. You have to estimate the extent to which each element regards itself as a part of the national complex, as well as its awareness of a sense of responsibility for the final resultant in any situation and its firmness in exercising that responsibility. In grave situations – in any national emergency involving peace or war or orderly or disorderly ways of viewing the credit of the nation – you always find in the end that, behind all the formal façades of governmental or political or business or financial organizations, the decision is made one way or another by a gradual process of interchange and calculation between the relatively few people who in each community across the country are informally recognized as leaders – that is, the resolute managing minds of the nation. They are men of all parties, some of them in active politics, some of them behind the public façade.

Consider for illustrative purposes the present case of the power contracts and bonds. You have an interplay between the political and the business and financial elements in the national complex. You have an extraordinary act by one group of politicians who are in a seat of governmental power. They propose to use that power, that machinery of government, as a force, a club, a weapon – and by force at least to whittle down the rights of certain elements in the country – elements who are not all even in their own province. It is a completely arbitrary exercise of governmental power. No opportunity has been or is to be afforded to show cause in an orderly way why the thing should not be done. Every doorway to such an elementary remedy has been banged and bolted. It is a violent assault upon the most ancient constitutional aspects of the common law of the land. If allowed to continue such a process would be tantamount to revolution. There is a certain calmness at the moment, but there is an undercurrent indicating that the realities are gradually forcing themselves upon men's consciousness.

What, in these circumstances, will be the effect upon the national credit if the power companies and security holders, with the consent of the leading financial and business groups, surrender to this arbitrary act of government, this loaded weapon – if they simply place themselves in the hands of the political colleagues of those who have loaded and pointed the weapon and through such a channel accept what is called a 'compromise' – if they fail to demand the most elementary right known to the common law of the land, the right to have the case alleged against them publicly exposed and determined by some impartial process, free from the menacing shadow of this new legislation?

If an individual hands over his pocket book at the point of a gangster's pistol, his credit is not affected. If a bank messenger in such a crisis hands over a portfolio entrusted to him, there is always theft insurance to be reckoned in.

But in this case there is no insurance fund and there cannot be. The only insurance is the awareness and firmness of resolve and responsibility of all those elements who – as we have seen – by the interplay of their behaviour at any crisis express the national character.

Any 'negotiated' revision of the contracts – any 'compromise' – under the guns of this legislation is seen upon analysis to be equivalent to arbitrary repudiation. If this surrender is made – if elementary rights are not insisted upon – will not the people of other countries as well as this country be driven to the calculation that in a moment of crisis you cannot count upon the awareness and firmness of resolve of the business leaders of Canada who are entrusted with a part of the responsibility for the management of the nation's economy and the savings of the people of this and other lands. Will it not in the end be said that in effect, because they disliked unpleasantness, they sat down and became accomplices to this violent act of repudiation? It has not been the fashion in the English speaking world to submit to arbitrary confiscation of rights by government without violent protest.

If such a surrender is made – if the power companies finally find themselves without support and decide to accept 'compromise' – if they fail to demand the orderly means by which alone they can hope to fulfil their simple covenant "to maintain the security", which appears in every Trust Deed – it seems clear enough that realistic observers inside and outside Canada will be forced to the calculation that Canada's credit is a most doubtful affair – that she is in for a prolonged and incalculable emergency. L.C.C.

April 23, 1935

ITEMS GATHERED BY AUTOLYCUS – SNAPPER UP OF UNCONSIDERED TRIFLES

1 Provincial Liberal Board of Strategy – Hepburn, Nixon, Slaght.

2 Hepburn visited north country; Roebuck, in his absence, to

throw dirt at Henry government; Roebuck, without authority from Hepburn or from Board, made his nine-hour speech declaring power-contracts void.

3 Previously to this there had been a fierce quarrel which nearly resulted in Roebuck's resignation.

4 Slaght consulted Hydro legal department before giving opinion that MacLaren-Quebec contracts were valid; now declares himself 'flabbergasted' by Roebuck's action. Capable Toronto counsel think he is sincere in this.

5 As indicated above, Roebuck forced Hepburn's hand; and the latter was compelled to submit.

6 Hepburn completely in Roebuck's power, as latter has knowledge of grave circumstances.

7 Roebuck aspires either to Provincial leadership, or preferably to Federal arena.

8 Roebuck and McQuesten are 'red' Communists and are in complete control of Hydro, Stewart Lyon being merely a sorry façade.

9 Twelve Liberal members were prepared to vote against repudiation but by some means, probably by the proclamation clause, they were quieted.

10 Many efforts have been made to sound Mackenzie King; but he has retired within the lines of Torres Vedras; and from him no sound, not even a sigh.

11 There is unrest in Liberal ranks. Ralston declares he must retire on account of business affairs; Euler threatened to repudiate Provincial Liberal party; Senator Hardy has put in vigorous protests.

12 Small groups in several Canadian cities may be organized to educate public opinion on the effects of repudiation. Presently a considerable majority of the Ontario electorate are said to favour Hepburn's policy. (Read an article in current *Atlantic Monthly* which describes the neolithic mass out of which a few human beings are occasionally produced.)

13 In responsible quarters there is an intense feeling that Hepburn should not find his policy profitable, either economically or politically.

14 But the Power executives are prepared to negotiate with him and they intend to make a bargain at the expense of the bond holders which will result in advantage to the executives in whom the common stock equity is vested.

15 There are indications that repudiation and legislation based on the Price Spreads Commission may divergently cut across party lines at the next election.

16 The following rumour is current. An Independent Liberal party

in Quebec, organized by Gouin, desires Gagnon as leader and offers to drop the word 'Liberal'. Senator Moraud strongly urges Gagnon to accept.

17 Taschereau is taking into his cabinet Bouchard who has warmly approved Ontario repudiation. He expects so far to lower the value of the Quebec power companies' properties that the Quebec government can acquire them at its own price.

18 The Gouin Independent Liberal Party is bitterly opposed to Bouchard's proposals.

19 An attentive observer suggests that the King-Taschereau-Hepburn-Roebuck tactics will string along negotiations until after the Federal election at which they confidently anticipate a Liberal triumph.

20 Conditions are in such a flux that these items may probably have become valueless before their receipt.

From 1933 until his death Sir Robert was president of the Dominion Drama Festival which was founded by Lord Bessborough early in his term as Governor-General.

The following two Limbo letters deal primarily with the Festival in April, 1935, and in April, 1937. The letter dated May 13, 1937, was the last dictated by Sir Robert, who died early the following month. It was not corrected or revised by him but I have included it in this volume and out of its chronological order for reasons which should be obvious to the reader.

April 29, 1935

DOMINION DRAMA FESTIVAL, 1935

Sir,

The Dominion Drama Festival opened a week ago today and continued until the following Saturday (April 27). During that week I was present at twenty-two plays. In nearly every instance there was a decided advance over the average of two years ago. The Little Theatre movement has created wide and active interest throughout Canada; and it cannot fail to have a good influence.

Mr Morley, who acted as regional adjudicator, told me that no less than one hundred and twelve plays had been performed in the various regional districts from Halifax to Vancouver. He spoke very highly of the standard of acting, although he admitted that in some cases performance was very poor.

The Bessborough Award was won by *L'Innocente*, presented by L'école de Musique et Déclamation de l'Université d'Ottawa. La Toca, the principal role was admirably played by Mlle Florence Gastonguay. *The Poacher*, presented by the Arts and Letters Club of Toronto, was awarded first place among English-speaking productions, although there were several plays of almost equal merit.

The prize for the best actor was given to Moray Sinclair as Smirnov in *The Bear*, the presentation of the Masquers' Club of Winnipeg; and Brenda Ferguson was selected as the best actress. She played Jeanne D'Arc in the trial Scene from *Saint Joan*, presented by the Embassy Players of Vancouver.

Her Excellency gave a special memento to Thora Adames for her performance of Ada Mason in *Vindication*, presented by the Theatre Arts Guild of Halifax, as well as to Vincent G. Perry for his interpretation of St Simeon, in *St Simeon Stylites*, produced by the London Community Drama Guild. In conversation with Miss Adames at Government House on Sunday afternoon when the awards were presented, I learned that she was born in Fiji and that she had come from New Zealand to Halifax with her father, who is an officer of a cable company and remains at each post only three years. Miss Adames told me that at the conclusion of the play she retired to the dressing-room overcome with emotion. While the tears were flowing through her make-up, Mr Massey arrived on the scene to congratulate her. She said that she was so wrapped up with the intensity of her role that she wept all through the following night.

On Friday evening (April 26), in response to insistent requests from Colonel H.C. Osborne, I spoke for about ten minutes while the adjudicator was summing up his notes. At the time, I was extremely tired. I recalled the experience of the famous Marquis of Hartington who was said to have delivered himself on one occasion in somewhat the following manner: 'I dreamed that I was making a speech in the House of Commons. I woke up; and by Jove I was.' I felt that my effort on this occasion was an utter failure but my wife assured me that I was mistaken. Subsequently, I received many congratulations, apparently sincere. My notes, as well as the press report, are appended. [The notes are not reproduced.]

The adjudicator, Mr Allan Wade, was highly regarded; and,

although his criticism was on occasion rather meticulous, it served a useful purpose.

At Government House on Sunday, Mr Massey showed me the Address to be presented to His Excellency that afternoon. It was admirable in many respects; but consisted chiefly of finely-phrased commonplaces. I remarked that, in my opinion, he had overlooked one very important feature – the more intimate understanding between those from distant points in Canada with their associates in the Festival.

During the greater part of the week we had as our guests two charming young men, Eric Aldwinckle and Andrew Allan, members of Toronto Hart House Theatre.

I remain, Sir, Yours appreciatively,

April 27, 1935

The *Ottawa Journal*

MOVING TRIBUTE

Last evening, the fifth of the festival, was another wonderful experience. Not only was each of the three plays extraordinarily well produced and presented, not only were Mr Wade's criticisms more revealing of his keen sense of perception, discernment, thorough knowledge of the theater and qualifications for his duties as adjudicator, but in all the tributes paid during the week to His Excellency the Governor-General, founder of the movement, none were so beautifully expressed or more moving than that of Sir Robert Borden last evening. His Excellency, declared Sir Robert, quoting from the Odes of Horace, could truly say: 'I have erected a monument more enduring than bronze,' which would stand for all the years to come.

'We are all such stuff as dreams are made of,' said Sir Robert, speaking of the movement inspired by the Governor-General, 'and the only reality is the spirit.' The movement had spread all over Canada but it was really only beginning and would go on for ever to even greater things. 'As long as rivers run to the ocean,' quoted Sir Robert. 'As long as mountains cast shadows across the valleys. As long as the stars nourish the heavens, the names of Their Excellencies will endure with Canadians in the truest spiritual sense. They cannot escape that. And when the time comes for their departure we can only say, 'Better lo'ed ye canna be. Will ye no' come back again?'

May 13, 1937

DOMINION DRAMA FESTIVAL, 1937

Sir,

In my recent letter I omitted to make any comment upon the Drama Festival which was held in Ottawa from April 26 to May 1, both inclusive. We attended only on the twenty-sixth, twenty-eighth, thirtieth April and on May first.

In the early part of the week I thought that the standard of performance had distinctly deteriorated; but towards the close of the week there was a vast improvement and some performances were given which compared favourably with anything in our experience of such festivals. Especially fine were the scenes from *David Copperfield,* presented by the Loretto Players of Hamilton; the scene from *The Barretts of Wimpole Street,* presented by the Strolling Players, Vancouver; *The House in the Quiet Glen,* presented by Toronto Masquers and the scene from *The Cradle Song,* presented by the Dramatic Club of the University College Alumnae Association, Toronto.

Herewith I attach press notice of the prize-winning plays and players. [Not reproduced]

M. Michel St-Denis, the adjudicator, is obviously a very able man and the audiences greatly enjoyed his comments which were very clever. However, I thought that he was too prolix; that on occasion his observations were too discursive and disjointed; and that sometimes his criticisms were rather trivial. He lacked the dignity and repose of manner which had characterized both Mr Grein and Mr Granville-Barker. Occasionally he mimicked the mannerisms of the players; and especially on Friday evening his posturing was of an unusual character, as he was sprawling all over the table in front of him.

I am delighted that Winnipeg is to be the scene of the next Drama Festival. Against my desire and suggestion, I was re-elected president of the Dominion Drama Festival. But I intend to resign before the next festival and to suggest that my friend Honourable W.J. Tupper (who was a student in my law office many years ago) should take my place.

Several years ago, I erected a bird-house in the hope that purple martens would occupy it; they have never done so. But, not infrequently, it has been occupied by the tree swallows, most beautiful birds. Their flight is more graceful, skilful and impressive than that of any bird I have observed.

On the north side of my house, just above a small stone verandah (upon which the door of the kitchen opens) there are two apertures which formerly were used for ventilating our cold-storage plant. They are round, about three inches in diameter. Yesterday (May 12), while these openings were uncovered, two purple martens became impressed with the idea that these apertures were entrances to a bird-house provided for their accommodation. Accordingly, they entered and proceeded to descend to the lower part of the interior from which they were unable to emerge until released by one of the servants. It appears singular that the martens were scornful of the bird-house designed for their accommodation and preferred this entrance to our abandoned cold-storage.

Yours, etc.,

May 17, 1935

OLIVAR ASSELIN–JOURNALIST

Sir,

The late Charles J. Doherty, who for nine years was one of my colleagues, had singularly faulty judgment with regard to personality. He had a high opinion of Olivar Asselin's ability and influence; and he strongly urged that we should take him to the Peace Conference at Paris as a member of the Canadian Delegation. A more unfortunate selection for that purpose could not be imagined. Morose and discontented, Asselin seemed to seek continually for some cause of complaint or criticism. From first to last during his attendance in Paris he never gave, so far as I am aware, one single hour of useful service.

Doherty was impressed with the view that Asselin exercised upon the youth of Quebec an important influence, and that his inclusion in the Canadian Delegation would strongly appeal to them.

An article on Sir George Foster, which appeared in *Le Canada* (5, Janvier, 1932) indicates Asselin's true character. He makes contemptuous reference to J.W. Dafoe,[28] to Mowat Biggar,[29] and to

28 President, *Manitoba Free Press,* Winnipeg
29 Prominent Ottawa lawyer

Loring C. Christie, although for any useful service he was not fit to tie the shoe-latchet of any one of them. His mentality ran in a grotesquely narrow and tortuous channel. One could never interpret his extraordinary diversity of moods.

On one occasion, in 1919, when I entertained at dinner at the Hotel Majestic in Paris, I requested that we should converse altogether in French and that no English should be spoken. Among other guests were George Campbell of Halifax and Miss Elizabeth Montizambert. Asselin of course was present. In the midst of the dinner he asked to be excused and left the table without any apparent reason, unless his action could be interpreted as a protest against the use of the French language. No one could have the faintest idea as to the reason for his departure.

... In recent years Asselin put forward a project for the creation of a new state comprising Quebec and the French communities of New England. This proposal was received with derision by his compatriots. He had lost touch with reality. It is said that he has now lost touch with everything.

I remain, Sir, Yours faithfully,

July 8, 1935

PRESIDENT CARLETON STANLEY

Sir,

On June 25, I had a call from President Carleton Stanley of Dalhousie University. We had a most enjoyable evening and discussed many phases of modern civilization, including tendencies in education and in the development of political ideals.

President Stanley is evidently a man of outstanding erudition.

He spoke with much appreciation of two members of his staff; one, a German, deplores with great earnestness the perversion of the true spirit of the German people by Hitlerism: 'you know we are not like that', said he to Stanley. The other professor of whom Stanley spoke highly is a young Englishman who has recently joined the university staff. It is said that he has made the best reply to Lord Hewart's attack on modern bureaucracy.

The latest number (July 6, 1935) of Toronto *Saturday Night* contains an article by President Stanley which sets forth ideas with which I do not agree. He fiercely denounces the Versailles Treaty as 'insane insanity'. I for one, had no admiration for that Treaty; but the wonder is that any Treaty was possible. Stanley is, doubtless, an able man; but if his ability had been raised to the *n*th power, if his individuality had been multiplied by a thousand, and if the intellectual and moral forces thus represented had been applied to the problems confronting the Peace Conference, it is extremely probable, indeed practically certain, that the Stanley aggregation would have made a worse mess of it.

He writes also in contemptuous terms of efforts made by the present administration to deal with the problem of unemployment. Is it possible that the professorial self-appreciation and lack of touch with practical realities which infests so many of our university leaders can have so taken possession of Stanley that he imagines himself better informed, better equipped, more zealous and more efficient than R.B. Bennett to grapple with this tremendous problem?

It seems hardly conceivable that so capable a man as Stanley could be so misled. However, professors and editors are prone to set up ideals and conceive achievement which they are utterly incapable of fulfilling or undertaking.

In these days of confused thinking and emotional outburst, such exaggerated lucubrations, unaccompanied by any reasonable or useful suggestion or purpose or of action, are to be deplored.

President Stanley's article is appended.

I remain, Sir, Yours, etc.,

July 6, 1935

Saturday Night

THE INCURABLE STUPIDITY OF THE HUMAN SPECIES

It is a wonted usage, for those who at this season of the year are called to the delivery of orations at University functions, to dwell on the mountain peaks of human existence: to quote such things as the exalted chorus in Sophocles on the marvelous nature of man, or Hamlet's outbursts. 'What a piece of work is man! How noble in reason! How infinite in faculty! ... in apprehension how like a god!' That has become almost a ritual: to refer to man at his best, his rational nature, his supreme mental achievements, and the outward evidence of this human greatness, to be found in institutions, laws, the triumphs of art, the structure of civilization.

Not out of any perverseness, but in what appears to me simply a sensible effort to see things as they are, I call attention, for once, to the irrationality, the incurable stupidity of the human species. If anything is obvious, if anything needs no proof, it is that in America and in Europe folly and not reason has been in the ascendant for the last twenty years or more.

As for the War, and the still more insane insanity of the Treaty which concluded it, and the mad political and social results which flowed therefrom, it is not wisdom to add words to the many volumes of words which have been written and uttered upon it. At most one might quote one of the greatest poets who has written in our time, who said eight or nine years ago:

We are getting to the end of visioning
The impossible within this universe,
Such as that better whiles may follow worse
And that our race may mend by reasoning.

We know that even as larks in cages sing,
Unthoughtful of deliverance from the curse
That holds them lifelong in a latticed hearse,
We ply spasmodically our pleasuring;
And that when nations set them to lay waste
Their neighbors' heritage by foot and horse
And hack their pleasant plains in festering seams,
They may again – not warely, or from taste,
But tickled mad by some demonic force –
Yes, we are getting to the end of dreams.

So much for the War and its aftermath. But in a hundred other ways, totally unconnected with politics, the folly and unconsidered rashness of men is evident. Think for a moment of the matter of health. Individually the race seems to aim more at health than it has for centuries past. Not since the fifth century BC has there been such a universal cult of sunshine and outdoor exercise. But, in the mass, human action has rarely been so destructive of health. In our cities, it is well known, the air is so charged with corrosive gases that certain metals are eaten away in a short period. It has recently been proved by actual measurement that in certain English and American cities, and in the country for miles distant, tons of carbon and other dust particles are deposited annually on every acre. At least a quarter of the people in this country drink water which they have first sown with disease, water that is so poisonous that only certain sorts of fish can survive in it. We have spent billions of dollars in proving to ourselves that most diseases are propagated by infections and contagions. Yet in nearly all our North American cities we force a large part of our population to live in the vilest hotbeds of disease.

In all these respects we sin against ourselves not in ignorance. We have seen the light. There is perhaps not a person in one hundred thousand in North America that regards disease superstitiously, as our ancestors nearly all did. We no longer believe that tuberculosis, diphtheria, typhoid, malaria, rickets, are visitations from God. We know not only how to avoid these things individually, we are conscious that we possess the means of wiping out these afflictions from the human race. Indeed we have spent great efforts in wiping them out – during part of the time. For the rest of the time we encourage them. We might compare ourselves with a farmer who keeps the weeds down in all the outer fields, but allows the wild mustard and wild oats and burdocks to flourish in his central field. As the wind changes, the centre field resows all the others with mischief. Indeed, such a farm is a good picture of most of our cities – healthy suburbs round a festering sore.

We boast of our inventions. Most striking of all recent inventions, though it may not be the greatest, is the radio. This might be made one of the most instructive and civilizing agents, and occasionally we do use it in this way; but perhaps it would be no exaggeration to say that over most of this continent, except for a few hours a week, we have allowed the radio to become a public nuisance. In most parts of this continent it has been turned over almost entirely to the most mercenary and most selfish of our fellow creatures. It used to be said by the bitterest opponents of private exploiters that if they knew how to bottle the sunshine and peddle it to their fellow men they would do so. But now the private exploiters, seizing upon the wizardry which tapped influences more viewless than the winds of heaven, have turned this marvelous alchemy into their own muddy canals, so that not a remote hamlet, nor even a ship at sea, can escape their slime.

Some have held that self-preservation is the intuitive wisdom of all animals. Certain philosophers have held that man is distinguished from other animals in seeking his own pleasure. We have seen that man, even aside from war, does not always seek his own self-preservation; we have seen that man sometimes turns his own pleasures into misery and plagues. Is he then more rational, or less, than the other animals?

If one really wished to establish that man is indeed the paragon of unreason, one might turn to his economic management or mismanagement. For the last hundred years most of the major discoveries have made for a widening of human travel, intercourse and trade. The steam engine and the steamship; the telegraph, the telephone, and indeed most of the applications of electricity; the labor-saving devices; photography; the automobile, and latterly the airplane have united the human denizens of this planet, as they have never been united before. I am one of those who had a golden youth. Without a passport, without credentials of any kind, and with only a scanty supply of British sovereigns in my pocket, I was able to travel about Europe on a bicycle, across half a dozen frontiers. Europe today is still the most civilized part of the world. But the restrictions on travel in Europe are now greater than those which Marco Polo encountered in the Turkish dominions and in China. As for international trade I have myself seen, over and over again, the bankruptcy and ruin of those who tried to conduct it. I have myself seen the price of a commodity imported into this country, increased fourfold by stupid tariff regulations. I have seen goods rotting in a customs warehouse which no one in this country manufactured, and which a dozen trades in this country were clamoring to have. The prohibition of these imports was of course tantamount to the prohibition of our exports. This country, geographically, historically, economically, is designed for foreign trade. By our own human action we have done nearly everything to stifle foreign trade.

Then there is the question of unemployment. This has always been a difficult business, as students of history know. In old days Englishmen grew sheep on their succulent pastures, ate the mutton themselves, and exported the wool to Flanders. Anything that happened in Flanders upset the balance in England. The student of history knows that, ever since the introduction of coinage, about 700 BC, anything that has seriously upset the balance of prices has meant that thousands of human beings have starved to death. I cite these things to show that unemployment is sometimes far beyond the skill of governments; whether the government is a prince or a democracy. And yet the unemployment of a large fraction of the population in Europe and America which has persisted for a decade is mostly a reflection of the stupidity and unreason of men. Everyone knows that it is a sin against Nature to keep a sheep dog in a city where there are no sheep to tend, or a hound where there is no hunting, or a water dog where there is no water. And everyone knows that men without work are denaturalized, devitalized creatures. Four hundred years ago one of the wisest of men proposed that, for heavy manual labor at least, six hours out of the twenty-four were sufficient for any man to labor. In the interval we have enormously increased labor-saving devices of all kinds. And yet men are laboring in the mine, in the factory, ten and eleven hours a day, while millions of their fellow creatures have no work to do. These labor-saving devices are the common property of men. By what legal title, by what right human or divine, do a few of us say to these unemployed: 'You are not working, therefore you cannot eat?' Yet so it is. I do not wish to raise ethical questions here; I am simply trying to show that all of us recognize unemployment on a vast scale as a menace to society at large. And yet, so irrational are we, that we do nothing, or next to nothing, to cure it. In this vacant empire, which we call Canada, there are only ten millions of people to be decently housed, clothed and fed. When, in history, have ten millions of people controlled so much wealth? What a confession must we make of ourselves if in such plenty some of us starve?

I have said these things without any desire to be satiric or cynical. The cynics have no reverence for themselves or their fellows. The cynic never exclaims about Man as Shakespeare makes Hamlet exclaim. On the other hand, self-knowledge as well as self-reverence is a virtue. And it is well to reflect occasionally at least on these aspects of human nature and life which I have illustrated. Not otherwise shall we understand by what exertions and slow toil Man can raise himself to power, felicity and virtue.

I come finally to the moral of my discourse: It is not the function of the educated to make gibes about the multitude. It is their duty, first of all, to see that they themselves really be educated, not sciolists. Of all stern words, the sternest perhaps is that phrase about 'the salt that hath lost its savor.' Their second duty is to remember humbly that they owe nearly all of what they are to society. The individual by himself is a barbarian, as Professor Einstein has lately reminded us. I see a connection, I may be wrong, but I think I see a connection between present follies and the fact that so many of our universities are hardly to be distinguished from the rest of society. So many university men and women seem to read pretty much the same stuff as anybody else. Their amusements so often are hardly distinguished from the amusements of the rabble. The rabble itself, as a great man once said, 'is generally mistaken in the particular instance, but almost never in the long run.' The question is how to abridge the period of popular delusions. I am inclined to think that one way of approach is for the universities to give over turning out a merely conventional product, and to attend rather to putting a cutting edge on those young men and women who have original ideas and the quality of courage.

July 12, 1935

CANADIAN-AMERICAN CONFERENCE CANTON, N.Y.

Sir,

A Canadian-American conference sponsored by the Carnegie Endowment under the direction of Dr James T. Shotwell [Professor of History, Columbia University] was held at St Lawrence University, Canton, New York, from June 17 to June 22, 1935, under the joint auspices of Queen's University and St Lawrence University.

I am a member of the Advisory Committee of the Project of Research on Canadian-American Relations, but in accepting this office I stipulated that I should not be called upon for any active work. Further, in correspondence with Dr Shotwell and Dean Corbett [Percy E. Corbett, Dean of Law] of McGill University, I emphasized the importance of bringing into such studies as might be undertaken on either side of the line men of practical affairs, who would temper unattainable ideals in which academic students are somewhat prone to indulge.

In connection with the conference it was arranged that a luncheon should be given in honour of the Honourable Elihu Root and myself. Correspondence (appended) relative to this proposal includes an interesting letter from Owen D. Young [Chairman, General Electric Company] in which are to be found very generous expressions respecting my public service.

My wife and I left Ottawa at 1.45 p.m. on June 17, and arrived at Canton in good time after a pleasant motor journey. Apartments allotted to us in the university were rather cramped so far as the bedroom was concerned but quite comfortable.

Canton is situate in a beautiful country and the university buildings are handsome and commodious. We renewed many acquaintances upon our arrival.

On Monday evening we attended the dinner of welcome at which the President of St Lawrence University, Dr Richard Eddy Sykes, presided and extended a graceful welcome. At the opening session that evening there were admirable speeches by the Chairman, Owen D. Young, Dr Shotwell and Principal Fyfe [Principal of Queen's University] who was especially happy in his address which was lighted with delightful flashes of humour.

On Tuesday morning the session on 'Tariffs' was opened by Professor W.W. McLaren, Williams College, who, in my opinion, was prolix rather than helpful. Professor McLaren was followed by Professor Jacob Viner of Chicago University. Both McLaren and Viner were originally Canadians but are now United States' citizens.

Viner's intellectual force was unmistakable. He is at least a great intellectual machine, probably something more. At one time he was in the service of the United States' government but he took pains to disclaim any present connection of that nature. However, to such an extent did he harp upon and emphasize alleged discrimination in Canadian tariffs against United States that, but for his disclaimer, one would have imagined him the paid advocate of that country's government.

Unfortunately, I was not present at the discussion (*in camera*) which took place after Viner's address; but I was informed that the Canadian side had not been very ably presented. Toward the end of the week this was remedied by John W. Dafoe, among others.

At the luncheon Honourable Alanson B. Houghton, former US ambassador at the Court of St James presided. After setting forth very cogently his views as to economic conditions in United States and throughout the world, he proposed my health in extremely generous terms. A summary of my reply is appended. Eloquent tributes were paid to Mr Root by Mr Young, Mr Houghton and Dr Shotwell. During the course of his address, Mr Young read a letter from Mr Root written in his own hand, copy of which is appended and which I value for its kindly reference to my public service. Subsequently I wrote to Mr Root; and I append a copy of that letter.

On Friday, June 21, Dr John W. Dafoe made an important and interesting contribution in an address on Public Opinion. At luncheon on the following day (June 22), he spoke warmly, frankly and bravely of United States' failure in 1919 and 1920 when that country, having acquired moral leadership of the world, sold for a mess of pottage inestimable opportunity for world service. The accompanying letter to Dr Dafoe explains more fully my agreement with him and my regret that so great a nation should have been inspired by so mean an ideal.

I remain, Sir, Yours faithfully,

May 10, 1935

570 Lexington Avenue,
New York, NY

My dear Sir Robert,

When I had the pleasure of lunching with you a few weeks ago at the invitation of Mr Bullock, I spoke to you about the Canadian-American Conference sponsored by the Carnegie Endowment under the direction of Professor James T. Shotwell, which is to be held at St Lawrence University, June 17 to June 22, under the joint auspices of Queen's and St Lawrence.

The Carnegie Endowment has been making for some years, as you probably know, a very thorough study of the historical, economic and political factors involved in the relations between this country and Canada. This, like all work under Dr Shotwell's direction, is being done carefully and thoroughly and not superficially. He has had for sometime now special students in both countries studying different phases of the problem. This conference has been called for the purpose of enabling these special students to meet and exchange views on different phases of their work and at the same time to bring to them the experience and observations of practical men of affairs. A very excellent program of serious work has been developed. There is to be no ballyhoo about it.

It is our wish to give a luncheon in our men's dormitory which is entirely adequate for the purpose on Wednesday, June 19, at one o'clock, in the joint honor of Sir Robert Borden and Mr Elihu Root. Mr Alanson B. Houghton, our former Ambassador in London, will be present and preside. I do not yet know whether Mr Root will be able on that day to come, but if he does not, some of his friends, like Dr Henry S. Pritchett, Mr James R. Sheffield, our former Ambassador to Mexico, will be present.

St Lawrence University is at Canton, New York, only about sixty or seventy miles from Ottawa, and the river crossing is very short at Waddington.

We would like very much to have you come to the luncheon. It will not take you more than an hour and a half or two hours to drive down, and you are at perfect liberty to say something if you wish, or nothing. We in no sense wish to burden you any more than we do Mr Root, but we do wish to have your permission to carry on the luncheon in honor of the two most distinguished men now living who have participated so importantly in Canadian-American affairs.

I shall act as general chairman of the conference, and I sincerely hope that you may find it not only convenient but pleasant to come to St Lawrence not only for the luncheon, but perhaps to listen to the exchange of views which these scholars as a result of special study may make.

Sincerely yours,
(Sgd.) Owen D. Young

Clinton, Oneida County, NY
May 30, 1935

My dear Mr Young,

I am warmly sympathetic with the proposed conference over Canadian-American affairs, and I should feel greatly honoured to be associated with Sir Robert Borden in the luncheon at Canton. I have admired and honoured him for many years, and I would not readily forego any possible opportunity to continue and cultivate friendship between us. I am compelled, however, to realize limitations upon the physical strength which advancing years have left me. I can start very bravely but grow tired very quickly; and some painful experiments have proved that the journey, the meeting, the luncheon, the delightful interviews with old friends – all put together would be too much for my strength, so I must stay at home. I hope that you may have a useful and delightful meeting and I am sure you will.

I beg you to present to Sir Robert assurance of my profound respect and friendship. I appreciate highly your kind invitation and regret very much that I cannot join you in person.

Always faithfully yours,
(Sgd.) Elihu Root

May 14, 1935

To Owen D. Young, Esquire,
Chairman,
Conference on Canadian-American Affairs,
570, Lexington Avenue,
New York City, NY, USA

My dear Mr Young,

Your letter of the tenth instant is before me; and I hasten to express my thanks. To be associated with the Honourable Elihu Root at such a luncheon I regard as a distinctive honour which I very deeply appreciate. At the Washington Disarmament Conference it was my privilege to be in intimate touch with him and with the other United States' delegates. The vivid impressions I received at that Conference will always remain with me.

So far as I can foresee, I shall be able to attend the luncheon and perhaps to remain for another day at least. In that case, I shall be glad to speak very briefly at the luncheon.

It will be most interesting and instructive to hear the observations of various students who have devoted themselves to the designated subjects.

Your words with regard to my public service are so kind and so generous that they almost overwhelm me. The warm thanks which I now convey must not be regarded as expressing concurrence therein.

With kind regards, I remain, yours faithfully,

SIR ROBERT BORDEN'S ADDRESS AT THE LUNCHEON IN HONOUR OF HON. ELIHU ROOT AND SIR ROBERT BORDEN AT THE ST LAWRENCE UNIVERSITY, CANADIAN-AMERICAN AFFAIRS CONFERENCE, JUNE 18, 1935

My warm thanks are due to Mr Houghton for his very kind but I fear too generous words in introducing me. His reference to a very brief introduction which greatly impressed him recalls an occasion during my political years when I was introduced in a speech of fifty minutes, although time was of the essence. When in England some years ago, while Mr Houghton was Ambassador of United States at the Court of St James, I had the privilege of meeting him on several occasions. Then as now I was impressed with his broad outlook and his keen insight into conditions that affect the relations between this great Republic and the British Commonwealth.

It is indeed a great honour to me that I should be associated in this luncheon with so distinguished a statesman and jurist as the Honourable Elihu Root whose service to his country in many fields has been conspicuous. He has indeed been a great servant of the state to whom is due the highest praise – that he has in every sense deserved well of his country. May happiness attend him in all his years.

Nearly fifteen years ago, I was brought into intimate association with him when he was one of the delegates from United States and I was the delegate from Canada at the Washington Disarmament Conference. I have a happy memory of that association and I retain a vivid impression of his keen desire that the relations between these two great democracies should be intimate and cordial and that they should work together for the peace of the world.

It was an interesting and practical conference. Its success was remarkable, as very little spade work had been done in advance. The announcement of the policy of the United States, set forth by Mr Hughes at the first session, was a complete surprise to the delegates of the other powers. Fortunately, United States' proposals were accepted in form and in spirit.

Perhaps the most remarkable feature of the conference was the circumstance that, certainly in United States and in some Dominions of the British Commonwealth, it would have been regarded as virtually a failure except for two treaties which were not in the first instance upon the agenda. I refer to the Quadruple Pacific Treaty which brought to an end the former Anglo-Japanese Treaty, and the Sino-Japanese Treaty which for the time quieted the differences that had arisen between these two great oriental powers.

To those who are engaged in the task of improving understanding and strengthening goodwill between our two countries I extend my very warm congratulations and my fervent wishes for success in these activities. He who lends his endeavours to so vital a purpose deserves well of each country. It was said by the ancients that the maxim 'Know Thyself' descended from Heaven. To these two adjacent countries, 'Know each other', is especially imperative. Do not forget that the scope of this purpose is greater than appears on the surface. Cooperation and sympathy between Canada and United States leads in a larger and higher sense to cooperation between United States and the British Commonwealth.

Such sympathy and cooperation seem more essential now and in the immediate future than at any time in the past. Cooperation between these two great powers should be not against other nations, not against any nation, but cooperation for all other nations to the end that public right may be enthroned and world peace be maintained. It should be a cooperation arising out of the growth of goodwill and better understanding. Cooperation such as was envisaged by Cecil Rhodes many years ago.

But such growth must measurably depend upon leadership. Let it be our trust and our prayer that in each country 'Greathearts' will arise to give such leadership, men whose 'glory of grace' will be of pure love, not for country alone, but for all nations, for humanity.

I recall now and I apply in a higher and broader sense words that came to my lips nearly twenty years ago in addressing the nations of the British Commonwealth. Let us pray that the governments, the leaders and the people of these outstanding world powers will so bear themselves in the years to come and especially in those that lie immediately before us, let us pray that they will so bear themselves that the future will not hold to their lips the chalice of vain regret for opportunity neglected and dead.

June 20, 1935

My dear Mr Root,

At the luncheon on Tuesday, I was highly honoured in the association of my name with your own. I was privileged to speak of your wonderful career, of your inestimable service to your country, to which eloquent tribute was paid by Mr Houghton, Mr Young and Dr Shotwell.

Your unavoidable absence was deeply regretted, but the considerations which made your attendance impossible were fully realized. I was greatly touched by your most kind reference to me in your letter to Mr Young. Pray accept my very warm thanks.

In looking over my diary during the Washington Disarmament Conference, I find the record of an interview with you on November 9, 1921; and, merely as a curiosity, I send you a copy.

If I should live to the twenty-sixth of this month, I shall then have completed my eighty-first year. It is a great age but by no means equal to your own. I have not felt the loneliness which is sometimes incident to advanced years. Joseph Choate once said to me: 'I am in my ninth decade and each has been more enjoyable than that which preceded it.' But I should hardly go so far.

However, I do try to preserve a youthful spirit; and I venture to send you my address (1932) to the students of Acadia University, situate in the beautiful Annapolis Valley, only three miles from the place of my birth.

May health and happiness attend you in all the years that lie before you.

With renewed thanks and very kind regards, I remain, dear Mr Root,

Yours faithfully,

July 12, 1935

To Dr J.W. Dafoe
Winnipeg Free Press Limited

Private
My dear John,

Thanks for your letter of the fifth instant. I have just returned from a short sojourn in Montreal where I was in attendance at the board meetings of two companies over which I preside.

My wife and I greatly enjoyed the visit to Canton and especially the opportunity of meeting you and Mrs Dafoe again. We regretted that our stay could not be longer.

I did especially want to see your address at the final luncheon on June 22. You did well and bravely to speak out. In her tragic surrender of world leadership through submission to the dominance of relatively petty domestic antagonisms, United States sustained a distinctive humiliation which will lower for all time her place in the world's history. This disastrous descent her people have by no means realized, perhaps they will never realize it.

Your address on public opinion I found extremely interesting and it carries my thought in many of its features. In one aspect, however, I disagree, but with great respect.

In twenty-five years of active public life I found the Senate a more efficient legislative body than the Commons and far more thorough in the work of its committees. On occasion it has been absurdly partisan; but I think in recent years one can discern the beginning of an independence which might realize the purpose of the framers of our Constitution. At present it stands, in my opinion, as a safeguard against the vagaries and extravagances of unscrupulous demagogues whose opportunity has arisen from conditions that expose manifest deficiencies in our social order, deficiencies that undoubtedly must be corrected.

Whatever may be said of varying forms of virtual repudiation as they have recently appeared, nothing has occurred so detrimental to a nation's credit as Ontario's legislative repudiation of the power contracts. The resulting impairment of credit and confidence abroad has been startling. If you have studied the proposals practically accepted in Great Britain for a series of conversion loans you must realize how vitally important they were to Canada's financial structure which, to speak very euphemistically, is far from satisfactory. A series of conversions into long-term securities would have made the position impregnable for such a period as to remove apprehension. An agreement had been prepared and approved and was about to be signed for the first conversion. The negotiations came to an immediate and untimely end when Ontario repudiated. By this conversion and those in contemplation there would have been a saving of about a million dollars per annum in interest charges. I venture to observe that even Hepburn comes high at that figure.

I entirely agree that there is an element of Fascism in democratic government as we practice it. In the first edition of Low's *Governance of England* (I have not the second at hand) this is clearly pointed out.

I am glad the conference proved more interesting as the days passed. Professor Jacob Viner greatly impressed me with his immense intellectual power, but not with his fairmindedness or his tact.

I should indeed have been glad to discuss with you matters of great moment that are pressing upon our country and will soon weigh heavily upon those entrusted with its governance during the next four years.

In writing recently to Rowell respecting other matters, I used this language,

> Without being concerned as to the party aspect, I do hope and pray that either before or after the next election we may have a strong, stable administration, backed by the best elements of our people, an administration disposed and able to deal effectively with pressing problems (especially railways and unemployment) and to lead Canada along a path of reasonable and effective readjustment of our social order.

However, there seems little reason why at my age one should not rather concern one's self with the varying moods of nature, the spring-awakening of Mother Earth, the beauty of the first wild-flowers, the lacery of the tree-tops in earliest Spring, the mystery of a cloud-continent as it floats below the morning star and above the dawn.

I hold him happiest
Who, before going quickly whence he came
Hath looked ungrieving on these majesties,
The world-wide Sun, the stars, water and clouds
And fire. Live, Parmeno a hundred years
Or a few weeks, these thou wilt always see,
And never, never any greater things.

In these days I derive from my wild-garden my greatest enjoyment, except from my books.

When next you come to Ottawa, pray do not fail to communicate with me in advance.

With kindest regards, I remain, Yours faithfully.

June 20, 1935

Associated Press Despatch, Canton, NY

DEFENDS THREE TARIFF SYSTEM
USED IN CANADA

John W. Dafoe Makes Spirited Reply to American Charge of Discrimination at Canton Parley

LIVELY DISCUSSION ON CONTROL
OF AIR WAVES

Graham Spry Advocates Complete Freedom of Opinion Over the Air

A spirited reply to an American charge of tariff discrimination was given today at the conference of Canadian-American affairs by John W. Dafoe, editor-in-chief of the *Winnipeg Free Press*, and two Canadian educationists – Prof Frank A. Knox of Queen's University and Prof Robert McQueen of the University of Saskatchewan.

Dr Dafoe said the charge of Prof Jacob Viner of Chicago, that Canada, with its three tariff system, was discriminating against the United States, had not been proved.

'Under our system of main, intermediate and Empire tariff schedules,' he said, 'we go to other nations and offer them the intermediate rate on their goods in exchange for a preferred consideration for our wheat. The Americans, with a single tariff, argue that we have been unfair because we have three tariffs, and the United States is not favored by our intermediate tariff.

'It is our contention, however, that concession should be given for concession,' which has not been done under the inflexible single tariff system.

Explains Point

After the session, Dr Dafoe explained his point by saying that it was possible the new United States tariff plan giving the President the right to change tariff schedules by 50 per cent, and the program of bargaining favored by Secretary of State Cordell Hull, would have an important bearing on this phase.

'I understand that negotiations have begun at Washington,' he said, 'out of which some small agreement is approaching. This is a favorable sign that the problems of the two nations are coming closer to solution, and I believe the agreement should be so looked upon.

'It is of course extremely difficult to arrange tariffs between the two nations. No attempt has been made to compose differences. A combination of manufacturers in Canada and agriculturists in the United States has always successfully blocked such plans.

Blames Single Tariff

Dr Dafoe said he believed the difficulties between the two countries could be composed if the United States did not have a single tariff system, but had variable tariffs.

'I understand, for example, that your protective tariff against Canadian stocker and feeder cattle, which American farmers would like to get, was not designed to keep out Canadian cattle, but if the United States lowered the duty on Canadian cattle, under the single tariff system, the duty naturally would automatically be lowered against Mexican cattle.'

Professors Knox and McQueen took up the technical argument where it was left off yesterday in the tariff section of the conference.

Control of Air Waves

Today's main session was devoted to radio. Public control of the air waves was advocated by Canadian and American observers in a lively discussion.

The names of Hitler, Huey Long, Father Coughlin and General Hugh S. Johnson figured prominently.

Graham Spry, former president of the Canadian Radio League, opened the subject with a vigorous argument for freedom of the air.

'I believe that radio broadcasting, both as it concerns international relations and international politics, should be operated on the principle that freedom of opinion should be given complete and unfettered expression,' he said, 'and that some form of public ownership can alone protect and extend that freedom of opinion over the air.'

Spry also proposed the setting up, in effect, of an international commission to 'hold in trusteeship the desires of the North American audience and recognize the different susceptibilities.'

Debate On the Air

In the ensuing private discussions, the question of public control was enlarged when the question was raised as to how the recent Huey Long, Father Coughlin-General Johnson debate got on the air.

Levering Tyson, director of the National Council of Radio in Education, said an invitation to Johnson to speak free of charge 'started the whole fight.' He said Senator Long and Father Coughlin demanded time and were given it free to reply, and the debate was then shut off because 'it was believed that the public was fed up.'

'French-Canadians are in favor of a national broadcasting system to secure adequate coverage of Quebec and enable 500,000 to 600,000 French people outside the province to hear their language on the air,' said Prof Henri St Denis of the University of Ottawa.

More than 28 per cent of Canada's population is French, he pointed out.

Praises Canadian Programs

Prof M.L. Bonham, Jr, of Hamilton College said:

'I want to pay a tribute to Canadian radio programs. I wish American ones were as good.'

Dr Dafoe declared radio advertising 'has not hurt newspapers.' He said newspapers supplemented such advertising, and added: 'we need supervision and control of the ether as a public commodity.'

June 29, 1935

The Ottawa Journal

A CANADIAN EDITOR
DISCUSSES LIBERTY [Address of Dr Dafoe at Canton, NY]

In a life which has covered all the transformations and material revolutions brought about by modern science, I have found little difficulty in adjusting myself to the resultant changes; but I confess myself completely stumped by the sight of young men, anywhere in the so-called civilized world, keen to renounce their rights of private opinion and of freedom of action, by pledging subserviency to some self-proclaimed leader, under the delusion that they will thereby obtain security, either temporary or permanent.

If security could be thus bought, the price would be much too high; but there never can be security, in terms of the needs of civilization, in serfdom.

I have been privileged in the past few years to speak to many audiences of young people. I have said to them: Don't give your allegiance to any proposed system of government, or to any suggested reconstruction of society, which will limit your right to continue to think about these matters and to act freely in the field of political action in keeping with your changing thought as your knowledge and experience grows.

This reservation of the right of private judgment as an inalienable personal possession, and the liberty to seek by legal means to give effect to it, if universally made, will very sharply limit and in many cases destroy projects highly publicized and skillfully camouflaged as reforms designed to widen the field of human opportunity. It preserves the right to reconsider and the power to retreat; it blocks the building of barriers on the road to yesterday.

It is therefore unacceptable to those who would like to make an induced declaration of public opinion irrevocable once it marches with their plans, who would use the privileges of freedom to destroy freedom, and would seek to end constitutional liberty by a perverted employment of constitutional methods.

Subject to this continuing right of freedom of thought and action, inquiry into things as they are, critical examination of existing beliefs, formulas and institutions, and extensive and daring experimentation, are not only desirable; they are imperative if mankind is to rise, generation after generation, to higher levels.

To the abstract claim that public opinion determines the form and the range of power of government, denial would be made by none of the newly established despotisms.

The mortal fear that the dictators have of free opinion is the handsomest tribute that could be paid to its dynamic power. Their method is, by the suppression of free discussion, by the destitution of all the agencies by which opinion is formed and expressed, by frightfulness directed against all who hold views discordant with theirs, to obtain at command manifestations of apparent popular approval, and in the period intervening between these demonstrations, submission abject and complete.

But the public opinion which sustains and directs popular government is not fashioned in this manner. The essential ingredient of public opinion is that it is the product of a long process of free discussion; to its making have gone the clash of divergent views, the contrast of theories, the pull and tug of interests, the consideration of its practicability and of the resistances that will be excited by its embodiment in action.

And when it emerges in this form it is nothing but the opinion of a majority possibly still faced by a vocal and unconvinced minority with a conceded right to convert itself into a majority if it can do so by persuasion, organization and propaganda.

It is at this point that the Fascist and Liberal-Democratic conceptions of government meet in a death grapple. The Fascist point of view is well expressed in a single sentence by F. Yeates-Brown: 'No country can benefit from a continual discussion of diametrically opposite points of view.'

This precisely is the issue. Under democracy diametrically opposite points of view yield in time to discussion, when it becomes established that behind one view there is a constant predominance of public opinion. Our constitutional history is full of cases of issues, once violently debated, which were ultimately settled by agreement.

Democracy is not likely to abdicate its functions. It is still less likely to be coerced by the overt acts of conspirators. But it may commit suicide through popular exasperation over the failure of government to meet the expectations of those who have exaggerated and absurd ideas of what the state can and should do for them.

It is conceivable that an ill-informed, inflamed, revengeful state of public opinion might, in a gust of passion, wreck the carefully balanced machinery of democratic government and turn over the direction of affairs to a government which would seize the occasion to vest itself with despotic power. But unless the people lost, or were coerced into renouncing, their traditional Anglo-Saxon instinct for freedom, the damage would be repaired, given time, with an increase in knowledge and experience that would be a safeguard against a recurrence of an emotional stampede of this nature.

Dr R. Tait McKenzie MD was born in Almonte, Ontario, in 1867. He was a physician and became an internationally recognized sculptor. At the time the following Limbo letter was written Dr McKenzie was Research Professor of Physical Education at the University of Pennsylvania. He had a most distinguished career.

July 24, 1935

VISIT TO MILL OF KINTAIL NEAR ALMONTE, ONTARIO

Sir,

Last week-end (July 20–22) we spent with the Tait McKenzie's at Mill of Kintail. They have made a delightful summer home of the old structure; and they secured it just in time as it was being rapidly dismantled. At the front door entrance there is a drawbridge, crossing what seems to be a castle moat. Below this is the ground floor used for various purposes; and on this floor are the living rooms, the bedrooms and bathroom, the kitchen and pantries, as well as a small verandah overlooking the Indian river on which the mill is situated.

Above is Dr McKenzie's studio in which he has gathered many of the articles used a century ago when the mill was in operation. During our visit he was engaged in leisure moments upon his sculpture, especially upon a large medallion of his father and mother designed from daguerreotypes taken during their early married life.

Above this is a half-story or large platform constituting a sort of open bedroom. This I occupied during our visit, leaving the guest-room on the first floor for the use of my wife. The very comfortable bedstead on this platform was of the type which a hundred years ago was called 'Hired man's bed' (freely translated by me, *lectus pueris aptus*) in contra-distinction to another type of bed called 'Master's bed.'

The elevated accommodation thus afforded was most enjoyable, as a splendid current of air swept in from two open windows and through the open doors of the studio.

Above the mill stream is a delightful pool into which we plunged at least twice a day. Along the river are picturesque walks and at various points there are bathing facilities conveniently arranged for those who do not care to plunge into the pool. Along the upper reaches of the pool, Dr McKenzie has established groups of very beautiful water-lilies of varied and resplendent colouring.

Dr Tait McKenzie is a most interesting companion. His fame as a sculptor extends over two continents. Probably his masterpiece is a wonderful war-memorial at Edinburgh – one of the most impressive war memorials in the world.

Mrs McKenzie, a woman of great culture, poetess, musician, artist, was beginning a poem descriptive of Klara Schumann's career which she related to us in most interesting detail.

Waking early in the 'hired man's bed,' I often pondered upon the century-old activities in that building; and I thought of a translation from the German in which is described an old, deserted mill. I can recall only fragments of the poem which I have not seen for half a century.

It stands in the lonely Unterthal
at the base of Elsberg Hill,
It stands as if it fain would fall,
the old deserted mill.

Its engines covered with mould and rust
bide silent all the day;
And its mildewed walls and windows old
are crumbling into decay.

Then follows a description of its quiet during the day followed by intense activities at night when the spirits of former occupants return to resume their work.

As soon as the daylight is no more,
the night's weird work begins,
The hoppers clatter, the engines roar
and the flour o'er flows the bins.

But before the morning's earliest sheen
the hellish tumult wanes;
And the death-pale face of a woman is
seen at the mill-dulled window panes.

She opens the sash and her words resound
in tones of unearthly power:
'Come hither good folks, your corn is ground,
Come hither and take your flour.'

So I thought of the pioneers of a century ago, of the bustle and activity around this mill which did a roaring business in those days. But spirits, returning to resume their former labours, would find most perplexing conditions, for Dr McKenzie uses the mill-wheel as a table in his studio and many other articles necessary for the mill's operation have been utilized for useful purposes.

However, no 'revenants' haunt the place, unless it can be surmised that they take the form of bats which occasionally frequent the upper courses of the mill.

I append a copy of a letter which, after our return, I sent to Dr McKenzie.

I remain, Sir, Yours faithfully,

July 23, 1935

To Dr R. Tait McKenzie
Mill of Kintail
near Almonte
Ontario

My dear Dr McKenzie,

Our best thanks to you and to your dear wife for three most delightful days which we shall always hold in happy memory. The morning walk, the plunge in the brimming pool, the intimate communion of thought, the delights of your studio, the charming visits to your neighbours at Almonte – these will always dwell in our thoughts.

What do you think of *lectus pueris aptus* as a free translation for hired man's bed?

With love and all good wishes to you both, in which my wife joins, I remain,

Yours faithfully,

In mid 1935 unemployment in the country was still a serious cancer in the body politic. There were many relief camps and men were becoming desperate.

In the following Limbo letter Sir Robert, inter alia, comments on marches of some unemployed on Ottawa.

August 21, 1935

MARCHES ON OTTAWA AND OTHER MATTERS

Sir,

August has brought such heat as has not been felt in Ottawa for many years. Under its influence I have given little thought to conditions at home or abroad.

There have been many excursions and alarums by men who have deserted relief camps and undertaken marches to Ottawa with the obvious purpose of intimidating the government of the day. Unfortunately, it seems clear that these movements have been organized by shrewd leaders whose intention was not revealed to the young men whom they induced to join therein. Their various futile marches reveal no purpose except disorder and disregard for law. Presently there are a few hundred in Ottawa who seek aid for returning to their homes or camps which they should never have left.

The press of the country has rendered marked disservice to the public interest in attaching importance and giving publicity to incidents that should have been accounted of little moment if not magnified by unfortunate recital.

For your information, I enclose an editorial from today's *Ottawa Citizen*, and another from the *Montreal Gazette* of the same date, together with a copy of a letter which I have addressed to Paul Bilkey, editor of the *Gazette*.

The firm conviction of the *Ottawa Citizen* that it could handle the affairs of state better than R.B. Bennett, or Mackenzie King, and could deal with civic affairs better than Paddy Nolan[30] is interesting but pathetic.

Mitchell Hepburn, Premier of Ontario, does not stand high in my regard as may be evidenced by the enclosed communications which on various occasions I have addressed to my good friend, John W. Dafoe, editor of the *Winnipeg Free Press*. But I commend Hepburn's outspoken resolution in declaring that men who refuse to engage in useful work shall be absolutely debarred from relief.

Having refused, since the beginning of the year, more than two-score invitations to deliver public addresses, I finally consented to open the Central Canada Exhibition on the nineteenth instant. You may be interested in the enclosed press report of my address.

Mussolini who signed the Paris Pact has openly announced to the world his firm intention of contemptuously violating its provisions by using war as an instrument of national policy in his proposed attack upon Ethiopia. My opinion of his purpose and his conduct is expressed in the following extract from a letter to the Canadian minister at Paris (August 16, 1935):

> There is anxiety on this Continent as to Mussolini's adventure in Ethiopia. 'Whom the gods would destroy they first make mad'. He may precipitate a world war out of which Italy may stagger, maimed and almost helpless.

30 Mayor of Ottawa.

Also I quote an extract from a letter (August 20) to my good friend Newton Wesley Rowell on the same subject:

> With Great Britain and France clouded in mutual suspicion and vacillation while Mussolini plays a swaggering role, caught from the example of Japan and of Germany, and with the League giving little occasion to hope for the only action that will preserve its remnant of prestige, one cannot fail to be discouraged.
>
> Germany scornfully defied the Peace Treaty; Japan politely sneered at the League; and now Mussolini publicly proclaims his utter contempt for the Paris Pact to which his country is a signatory.

I remain, Sir, Yours, etc.,

August 21, 1935

The Citizen

NO SECOND REGINA WANTED

Ottawa at this moment stands in danger of being made into a second Regina. The trekkers and the police may at any moment come in conflict, and it is almost certain that if they do a similar tragedy to that which was enacted in the Saskatchewan capital when trekkers met armed forces will be witnessed.

On Monday night the vicinity of Plouffe Park resembled an armed camp. City police patrolled the region with tear-gas bombs and other weapons in readiness. Awaiting call in case of trouble were RCMP detachments, armed with deadlier weapons, according to a report.

It was all to prevent a parade of the trekkers. The parade was forbidden presumably in the interests of public safety, but that this had to be done suggests the somewhat dubious state to which we have come in Canada, where the right to hold a peaceable procession has long been established.

Fortunately, the trekkers are under moderate leaders. Those leaders have insisted that the marchers commit no act which might lead to law-breaking or collision with the police or military. Had it not been for this fact a different story might have been told.

If the trekkers had been handled diplomatically from the beginning of their march, the probability is that they would have returned to their homes or camps long before now. But 'bluntness' aroused feelings and left the trekkers in a more resentful mood than might otherwise have been the case. Mayors and ministers have refused food and shelter – but have caused as much to be spent on extra police precautions than would have been spent on the other things had the march been more tolerantly dealt with.

Official policy seems to be to do nothing but hold the police ready to shoot. It is an aggravation of the situation. But the trekkers have been here nearly two weeks and it is time the matter was taken out of the sphere of police tactics and transferred to that of human relations. The men ought to be sent back, both for safety and for conscience' sake.

It is said that private agencies are endeavoring to provide the means of transportation. If they succeed, all well and good. But if they fail, then something more will have to be done than play the present cat-and-mouse game. We suggest that the provincial government – which escorted the men to Ottawa's door – ought to be prevailed upon to do something. If Toronto will do nothing, then the Ottawa government ought to unbend sufficiently to provide the means – on economical if not common-sense grounds.

The situation is getting ticklish, and Ottawa wants no bloodshed. It is time the authorities got back to reason.

August 21, 1935

The Montreal Gazette

ORGANIZED TROUBLE-MAKERS

For the past few weeks an army of trekkers, who marched upon Ottawa despite warnings from the authorities, have been living at the public expense in a camp provided for their accommodation at the capital. These men have been pestering the citizens in various ways and have been making threats against the municipality and the government. The opening of the Exhibition was regarded as a favorable opportunity to harass the public and the law officers and it was announced that the crowd would march to the fair grounds and there hold a public meeting. When police were sent to the camp to prevent such a demonstration pickets attempted to prevent them from entering. As the officers persisted in carrying out their instructions there was a skirmish, which resulted in a victory for them. The disturbers then held an open meeting, at which speakers denounced the

Dominion government, the city police, the RCMP, the municipal authorities and the two major political parties. Premier Bennett was denounced for appropriating millions of dollars for his 'peace, order and good government plan,' and the height of absurdity was reached when one leader threatened the city with trouble unless the campers were furnished transportation back to their homes. Thus, Ottawa, which tried to keep the trekkers away, is requested to pay for their departure on pain of physical attack, for that is what the threat conveyed.

The attitude of these trekkers bears out the statement made by Premier Bennett in the House of Commons on June 24 last, when he remarked that 'the movement of marchers upon Ottawa in defiance of the law, is in reality an organized effort on the part of the various Communist organizations throughout Canada to effect the overthrow of constituted authority in defiance of the laws of the land.' The Prime Minister went on to say that propaganda, not confined to Canada, was being carried on by well-organized forces, the leaders of which did not hesitate to threaten to resist to the full any effort to maintain law and order.

The men who planned the descent on the Ottawa Exhibition on Monday actually defied the city police and openly denounced all authority. Their spokesmen condemned the older political parties and showed no appreciation whatever for the government's work in alleviating distress, making no mention of the hundreds of millions of dollars that have been spent in the last few years. By their actions they confirm the impression that their mission is to annoy as much as possible all municipal and governmental authority and do their utmost to destroy the present system. It is significant that scores of youths between the ages of 20 and 25, residents of the capital, have pledged themselves to assist the Ottawa police, if necessary, in preserving the peace during Exhibition time. This is a visible sign that the public have become tired of the trekkers and their extravagant demands and are determined that an ungrateful and disgruntled minority shall not have their way at the general expense. The challenge of the wreckers is to be met by the authorities, who will have popular support.

Sir Robert Borden, in an address at Ottawa, called upon Canadian youth to strive to maintain an indomitable spirit even in face of the present discouragement, and ventured to prophesy that in the very relief camps there are today young men who in years to come will serve Canada with distinction. Canada's grand old statesman has seen more than one depression in his long and honorable career, and has known many men who have risen from the lowest ranks to the highest, in more than one sphere of activity. He has faith in the youth of today and is confident they will overcome all obstacles, just as their fathers did. His counsel to 'hope, not despair,' comes from sincere conviction, and is good.

Ottawa
August 21, 1935

To Paul Bilkey, Esquire
Editor
The Gazette
Montreal, P.Q.

Private and personal

My dear Paul,

I write not so much to thank you (although I do thank you) for the personal reference in today's *Gazette*, but rather to convey my congratulations upon the editorial 'Organized Trouble-Makers' in the same issue. It is reasonable, well-conceived and cogent, in marked contrast to an editorial in the *Ottawa Citizen* this morning.

I have the highest opinion of Harry Southam, a splendid citizen in every aspect, a man of fine purpose and high ideals. Bowman, the Chief Editor, is also a worthy and well-intentioned man, although of unbalanced outlook. But the *Citizen*'s editorials do on occasion exasperate me. I cannot and do not believe that they are intended to foment and increase discontent, disorder and disregard of law, but if such were the intention these editorials could not have been better conceived. Any person with an admitted criminal record seems to have an especial appeal to the *Citizen*'s sympathies which invariably pass by the hundreds of thousands of honest, industrious, well-behaved men and women in Canada who have endured hardship without murmur, who have resisted temptation and who plod along a weary path in fulfilment of their duty as God gives them to see it. So far as the *Citizen* is concerned, the convict and criminal absorb the sympathies which rightfully should go forth to the splendid people I have described upon whose firm fibre the fabric of our national life and destiny rests secure.

With very kind regards and all good wishes, I remain,

Yours faithfully,

EXTRACTS FROM LETTERS TO JOHN W. DAFOE

April 15, 1935

The outburst of the Mayors and Hepburn's policy of repudiation have created a most unfortunate impression in United States and have dried up US investments in Canadian securities; although their businessmen preface their comment by confessing that, having regard to their own policies, they should best be silent. The comment from Great Britain is extremely acrid. Hepburn had reason for seeking some modification of the contracts but his manner of approach seems to me maladroit, clumsy, malevolent and highly detrimental. Gladstone carried even to excess the principle that engagements made by a previous administration must be faithfully observed. If I remember correctly, he carried this principle into practice even when understanding had been reached before the engagement had assumed final form.

July 12, 1935

Whatever may be said of varying forms of virtual repudiation as they have recently appeared, nothing has occurred so detrimental to a nation's credit as Ontario's legislative repudiation of the power contracts. The resulting impairment of credit and confidence abroad has been startling. If you have studied the proposals practically accepted in Great Britain for a series of conversion loans you must realize how vitally important they were to Canada's financial structure which, to speak very euphemistically, is far from satisfactory. A series of conversions into long-term securities would have made the position impregnable for such a period as to remove apprehension. An agreement had been prepared and approved and was about to be signed for the first conversion. The negotiations came to an immediate and untimely end when Ontario repudiated. By this conversion and those in contemplation there would have been a saving of about a million dollars per annum in interest charges. I venture to observe that even Hepburn comes high at that figure.

July 20, 1935

More than once I have set forth my opinion of Mitchell Hepburn in extremely uncomplimentary terms which I do not in the least withdraw. His outrageous attack upon public faith and credit, not only of this Province, but of Canada, his indecent treatment of efficient and respected public officials, his clownish vindictiveness, his utter lack of dignity, his smart-Aleck antics and the extremely undesirable characteristics which credible rumour attributes to his habit of life, have not roused my admiration.

For the first time I find something to appreciate and indeed to admire. I allude to his pronouncement that every person physically capable who refuses to work when work is available shall be debarred from relief. In my opinion, this is the most direct and unequivocal statement of sound policy in such matters that has come under my notice.

However, I deeply regret that it is merely a pennyworth of bread in so much sack.

The following four Limbo letters written in September and in October, 1935, deal principally with the general election of 1935, in which Mr Bennett's Conservative government was defeated and Mr Mackenzie King was returned to office after being in opposition for five years; the departure of the Governor-General – Lord Bessborough – and a visit to Canada of the Dean of Canterbury 'for the purpose of instructing the Canadian people in the mysteries of Social Credit'.

September 9, 1935

BEGINNING OF THE 1935 FEDERAL ELECTION CAMPAIGN

Sir,

The political leaders have gone into action. We listened last week to Mr Bennett's broadcast which was very good, except that he struck too much the personal note and made too extended references to parties and party controversies. Almost immediately he is setting out for a tour of the western provinces where he will be followed by Mr King.

On Friday, the sixth instant, Mr Lascelles [A.F. (Tommy) Lascelles – at that time secretary to the Governor-General] called to consult me on behalf of Lord Bessborough with regard to the proposal that the Prime Minister should return at the date of the Governor-General's departure from Ottawa. Mr Bennett's arrangements would take him to Edmonton on that day. I strongly advised against his return; and I pointed out to Mr Lascelles that such an eventuality might be not only unfortunate for Mr Bennett – by reason of his having to disregard arrangements already made – but unfortunate also for the Governor-General to whom Mr Bennett's return would be attributed and who would be regarded as inconsiderate in exacting the Prime Minister's attendance when public duties called him elsewhere. Further, I suggested that, in the midst of a general election, due respect for the Governor-General and his office would be sufficiently indicated if Mr Bennett should dispatch an appropriate telegraphic message of farewell. Lascelles fully concurred in my view.

Presently the situation at Geneva is undoubtedly critical; it may result in strengthening and preserving the prestige of the League. On the other hand, it may have a disastrous result. In any case it exemplifies the terrible danger of dictatorship.[31] It has been rumoured that Mussolini is a paranoiac; certainly his policy and his speeches indicate either an unbalanced mind or the existence of grave internal difficulties in Italy necessitating impetuous and violent external action to distract the people and to arouse patriotic fervour.

Meanwhile, the autumn colouring of the leaves on shrubs and vines in the wild-garden is most beautiful.

I remain, Sir, Yours, etc.,

September 28, 1935

DEPARTURE OF THE GOVERNOR-GENERAL

Sir,

The political leaders are now in full cry. No less than six parties have entered the field – Conservatives, Liberals, Reconstructionists, CCF's, Social Credit and Labourites.

The situation is more confused and more uncertain than at any time since confederation. There is absurd discrepancy in the estimates of the outcome. The anticipation of the Stevens' following [Reconstruction party led by Hon H.H. Stevens] ranges from 10 to

31 The reference is to the crisis created by the contemplated invasion of Abyssinia by Italy (Mussolini) which occurred almost four weeks later, i.e. October 3, 1935.

50 seats; he will have the largest group; the Conservatives will have the largest group; the Liberals will have the largest group; the Liberals will have a majority over all; Bennett is gaining ground; he is losing ground; King is gaining ground; he is losing ground, etc, etc.

The autumn colouring is more varied and more beautiful than ever before. One cannot put into words the loveliness of the leaves on the vines, the shrubs and the trees.

The Earl and Countess of Bessborough took their departure from Ottawa on Thursday, September 26, after a round of festivities that must have been not only tiresome but extremely exhausting. However, they have played well their part.

Both at the Rideau Club dinner and at the government dinner Lord Bessborough spoke more feelingly than ever before and with fuller acceptance by his audience. At the government dinner there was an eloquent faltering in his voice when he alluded to his Canadian son, George,[32] a faltering that greatly moved all who listened. ... He made a very kind and most generous reference to the writer.[33]

On September 17, his little son, George, came to visit me and I took some photographs, one of which was so good that Lady Bessborough said she had it framed and kept it on her dressing-table. George gathered various kinds of wild and cultivated flowers, and asked for 'another rose', so that he had three in all. He was particularly taken with the Scarlet-Runners of which he acquired about eight or ten, informing his nurse that he would have them for his 'nice dinner.'

For some days the lady of the household was, unfortunately, *alitée* by reason of a tiresome although mild attack of grippe. Three

32 Four months after their arrival in Canada in 1931 Lady Bessborough gave birth to a son named George St Lawrence Neuflize Ponsonby.

33 The *Ottawa Evening Citizen* of September 26, 1935, made the following reference to Lord Bessborough's remarks at the government dinner the preceding evening:

SAYS SIR R. BORDEN GRAND OLD MAN OF CANADA AND EMPIRE

Sir Robert Borden is not only the Grand Old Man of Canada, he is the Grand Old Man of the British Empire, said His Excellency the Earl of Bessborough in his speech at the dinner given by the Canadian government at the Chateau last night.

His Excellency spoke feelingly of the regard he had for Sir Robert and the intimate friendship which had sprung up during the past four years. He would never forget, he said, the counsel and close companionship he had enjoyed with Sir Robert.

formal and important dinner-parties I was obliged to attend *en garcon*. Fortunately, she has now almost recovered and I hope to take her away for a brief holiday next Monday. Perhaps I should regret this absence as an unfortunate deprivation of opportunity for political activities. However, I shall endure it with great equanimity.

I remain, Sir, Yours, etc.,

September 30, 1935

DEAN OF CANTERBURY AND SOCIAL CREDIT

Sir,

The Very Reverend Hewlett Johnson, Dean of Canterbury, has recently paid a visit to Canada for the purpose of instructing the Canadian people in the mysteries of Social Credit. Beyond question the Dean would have done much better to remain at home and give wholehearted attention to the religious duties that ought to engage his time and his energies. His intrusion into an election campaign was not only stupid but offensive.

At Ottawa his speech comprised a flood of eloquent generalities and airy nothings, coupled with absurd mis-statements. At Toronto, he delivered himself of this gem:

> Bankers create money out of nothing. Bankers lie when they say they borrow money and then lend it out again. They make money out of the blue.

As a rule, English ecclesiastics visiting Canada are quite unaccustomed to their environment and their speeches usually do more harm than good. Some years ago the Bishop of London, at an outdoor gathering in Lansdowne Park, [in Ottawa] exhorted his audience to maintain the dominance of English influence in Canada. About a third or a fourth of his audience was French. Immediately in front of us sat a French mother whose attention was largely engaged with two young children. Her elder child of about eight, following the example of some who sat near, innocently gave warm applause to this maladroit exhortation!

Apparently the Dean of Canterbury is somewhat of the same mental calibre as a former Dean of Windsor of whom this story is told. Upon the birth in 1841, of the late King Edward, [son of Queen

Victoria] he called a meeting of the Dean and Chapter of Windsor to approve and authorize an address of congratulations to the Queen. The address was curiously phrased in many respects. It purported to emanate from 'The Dean and Chapter of Windsor, The People of Windsor and The Other Inhabitants of Europe.' It conveyed to Her Majesty warm congratulations upon the birth of a son which, as the address expressed it, 'would save the Kingdom from the unspeakable calamity of a female succession!'

I remain, Sir, Yours, etc.,

October 19, 1935

FEDERAL ELECTION RESULT, 1935

Sir,

Hitherto you have refrained from comment upon the result of the recent election in Canada; and thus I am disposed to set forth my own impressions.

Six months ago the result was regarded as a foregone conclusion. This view was greatly modified by the remarkable, one might say 'whirlwind', campaign which Mr Bennett carried on for about six weeks before polling-day. His meetings were larger and seemed to be characterized by more wholehearted enthusiasm than those addressed by Mr King. Although still under the shadow of a serious illness, Mr Bennett apparently surpassed his opponent in his activity and in the tremendous energy of his utterances.

The situation was beclouded or bedevilled by the desertion of Mr Stevens who foolishly attempted the establishment of a new party (christened 'Reconstruction Party') for which, with assistance drawn from different parts of the country, he succeeded in creating some sort of organization. In several constituencies his candidates were persons of some standing; in others, they were obviously men of straw.

Grave doubt existed as to the strength of Mr Stevens' movement. The estimate of his probable following in the next House of Commons varied from 10 to 70 seats. In the actual outcome, out of his one hundred and seventy-three candidates only one (himself) was elected. He and his lieutenants had displayed marked activity; and my own personal estimate gave him twenty-five seats.

Stevens is a very clever speaker, adroit, forceful and by no means scrupulous. He dwelt with considerable effect upon some weak spots and some unfortunate tendencies in our social order. But foolishly and perversely, he overshot the mark and attacked banks, corporations, and the general conduct of business with a perverted zeal designed to create in the electorate an unfortunate and dangerous mistrust.

... Each of the major parties seemed quite confident of success. In the result the Conservative following has no more than forty members in the new parliament. Twelve of their ministers were defeated. In Nova Scotia and Prince Edward Island the party did not gain a single seat; and in New Brunswick only one.

On the other hand, the Liberals came into power with a following of about 171, which gives them a majority of nearly 100 over all other parties combined.

The Conservative debacle is due to many causes; the depression, unemployment, lack of organization, inefficient press. Any government, after five years' service in the severest depression ever experienced, faces the electorate under a heavy handicap.

But for the desertion of Mr Stevens the Conservatives would probably have won at least 80 seats. Several of the ministers who failed to secure re-election publicly ascribe their defeat to the candidature of Mr Stevens' followers.

It seems clear that this gentleman suffers from the vice of ingratitude. Mr Bennett had treated him most kindly, and indeed saved him from difficulty even danger at some risk to himself. But Stevens was not only ungrateful, he was unbalanced and disloyal. His temperament led him to destroy himself. With greater balance and even a modicum of loyalty, he would have remained in the cabinet and inevitably he would have become successor to Mr Bennett. As it is, he ceases to be a force in public affairs for some years to come. Meantime, it is probable, and indeed it is greatly to be hoped, that another leader will arise in the Conservative party to succeed Mr Bennett upon his retirement.

From a Conservative standpoint, the result seems disastrous; but there is compensation in the fact that the party has been spared Mr Stevens' leadership. His outlook, his tendencies and his qualities clearly indicate that he would have been a danger to the Conservative party as its leader, and a still greater danger to the country as its prime minister.

And there are other compensations. The country emerges from the election with the two major parties in the ascendant. Any threat of group-system has been removed for the present. The CCF has been reduced to a negligible proportion, while the Social Credit candidates, of whom seventeen were elected, will disappear with the disappearance of their party before the next federal election.

The Liberals, holding two-thirds of the seats in the House of Commons, are in a considerable minority of the popular vote. Absolute figures are not yet available, but the present estimate gives approximately one million, five hundred thousand votes to the Liberals and one million seven hundred and fifty thousand to other parties.

The Conservative party has no reason to be discouraged. In 1904, under my leadership, it sustained an overwhelming defeat. More than one hundred thousand dollars were employed to defeat me in Halifax; and we lost every seat in Nova Scotia. The purpose of the Liberal ministers was to drive me out of public life and to compel Conservatives to elect another leader. Seven years later we won a decisive victory and defeated the two Nova Scotia ministers who had plotted my overthrow.

Just a few words in conclusion. The roles of the two major parties have greatly changed. At the moment, the Liberal party, under Mr King, really occupies the Conservative seat, while Mr Bennett has conducted the Conservative party into extreme, even radical paths.

On the day following the general election (October 15), at a directors' meeting of Barclays Bank (Canada) in Montreal, I observed to Mr Taschereau that doubtless we would now have four or five years of good tory rule, such as Quebec had enjoyed for many years. About two years ago, when political affiliations of the directors were under discussion, I said to Mr Taschereau that I was not concerned as to the nominal Liberal majority on our board. 'With the exception of the late Sir Wilfrid Laurier and the late Sir Oliver Mowat, I regard you, Mr Taschereau, as the most outstanding, thoroughgoing tory that Canada has ever produced.'

We are not yet out of the woods and the new Prime Minister is confronted with a situation the difficulties and perils of which are by no means realized by the majority of our people.

Apart from questions relating to the tariff, to the railways and to the unemployed, the main considerations to be kept in mind are stability, non-interference with legitimate business, sanctity of governmental contracts and prevention of provincial inroads upon the federal treasury.

In troublous days the people sometimes place in power men whose desire to retain power far exceeds their sense of responsibility.

In saying this, I speak without distinction of party. A provincial premier, under the urge of demand for wasteful or extravagant expenditure which involves borrowing, realizes that the federal government cannot permit any province to default. In my opinion, this aspect discloses a very grave danger to the financial structure of Canada.

Whether Mr King realizes the actualities of the situation, I do not know. His views publicly expressed as to helpful cooperation between Liberal provincial governments and the Liberal federal government, do not impress me. It is highly probable, practically certain, that the provincial administrations will seek to retain all their powers and to avoid some of their responsibilities.

Within the confines of Laurier House Mr King is presently engaged in the formation of his administration. If he selects able men of broad outlook, strong common sense and real patriotism, men willing to put country above party in the present emergency, I shall be content; but in his immediate following there are some nincompoops, some wild men and some dreamers who may make trouble not only for him but for the country.

I remain, Sir, Yours, etc.,

October 26, 1935

ON THE PASSING OF LORD CARSON AND RT. HON. ARTHUR HENDERSON

Sir,

Since my last letter, two men have passed away in Great Britain with whom, during the War, I was in more or less close association.

Lord Carson has been described so vividly and so often in current literature and his life has been so fully written that any portrayal by me would be superfluous. While in attendance at the Imperial War Cabinet and the Imperial War Conference in 1917 and 1918, I met him many times. He was a picturesque and, in some aspects, a most attractive figure. His resolution was like granite, his courage unfailing and unfaltering. Notwithstanding his fierce antagonism to the roman catholic church leaders and people of the south of Ireland, they admired him, although they abhorred his policies.

Prepared for armed rebellion in Ulster and presiding at a stately ceremonial when the Covenant was signed, he made no secret of his purpose and challenged the British government to arrest him. Birkenhead, as one of his lieutenants, was known as 'Galloper Smith.' The Irish leaders of the south strongly urged the British government not to arrest Carson: 'He is immensely popular in the South, because he is fighting the Government; if he were arrested he would become the most popular man in Ireland.' So he went unscathed, so far as the law was concerned, although his defiance of the law was notorious.

Like Balfour, he was not a commanding figure at the admiralty where he remained only a short time. It is said that his administrative ability was not conspicuous.

At the bar, in the House of Commons, as advocate, statesman, revolutionary-leader, he was the most picturesque, stormy and resolute figure that his century had known for a generation or more.

Arthur Henderson was of a different type, a Labour leader who steadily advanced in influence and outlook. He became a member of the Imperial War Cabinet where I was brought into close association with him. On one occasion I won his esteem by declaring, in connection with proposals for preferential tariff, that Canada would not seek or desire any arrangement which would be regarded by the people, and especially by the labouring classes, of the United Kingdom as imposing an unfair burden.

At the request of Sir Eric Drummond, as chief Canadian delegate at Geneva in 1930, I opened the debate on the Secretary-General's Report to the Assembly, and strongly urged that material disarmament should follow moral disarmament which as I thought had been attained. After the conclusion of my address, Brian observed to me: '*Vous avez facilité ma tache.*' And Henderson told me that I had given him a useful text. I venture to enclose a copy of my remarks on that occasion.

Henderson's long struggle as chairman of the Disarmament Committee, the intensity of his effort, his keen disappointment at failure, which was in no wise due to him; all this inevitably sapped his strength and led to his passing at an early age. Those who had the privilege of association with him in his notable activities must honour his memory; a strong, earnest, capable and patient man imbued with the highest ideals of service, not only to his country but to humanity.

I remain, Sir, Yours, etc.,

ARTICLE IN THE SEPTEMBER, 1930, ISSUE OF *Interdependence*

ADDRESS DELIVERED BY RT. HON. SIR ROBERT BORDEN TO LEAGUE

It is with very great diffidence that I rise to address men whose long experience in the work of the League of Nations enables them to speak with an authority which I cannot claim to possess. But, as I had been present at the birth of the League, eleven years ago, and as this is the first occasion when I have had the honour to be present at an Assembly, it was suggested that I might venture to give my impressions of present conditions in contrast to those which prevailed in 1919.

The League was indeed born in a tempest-scourged world, and there were then not a few who trembled for its future and feared that it would succumb to the forces of jealousy, antagonism and hatred. It faced fearful odds, and it would have been no great surprise if its purpose had failed; but looking back over its first decade, which is but a moment in the life of nations, we have indeed great joy in realizing what it has accomplished; and there is confident hope that this is but a prelude to a still more glorious future. All honour to the men of high purpose and firm heart who guided it during those eventful and anxious years. Well may it be said that they who went forth weeping, bearing precious seed, have surely come again with rejoicing, bringing their sheaves with them.

The atmosphere of the world ten years ago was oppressive, almost stifling. In 1919 I returned from Europe to my own country with a feeling of profound depression. It seemed to me that men cried 'peace, peace,' when there was no peace.

To-day, in the clean and wholesome atmosphere of good-will, understanding and co-operation, I am inspired to see this Assembly of the nations in full and intimate conference, consecrated to the cause of peaceful arbitrament and the enthronement of public right between the nations. I should be the last to minimise the wonderful concrete results that have been accomplished during the first ten years of the League. To abate the threat of war on more than one occasion, to induce whole-hearted co-operation, to create great organizations for curing the ills of mankind, to aid the helpless, to strengthen the weak, to raise the fallen: all these and many other achievements are indeed memorable and the world owes its beatitude. But in my conception the highest service of the League to humanity lies in the constant association and co-operation, in the resultant education and training, of the nations. They are here in the kindergarten of peace and already they have learned many a useful lesson. There are others still harder that must yet be learned.

Is it not idle to conceive that the peace of the world may be maintained by force? Can we even imagine that it may be maintained by treaties and conventions unless behind them lies the will for peace? We must seek for the world's peace in the domain of the spirit. This was emphasized to you yesterday in the inspiring address of my fellow-continental, may I not say my fellow-countryman, the President of the Council. And I recall an impressive speech of most moving eloquence delivered at Washington nearly nine years ago by the great orator and statesman who was then Prime Minister of his country and who is now its Foreign Minister. In words that I have never forgotten, M Briand dwelt upon the need of moral disarmament as a condition precedent to practical disarmament. Do we not all admit the need and has not he, in conjunction with Mr Kellogg in the great Peace Pact of Paris, taken a memorable and momentous step towards moral disarmament in leading the nations to renounce war as an instrument of national policy. The world owes to him a debt of profound gratitude for that wonderful gesture of imperishable significance. Now, if we have in truth renounced war, what do we lack of moral disarmament?

Yet, while there has been this splendid moral renunciation, armaments continue to oppress the nations. It would be monstrous to believe that they are a preparation for war that has been renounced. I realize the difficulties and complexities of the problem of practical disarmament and the earnestness of the effort for its solution. Let us not forget that vast armaments are not only oppressive, but dangerous. To-day the world is expectant. War has been renounced. Why has there not been a like renunciation of armaments? This is the hardest lesson of all.

I have said that we are here as children in the kindergarten of peace. Is it conceivable that we can advance beyond the kindergarten until the world shall have been freed from the menace of armaments. Do I hear a whisper that this is vain idealism? Let us thank God that the idealism of one generation becomes the achievement of the next. In my country there are thousands of worthy and contented citizens from every nation in Europe and from many other nations. If I might interpret their message, they would bid you look forward and not backward. May not the dead past bury its dead? Let our faith have vision to look beyond, to behold the day when war shall be oustide the pale of thought or imagination, when it shall be cast forth forever into the outer darkness of things accursed, its brow seared with the brand of eternal infamy.

October 28, 1935

APPOINTMENT OF JOHN BUCHAN AS GOVERNOR-GENERAL

Sir,

Mr John Buchan has been elevated to the peerage and has taken the title of Lord Tweedsmuir. Before this honour had been conferred upon him, he had been designated as next Governor-General of Canada.

On Saturday night at Quebec he will be sworn into office by the Chief Justice. The Prime Minister has kindly sent us invitations for all the functions at Quebec which are very numerous and which have been detailed with meticulous care ... Unfortunately we find ourselves unable to accept.

The selection of John Buchan was something of a mystery. It was my intention to ask information from Bennett; but his pre-occupations during the election have prevented me. From Perley I once heard of negotiations or discussion with Mackenzie King when Bennett was ill. He said that a person of the James Bryce type was desired; that Buchan was known both to Bennett and to King and each believed he would fulfil this ideal.

The important post of Governor-General has hitherto been occupied by some member of an ancient and historic family; and Buchan's selection did not particularly impress the Canadian people. Certain eminent citizens of Toronto when asked for their opinion of the selection declared that they had never heard of Mr Buchan. This, however, indicated a remarkable inacquaintance with current literature.

During the War, Buchan produced many entertaining works of fiction of the type usually described as 'pot-boilers.' Afterwards he wrote a Life of Lord Minto, at the request of Lady Minto. His description of Minto's career in Canada and of Canadian conditions is not especially happy or accurate. On this subject, I addressed to Buchan (on July 28, 1932) a letter [copy attached] which speaks for itself.

But later, Buchan has produced three works of outstanding

merit. Two of them, *Life of Scott*, and *Life of Cromwell*, I have read with real appreciation. His *Life of Montrose*, which I have not yet read, is said to be excellent.

A few years ago when reform of the House of Lords was under discussion, Buchan, then a member of the House of Commons, made a speech of conspicuous merit and distinction, a speech that attracted marked attention and elicited warm approval.

Being human he has, doubtless, his weaknesses and foibles. Dr George M. Wrong of Toronto expressed considerable surprise at Buchan's selection and delivered himself of this opinion: 'he is a bit of a snob and he will lap up, as a cat would lap up warm milk, all the ceremonial that usually attends the various functions of his office.'

An Englishman of outstanding ability, Mr W.M. Goodenough, in allusion to the characteristics of Buchan and his family observed: 'They will dress for the part and they will play the part, but people will realize that they were not cast for the part.'

However, I am convinced that Buchan will fulfil with credit to himself and with general acceptance the duties of his high office.

I remain, Sir, Yours hopefully,

July 28, 1932

To John Buchan, Esq., MP,
House of Commons
London, England

Dear Mr Buchan,

I venture to offer my impressions respecting your criticism of the late Sir Frederick Borden, Minister of Militia in Sir Wilfrid Laurier's Cabinet from 1896 to 1911.

When *Lord Minto: A Memoir* first appeared I was disposed to make a public protest but refrained from doing so as evidently your attack upon Sir Frederick had not come to the notice of his widow whom it would have greatly distressed.

In political life I was vehemently opposed to Sir Frederick Borden; and in 1904 I suffered a humiliating defeat through his efforts and those of Mr Fielding. These two ministers represented Nova Scotia in the Laurier government and my defeat, in the early stage of my leadership, was intended to drive me from public life.

Whether fortunately or unfortunately the attempt failed. Seven years later I was able to return the compliment by defeating both Fielding and Borden. The latter never re-entered public life as he died January 6, 1917.

However, Sir Frederick Borden was my near kinsman – our fathers were brothers and our mothers first cousins. There was no physical resemblance between us and, perhaps, little intellectual resemblance. Notwithstanding our political controversies, we were on terms of personal friendship. And I deem it my duty to point out certain considerations that apparently you have overlooked.

First, as to Borden's personal characteristics. He was a man of reasonable ability, although I would not consider him in the first rank. He was an indefatigable worker and a good administrator. His courage was never questioned and never failed. He possessed in a marked degree the confidence and friendship of Sir Wilfrid Laurier and was respected on both sides of the Commons.

I regret that you should have applied to Borden, Rosebery's rather cheap sneer at Addington. Whatever may be said of Addington, he probably made better use of his abilities and opportunities than did Rosebery whose wonderful intellectual endowment, splendid position and great wealth gave him an opportunity of usefulness in public life which he certainly failed to grasp. Apparently he lacked the essential qualities of courage, patience and (although he was a wit) the saving grace of humour. It is fortunate that at a certain critical period in the Empire's history Campbell-Bannerman was in the saddle and not Lord Rosebery.

You will permit me to express my confident opinion that the similitude of a village apothecary inspecting the tongue of the State is no more appropriate to Borden than to Rosebery or to Minto.

Then, as to his career as Minister of Militia, Borden's one great mistake, which did not occur during the regime of Lord Minto and therefore was not noticed by you, was the substitution in 1905 of the Ross rifle for the British service rifle. This change was vigorously opposed by the opposition. Borden's action was probably due to the insistence of Sir Wilfrid Laurier who desired to establish a great factory in Quebec for the production of a Canadian service rifle. For many purposes the Ross rifle was an admirable weapon but it proved unserviceable during the War and the Canadian government was obliged to replace it by the British service rifle. Fortunately, although the Ross rifle was unserviceable in the trenches, it was useful for other purposes and eventually, I believe, it proved an excellent weapon for use on board naval craft. It is clear that the forces of the

Empire should have been furnished with the same type of arms and equipment but the selection of the type should have been made after consultation with the Dominions.

With respect to party patronage, I imagine Borden was not immune to a system that had prevailed pretty widely in the Laurier administration. However, his secretary informs me that on many occasions Borden refused to exercise party patronage although pressed to do so.

You lay stress on Borden's lack of military knowledge and experience. At the age of sixteen he enlisted in the Militia of Nova Scotia in 1863, four years before Confederation, and served in various ranks until he finally attained that of Surgeon. No one would pretend that he had any special military knowledge; neither did Lord Haldane whose service as Secretary of State for War was generally regarded as very valuable.

Your estimate of the circumstances that led to the retirement of General Hutton and afterwards of Lord Dundonald gives an impression that I do not altogether share. Dundonald certainly had great provocation in the partisan interference of Mr Fisher, the Minister of Agriculture, who was acting in the absence of Borden. I attacked the government on that occasion although I agree, that, under the circumstances, it was impossible for Dundonald to continue.

There was little debate in parliament respecting the resignation and retirement of General Hutton. I have made pretty careful inquiry as to the incidents of his career and as to his temperament. You liken him to a 'gadfly', but I should be disposed rather to compare him to a bull in a china shop. He had an excessive self-appreciation and an astonishing sense of superiority to 'Colonials'. He was guilty of incivility to the point of sheer insolence. Of this, Sir Frederick Borden's secretary, who is still in the public service, has given me some cogent illustrations. He was devoid of tact and possessed of an exceedingly domineering spirit. That he should have failed to realize the limitations of his office is not unusual in a soldier of his type. At a later date I found it necessary to quell the spirit of a military secretary who was possessed of fantastic ideas as to the proper functions of a Governor-General and as to his own official importance.

In speaking in the House of Commons on February 19, 1900, Sir Wilfrid Laurier used the following language:

> General Hutton in his speech has insinuated that his differences with the Government are due to a desire on the part of the lat-

> ter to exercise improper political influence on the Militia organization of the country. I desire, on the part of the Government, to say that there is absolutely no foundation for such a statement.
>
> The causes of difference between the Government and General Hutton were not over any particular questions of general policy. The causes of difference were that General Hutton was insubordinate and indiscreet, and deliberately ignored the authority of the Minister in the administration of the Department ... Such an officer is to be regarded as the adviser, but not as entitled to control the Department of Militia ... The Government would be derelict to their duty if they were to permit any subordinate official in any circumstances to take upon himself to disregard the instructions he may receive from the constitutional head of his department. (1. *Hans.* 1900, pp. 595–6).

At page 148, you quote Mr Chamberlain's despatch of April 17, 1900, but not the very firm reply made by the Canadian government. ...

General Hutton's service in Canada began on August 23, 1898, and ended February 1900. He made two annual reports; and his recommendations have been summarized as follows by an officer of the Department of National Defence:

1 Annual training for all the Militia; Company, Regimental and Brigade training. Period to be increased from 12 to 16 days.
2 Creation of a trained General Staff.
3 Provision of Regimental arms and equipment stores buildings.
4 Pension scheme for officers.
5 Creation of military administrative branches, viz., Army Service Corps, Ordnance Store Corps, Army Medical Corps, Army Pay Corps, Engineers, and Veterinary Department.
6 The duties of the General Officer Commanding to be more clearly defined.
7 Provision of Artillery and Rifle Ranges.

I am informed that several of these recommendations had been made by predecessors of General Hutton. The entire programme was put into effect a few years after his departure with other changes and improvements which he had not suggested.

I have procured from the Department of National Defence the following partial list of these changes and improvements which has been compiled from the annual reports of the General Officer Commanding Militia or of the Inspector-General of Militia.

O'Grady-Haly
1900 Army Medical Corps authorized and established
1901 Militia Pension Act passed

Lord Dundonald
1902 Army Service Corps authorized and established – Rockcliffe Rifle Ranges
1903 Ordnance Store Corps authorized and established
Engineer Services authorized and established
Intelligence Department authorized and established
War and Peace establishments prepared
Arrangements for improvement of military instruction
Signal Corps authorized and established
New Regulations for Cadet organizations
Military Library at Headquarters established
Canadian Officers admitted to Imperial Staff College

Sir Percy Lake
1905 Trained General Staff organized
Garrisons at Halifax and Esquimalt taken over
Operations and Staff Duties Branch created
Corps of Guides authorized
Efficiency pay authorized and immediately effective
Militia Council created
Subsequent re-organization of military command
Central Artillery Camp at Petawawa
16 days training for Artillery
Re-organization of camp staffs
Re-organization of Field Artillery
1906 Pay Corps authorized and established
Veterinary Department authorized and established
Survey Division authorized and established
Organization of Cavalry and Artillery into brigades
1909 Military training in Universities
New Rifle Ranges, Kingston and Niagara
Improved sanitation of camps
Improved quality of rations
Purchase of 18 pr. Q.F. Guns
1910 'The Inspector-General of the Imperial Forces, Sir J. French, considers that the Permanent Force has reached a satisfactory

standard of efficiency.' (Extract from Report of General Lake, Inspector-General of Canadian Militia, 26.10.10)

Between 1904 and 1910, the following Regulations were prepared and issued:

King's Regulations and Orders, 1910
Pay and Allowance Regulations
Equipment Regulations, Parts I and II
Clothing Regulations
Regulations for Engineer Services
Regulations for Supply, Transport and Barrack Services
Regulations for Medical Services
Regulations for Ordnance Services
Regulations for Rifle Associations
Regulations for Cadet Corps
Dress Regulations

With respect to the various improvements alluded to, I have procured from the Assistant Deputy Minister of National Defence the following memorandum:

> In all these cases, not only was authority given, but the units were actually created, organized and set to work. These were all new organizations, excepting the Ordnance Store Corps and the Engineer Services, which had previously existed as small civilian branches, but which were greatly re-organized, enlarged and improved when they became part of the Permanent Corps.
>
> The dates given indicate the actual beginnings made, and the report of the General Officer Commanding usually details what has been done to put into effect the authority given. He tells what units have been organized, what work they are undertaking, and in some cases what officers are being sent away for special courses of instruction. In almost all these cases development continued through the years. More units were authorized, larger establishments approved, and more work undertaken. The work of the various administrative Corps was generally praised by the General Officer Commanding; and this, notwithstanding that the report of the General Officer Commanding was, in the main, highly critical in tone.
>
> The present Army Medical Service Corps, Army Service Corps, Ordnance Corps, Engineer Services, Intelligence Service, Signal Corps, and Veterinary Corps have all developed from

these small beginnings. The Guide Corps was discontinued after some years. The Army Pay Corps has lately been disbanded, and its duties taken over by the civil accounting staff. The Survey Division is now represented by the Geographic Section of the General Staff; and is, in effect, a section of the Intelligence Service. The change is merely a change of name, and the Section turns out excellent maps.

In relation to your assurance of Borden's inefficiency and lack of zeal, it might be useful to note that when he took office the total expenditure on Canada's Militia was less than two and a half million dollars. In the face of strong opposing and antagonistic forces within his own party, he increased this annual expenditure to more than seven millions before he retired. This advance was not attained without a hard struggle against fierce opposition and passive inertia. The man who accomplished this result was no coward, nor was he devoid of ability, nor was he, as Minister of Militia, primarily a politician. He was a man earnest and enthusiastic in his work, a diligent student and advocate of progress who fought hard for the good of the Canadian Militia, as he saw it, and who feared not to oppose even more formidable personages than General Hutton when he thought the public good required it.

The suggestion that to General Hutton's inspiration was due Canada's aid to the British Empire in the South African War is, in my opinion, absolutely without foundation and wholly imaginative. That effort was no more due to General Hutton than was Canada's response in 1914, of which I can claim to have some knowledge.

So far as I can ascertain, the relations between Borden and the successors of General Hutton were entirely satisfactory. ...

In contrast with what I have placed before you, I quote your conclusion at p.155. You lament General Hutton's departure in these words:

> Canada relapsed into a provincial system of a small permanent Militia, an imperfectly trained active Militia, and a water-tight staff. She did not even, like Australia, have any custom of universal training.

Then, in referring to Canada's response in 1914:

> But everything had to be improvised, and improvisation takes time. It was eight months before the First Canadian Division could take its place in the field, and meantime the whole burden of the defence, not of Britain alone but of Canada, fell on the worn ranks of the British regulars.

The British Regular army in 1914 was probably the most effective fighting force in the field. But it was hopelessly outnumbered; and so improvisation had to begin in Great Britain as in Canada. What is the record? The Princess Patricia's Canadian Light Infantry arrived in France December 1914, and nine-tenths were dead or wounded before the following summer. The remainder of the First Canadian Division arrived in France on February 8 and 9, 1915; and on April 23, it sustained the shock of the first gas attack. And it did not fail.

From the Official History of the War, Volume 3, page 331, is taken the following quotation:

> On the 9th May (1915) the 9th Scottish Division, *the first of the new Army Divisions*, began to detrain in St Omer District.

Would it not have been appropriate in your criticism of Canada's effort to contrast these two dates?

I do not overlook the fact that the North Midland Territorial Division arrived in France on February 24, 1915, but this was not one of the 'new' or Kitchener Armies.

If I were at liberty to quote certain observations which I found it necessary to address to the Imperial War Cabinet on the thirteenth day of June, 1918, you might, perhaps, receive a fresh impression as to the efficiency of organization in the Canadian as compared with the British forces. Lord Milner said that these observations would be answered. They never were answered. In the provision and utilization of machine-guns, barbed wire entanglements, Corps Artillery and in many other respects, Canada's war organization was certainly not at a discount with that of the Mother Country.

The Duke of Connaught, at the outbreak of War, told me that many years previously, after he had attended the German military manoeuvres, his report strongly urged a large increase in machine-guns. Apparently his report was pigeon-holed in the War Office, with disastrous results when war broke out.

Mr Lloyd George in the summer of 1915, while I was endeavouring to obtain information as to Great Britain's preparation and as to the date when the Empire would be prepared to throw its full strength into the War, gave me a most impressive account of outrageous and scandalous neglect, delay and lack of foresight in the provision of machine-guns, munitions and otherwise. Speaking of a highly placed official in the War Office, he said: 'I do not say that ——— is a traitor. But I do say that if he had been a traitor he would not have acted differently.'

An English civilian who enlisted in Kitchener's army and eventually attained the rank of Colonel and who is now a highly placed official in the British civil service, communicated to me a few years ago, at a personal interview, an extremely vivid denunciation of the 'trade unionism' of the British Regular army. His language was passionate; and indeed certain incidents that came to my knowledge during the War indicated that on some occasions the retention of his 'job' by a regular officer was regarded as more essential than the efficient discharge of an important duty.

Lord Minto was obviously impressed with certain unfortunate tendencies of public life in Canada, especially party patronage and graft. Unfortunately this country has no reason to be proud of its record in this respect. Sir Wilfrid Laurier and the majority of his Ministers were above suspicion; but there were some dark exceptions, and in the rank and file of the party there were sinister figures. During the seven years preceding 1911, we, in opposition, exposed and denounced every case in which we could secure reliable evidence. These exposures had some effect upon the result in 1911.

Apart from this I am convinced that public life in Canada does not especially suffer in comparison with that of Great Britain. And there are some blots upon the political escutcheon of Great Britain herself.

During my absence at Paris in 1919, a resolution was passed in the Canadian Commons for the abolition of titular distinctions, with certain exceptions. If I had been present, I am confident that the motion would not have carried. The result was largely due to press reports of the systematic sale of titles in Great Britain for raising party funds. These reports may have been exaggerated; but, if my information is correct, there was a considerable sub-stratum of truth. Mr Lloyd George has always been defiant as to the source of his party war chest; and, as I understand, he claims he made a fair division between the Conservatives and the Liberals. There has been no investigation; but I understand that the former functions of the Patronage Secretary of the Treasury have been curtailed or perhaps abolished in this respect. It would be interesting to know Minto's reaction to this system of which he must have known.

While I both appreciate and admire your excellent work in *Lord Minto: A Memoir*, I do not altogether share certain conclusions which Lord Minto reached and which you have set forth with approval. An undue importance is sometimes given to superficial impressions. Lord Minto, notwithstanding his fine ability and vigorous grasp of affairs, was not entirely immune to this tendency.

I am not sure that he grasped the essential spirit and general outlook of the Canadian people. In this respect he did not differ from other Governors-General. For example, his successor, Lord Grey was thoroughly convinced that the reciprocity proposals of the Laurier government would receive the warm approval of the Canadian people in 1911. It seems singular that a man of his strong imperial outlook did not appreciate the probable result of those proposals in reducing Canada to commercial and industrial and, possibly, political vassalage to the United States. In this regard Lord Grey was in the company of Mr Asquith and Mr Lloyd George who, supremely confident that Reciprocity would carry, concerned themselves only with the result as affecting party fortunes in the United Kingdom since they believed it would finally defeat Chamberlain's scheme of mutual preferences within the British Empire. Apparently they neither knew nor sought to learn the real basis of protection in Canada which was not only economic but political in the higher sense. Lord Rosebery was of the same ilk, as I recall one of his public utterances.

The professional soldier is not an ideal selection for the office of Governor-General. That Minto had so great a success is a tribute to his ability, tact and sound common sense. Very early I discerned his outstanding qualities which were not fully realized by the Canadian people because of his lack of oratorical gifts. In this respect he made a great advance during his tenure of office; and before he left Canada I regarded him as an effective speaker.

In connection with the Alaskan Boundary arbitration, you might be interested in reading Dafoe's *Clifford Sifton in Relation to His Times*, at pages 211–243. The course and conduct of Theodore Roosevelt in that affair stain his memory; and both Root and Lodge acted no creditable part in accepting appointments to that Commission. It seems apparent that between Great Britain and the United States the result of the arbitration was pre-determined; and Canada was treated as a child who had to be humoured by a pretence while in the background hovered humiliation.

I trust you will accept these observations in the spirit in which they were made. It is my desire to set forth dispassionately conditions and circumstances as I see them.

Sir Frederick Borden's only son, a young man of magnificent physique, was killed in action during the Boer War on July 16, 1900. After Sir Frederick's death, a letter from Mr A.J. Pretorious which came to me was forwarded to Sir Frederick's widow ... It was a great satisfaction to Lady Borden to know that, beneath those distant southern skies, Harold Lothrop Borden's grave will be cared for by one who fought against Britain in 1900, but who fought with her little more than ten years later in the days of her trial. ...

With apologies for what I have inflicted upon you in this too prolix letter, and, with kind regards,

I remain, dear Mr Buchan, Yours faithfully,

NOTE: While Sir Robert did not mention it, it is only fair to the memory of Lord Tweedsmuir to record that he wrote, under date of August 25, 1932, the following letter to Sir Robert in reply to the latter's letter dealing with Tweedsmuir's book *Lord Minto: A Memoir*:

25th August, 1932

Elsfield Manor, Oxford

My dear Sir Robert

My warmest thanks for your letter of July 28th, which I found on my return from an expedition to the Faroe Islands. I feel very much in your debt for so full and wise an exposition of a matter which I fear I handled very perfunctorily in my book on Minto. Since that book was published I have come to the conclusion that I have been unjust and captious in many details, and from what you write it is quite clear that I was unfair to Sir Frederick Borden. My difficulty in writing it was that I was dependant almost entirely upon Minto's own notes and correspondence, and was compelled to see everybody through his eyes and the evidence of no one man can be final. I knew General Hutton slightly, but he was dead before I wrote the book, and I had no knowledge of the Canadian background to correct my view. It was different with the Indian chapters, where I had a good deal of supplementary knowledge.

The book is now out of print, and I do not suppose will ever be reprinted. But if it is I will certainly tone down my narrative in the light of your information.

My kindest regards and warmest thanks.

Yours very sincerely,
(Sgd.) John Buchan

December 2, 1935

THE NEW FEDERAL CABINET – COMPARISON BETWEEN MR KING AND MR BENNETT

Sir,

Several weeks ago Mackenzie King completed the formation of his cabinet; and, on the whole, he has done well, especially in passing over some of the old 'war-horses', and in selecting at least three young and active men for important positions.

Mr C.D. Howe, Minister of Transport, I do not know personally; but he enjoys a fine reputation. On all sides I have heard good reports of his ability, his character and his outlook.

The Hon. Mr Norman Rogers, who like Mr Howe enters the cabinet immediately after his entry into public life, is a young man of high ability and immense industry. Apparently he is rather academic, more theoretical than practical. As Minister of Labour he will be brought into close and sometimes disagreeable touch with the realities of life. It is probable that this experience will modify his outlook and correct academic tendencies.

Hon. Mr James L. Ilsley, who becomes Minister of National Revenue, is from my native County of King's. He is said to be able, industrious and courageous; and it seems probable that a fine career in public life awaits him.

Upon the Hon. Mr Charles A. Dunning, during the past three months, I have repeatedly urged the duty of re-entering public life in case the Liberals should come into power. Two days after the election, he called upon me in Toronto; and once more I urged upon him this duty. At that time, I observed that apart from the tariff, the railways and the unemployed, the government should take into consideration stability, non-interference with legitimate business, sanctity of governmental contracts and prevention of provincial inroads upon the Federal treasury.

On October 18, four days after the election, I addressed to Mackenzie King the appended letter. Shortly afterwards he expressed his acknowledgment in a telephone message; and later I received from him, while he was recuperating at Sea Island Beach in Georgia, a letter in which he explained (what I perfectly understood) the tremendous preoccupations in which he had been involved after forming his administration. After speaking of his desire for an interview with me, he continued as follows:

> No one realizes more than I do how difficult and many-sided are the problems with which our country and the British Commonwealth of Nations are faced. I think I may also say that I appreciate to a greater extent than some others the value of experience in dealing with public questions. It has meant much to me in the past to know that I could feel free to talk without reserve with you on many matters of state. I value that privilege, if I may say so, even more today than at any time in the past.
>
> From my attitude throughout the campaign, I think you will agree that I am at one with you in believing that, at the present time, no considerations could be more important than those mentioned in your letter, namely, stability, non-interference with legitimate business, sanctity of government contracts, and the prevention of provincial inroads upon the Federal treasury. Indeed for some time past, I have increasingly felt that, unless we speedily get back to the bedrock of common sense, and the application to public affairs of a few basic principles, which to our ancestors, were so all important in the affairs of state, there can be no telling how deep may be the abyss towards which the country is heading. Long before the campaign started, I made up my mind that, win or lose, I would not seek to gain office by mischievous appeals, and, above all, by methods which meant waste and extravagance of public funds. That the electorate were not carried away by what was attempted by other parties, in this way, ought to be a source of strength and comfort to public men in our own country, and indeed to all who have to do with government.

It is evident that the Prime Minister does not intend to assume the role of dictator. He has less intellectual brilliancy than Mr Bennett. He lacks Bennett's experience and grasp of business conditions, both in a national and an international aspect. It is questionable whether he is endowed with the like courage and resolution. But, on the other hand, he is more sure-footed than Bennett, a more adroit politician, in some respects, is happier in his relations with press gallery and generally with press representatives, is much less temperamental and impulsive, never loses the good manners and courtesy which, on occasion, deserted Bennett.

Bennett might be described as a man of unbalanced and erratic brilliancy; arbitrary, but lacking decision in important incidents of public affairs; impulsive, vacillating, unable to work with colleagues, capricious. His faults have been those of the qualities with which nature has endowed him. In the use of time, he has been utterly lacking in system and in any sense of proportion. His manner towards his colleagues and towards the press has been, on occasion, abrupt and even insulting. On other occasions, perhaps within a few days, he greets the same persons with utmost graciousness.

But his splendid ability, his keen grasp of general conditions, both national and international, his complete devotion to public duty and to the welfare of our country, the admirable resourcefulness and fine courage with which he has faced the overwhelming difficulties of the past five years, entitle him to the respect, admiration and gratitude of all right-thinking Canadians.

Bennett will continue to lead the Liberal-Conservative party in the House of Commons. Before making such announcement, he should have called together his parliamentary following and placed his resignation in their hands. His continuance involves a serious danger, as it cannot be confidently predicted whether he will continue until the next general election or for what period. His highly impulsive temperament might occasion his sudden retirement at a most inopportune moment, leaving his party in perilous condition. On the other hand, his splendid courage and self-sacrifice were evinced in his resolution to continue as leader in the face of desperate ill-health rather than to permit the succession to pass to Stevens ...

I remain, Yours, etc.,

October 18, 1935

To the Right Honourable W.L. Mackenzie King, PC, CMG, &c,
Laurier House Ottawa

My dear Mr King,

While the result of the recent election was profoundly disappointing to many Conservatives, the more thoughtful will realize that a return to the two-party system is most fortunate and that an adequate working-majority for the successful party is equally fortunate.

Doubtless you were disappointed in 1930; but as it transpired your defeat at that time was a blessing in disguise.

We are not yet out of the woods and you are confronted with a situation the difficulties and even the perils of which are by no means realized by the majority of our people.

Apart from questions relating to the tariff, to the railways and to the unemployed, it seems to me that the main considerations to be kept in mind are stability, non-interference with legitimate business, sanctity of governmental contracts and prevention of provincial inroads upon the Federal treasury.

In troublous times the people sometimes place in power men whose desire to retain power far exceeds their sense of responsibility. In saying this I speak without distinction of party. A provincial premier, under the urge of demand for wasteful or extravagant expenditure which involves borrowing, realizes that the federal government cannot permit any province to default. In my opinion, this aspect discloses a very grave danger to the financial structure of Canada.

I should like to have the opportunity of calling upon you at some convenient time and of mentioning one or two other matters to which I have not alluded. But I realize the insistent demands upon your time and energy and I shall not be surprised if you find yourself unable to give me an appointment.

Meantime, with warm congratulations and best wishes, I remain,

Yours faithfully,

Early in 1960 I sent a copy of the foregoing Limbo letter to Mr Howe. In acknowledging its receipt he wrote in part as follows:

> 'Sir Robert and I became very good friends, and I always looked forward to a talk with him, whether at lunch, dinner, or when we met casually. He had mastered the art of divorcing himself completely from political controversy, and his advice was sought by members of the Government, as well as by members of his own party. I will always remember him with affection.' ED.

January 22, 1936

ON THE DEATH OF KING GEORGE V

Sir,

Less than a week ago, press despatches indicated that King George's condition was becoming serious. He died shortly before midnight, Monday, January 20.

Never, within my recollection, has there been so universal an expression of sorrow. Not only throughout the Empire but in all the nations and among all the peoples of the world the tidings of his passing have been received with profound emotion. Especially is this true of the United States where the President and his Cabinet, the House of Representatives and other official bodies have cancelled their functions and activities in honouring the memory of our King; and generally the people of United States have testified to their respect for him and to their sorrow for his passing.

> On Monday evening I gave to the press the following tribute: Friend of peace and exemplar of goodwill to all mankind, our King has passed; and upon the Empire rests the shadow of profound sorrow which will extend far beyond its borders.
>
> Nurtured in the ideal and tradition of duty, the King deemed himself from the first the servant of his people. To this true conception of service he was faithful throughout his reign. The people of the Empire, diverse as they are in race, creed, faith and outlook, he regarded as one united and inspiring brotherhood. At each Christmastide he made to them moving appeal in the simple faith whereon rests his true greatness. His devoted love which never failed for all who owed him allegiance has raised for him an imperishable memorial in all our hearts.

In 1901, upon the death of Queen Victoria, and in 1910, upon the death of King Edward, I gave messages to the Press. [The 1910 message is appended.]

King George was not a man of unusual ability; but throughout his life he was inspired by the keenest sense of duty and he was guided by strong common sense which enabled him to pass safely through more than one critical period.

During the War, I was brought into very close touch with him. On many occasions I was received in audience. In April, 1917, I spent a week-end at Windsor Castle during which, after consultation with Colonel Clive (now Lord) Wigram, I expressed to the King my conviction that if the Prince of Wales should marry, he should marry within the Empire. This feeling was strong and practically unanimous in Canada. My diary for April 16, 1917, notes:

> H.M. became quite interested and a little excited. He said he and the Queen had considered that question more than once, that it was their strong opinion that the Prince should marry

> within the Empire. He further said that while he wished me to make no public statement on the subject, I could privately inform any of my friends of his opinion on the question.

When I told Lloyd George that I had spoken to the King respecting the marriage of the Prince of Wales, he seemed very much surprised and remarked that it was a plucky thing to do.

In 1920, after I had broken down in health and had crossed the ocean in the battle-cruiser *New Zealand* with Admiral Lord Jellicoe, the King, knowing of my condition, invited me to a quiet luncheon at which I met only the King, the Queen and Princess Mary. Again in 1927, while I was in residence at Oxford for the first series of the Rhodes Memorial lectures, I had the honour of lunching with the King and Queen alone. On this occasion I found His Majesty in a rather excitable and nervous condition. He talked incessantly and rather discursively; and it was apparent that his nervous system had been impaired.

In sheer intellectual force he was by no means the equal of the Queen; and this he probably realized. There was a rumour that the Prince of Wales once alluded to his parents as, 'George the Fifth; Mary the Four-Fifths.'

I remain, Sir, Yours faithfully,

PS Also annexed is a copy of my radio address delivered on January 29, in a nation-wide memorial service.

SIR ROBERT BORDEN'S MESSAGE TO THE PRESS ON THE DEATH OF KING EDWARD VII, MAY 6, 1910

The tidings of sorrow which have just been flashed across the ocean come to the people of Canada with startling suddenness. Words of foreboding had hardly reached us before the last message came. 'God's finger touched him and he slept.' To the people of the Overseas Dominions the Crown personifies the dignity and majesty of the whole Empire. But today's untimely tidings bring to the people of Canada the sense of a still deeper and more personal bereavement. They gloried in their King's title of Peacemaker, and they believed him to be the greatest living force for the right within the Empire. In him died the greatest statesman and diplomat of Europe.

SIR ROBERT'S RADIO ADDRESS OF JANUARY 29, 1936

Yesterday the peoples of the Empire in solemn mourning honoured the memory of a great King who had passed into the Eternal Peace. To their sorrow was joined that of all the nations for one in whose thought and life goodwill to all mankind had true expression.

More than any preceding Sovereign, King George was of the people. At the Jubilee, splendid pageants expressed the Empire's majestic tribute to him and to the Queen. Not the least memorable event of that wonderful celebration was their visit, at its close, to the working people of East London among whom they drove, unescorted and unattended, in token of intimate friendship and warm affection. The moving response of these people, not rich in this world's goods, but of sturdy and independent outlook, transcended in significance the ceremonial of the Jubilee.

At the very beginning, the late King was confronted with extremely critical conditions in the urge for constitutional change. Then came the supreme catastrophe of world-war; later the challenge of more far-reaching constitutional changes. Through these ordeals the King's balanced judgment and wise foresight guided him and influenced his ministers along the path of tolerance and unity.

Out of the paramount authority and power of feudal Sovereigns was evolved the moral authority and influence of later years. In the late King, this evolution had its perfect fulfilment. This man was King in the noblest sense. From the first he owned fealty to his people and held himself consecrated to their service. This conception determined his course throughout his reign, until at midnight in the quiet of that Norfolk village, 'God's finger touched him and he slept.'

I was received in audience by the King on many occasions when matters of intimate and grave concern were under consideration. Throughout the long-drawn agony of the War his courage never failed, and he never doubted the outcome. But I know how deeply he sorrowed for the hardships, the sufferings, the sacrifices of his people. A spiritual outlook, afterwards voiced in his messages at Christmastide, dominated his thought and its expression. He often spoke of 'our brotherhood.'

Of the King's tender solicitude and most considerate kindness, I have vivid memories, one of which I may recall. After my collapse in health in the autumn of 1919, I crossed the Atlantic with Admiral Lord Jellicoe. Weary in mind and body to the point of utter exhaustion, I remained in complete seclusion. A most sympathetic message from the Palace bade me to a family luncheon at which I met only the King, the Queen and the Princess Mary as she then was.

Seven years later I had the honour of lunching with the King and Queen alone. Although his fortitude was unshaken, I felt that his strength was greatly impaired. But his interest in all that concerned the Empire's welfare was never keener.

Lonely in spirit, but firm of heart, the Queen Mother remains to carry on her duty, as in the past, in loving memory of him who has gone before.

King George sleeps with his fathers; the Crown continues, symbol of the unity, power and majesty of the Empire. Its ancient prerogatives have become the nations' liberties, since their exercise is determined by the advisers upon whom, from time to time, the people bestow their mandate. Upon this convention rests the political union between Crown and people; but there are spiritual ties of far deeper import.

Apart from these, the formal compact between Crown and subject is expressed in the Sovereign's oath of fidelity and the subject's oath of allegiance. Edward, Prince of Wales, had won the hearts of his people long before he took the Sovereign's oath as King Edward VIII. Having taken it, he gave to the Commons of Britain and to the entire Empire the memorable pledge that, throughout his reign he will follow in his father's footsteps. There could be no finer purpose, no nobler pledge. And it will be honoured. So, may God save and guide our King.

February 17, 1936

LETTER TO KING EDWARD VIII

Sir,

For your information I enclose copy of a letter which I addressed to King Edward VIII on February 6. A full description of the incidents of his visit to Canada in 1919, to which this letter alludes, will be found in my *Memoirs*.[34] Today, in reply to my letter, I received the following telegram from the King:

MY SINCERE THANKS FOR YOUR KIND LETTER. EDWARD R.I.

I remain, Sir, Yours faithfully,

34 Vol. 2, pp. 985–991.

February 6, 1936

His Majesty
The King Emperor

Sir,

With our humble duty, my wife and I have the honour to convey to Your Majesty upon your accession our heartfelt wishes and our firm confidence that under Your wise guidance the unity of the Empire's nations and dependencies may be maintained and strengthened.

Many years have elapsed and great events have occurred since in 1919, I had the honour and the privilege as Prime Minister of welcoming You upon Your first visit to Canada. Of Your considerate kindness at that time and on many subsequent occasions, I have a most grateful memory.

During that visit there were many happy incidents and some which, I imagine, you may recall with amusement. Perhaps you may remember an eccentric Mayor who was a guest at the luncheon which You gave at Halifax on the eve of Your departure. Arriving very late and in full evening dress, he proceeded to chat affably with You and with the Duke of Devonshire until gently persuaded to take his seat. Opinion was divided as to whether he had been out all night, or whether he regarded that attire as appropriate for the occasion; but there was general agreement that he had visited *les vignes du Seigneur.*

There were other happy and occasionally amusing incidents of that visit. But its outstanding and controlling feature was the warmth, sincerity and spontaneity of Your welcome throughout the length and breadth of our country.

Yesterday, at a luncheon given by the Engineering Institute, I sat beside Lord Tweedsmuir, who was the guest of honour. He is most earnest in his desire to gain a thorough insight into the conditions prevailing in his new environment, and to comprehend the difficulties and perplexities of those responsible for the governance of Canada's vast territories and scattered communities. During his visits to Montreal and Toronto, as well as in Ottawa, he has been most happy in his public addresses.

It is nearly sixteen years since I laid down my duties as Prime Minister. Although I eventually recovered from the collapse which compelled my retirement, I have had no desire to re-enter public life. However, I still take a keen interest in all that concerns the welfare of our country and of the Empire; and above all I am profoundly thankful that in the vicissitudes, trials and suffering of the past five years, the spirit of our people has never faltered. I know that it will remain firm to the end.

I have the honour to be, Sir,
Your most obedient, humble servant

February 18, 1936

OPENING OF PARLIAMENT, 1936

Sir,

Parliament opened on February 6th. Mr Bennett took a courageous stand in opposing the election of Mr Pierre Casgrain, although he did not press for a division. It is apparent that Casgrain proposed to make practically a clean sweep of all the employees of the House and to appoint in their stead officers selected from a horde of hungry Liberal applicants. The announcement of impending dismissals was sent out by Casgrain after he had been named but before he was elected Speaker. It seems clear that this unworthy programme was eliminated by the Prime Minister, or by the government, as the dismissals have been reduced to about a half a dozen.

Mr Bennett spoke for about four hours in the debate on the address. His wide range of knowledge and his facility in speaking sometimes prove a handicap. And so it transpired on this occasion. Further, he did not maturely consider some aspects of his attack. His reference to the large number of Liberals elected by the minority vote, was turned upon him with deadly effect by Mackenzie King who showed that if members elected by minority vote should not be considered, the Conservative members would be reduced to four.

The Prime Minister did not quite equal Mr Bennett in the length of his address; he occupied barely three hours which for Mr King is very moderate. But it is probable that very few will ever read either speech.

... It is apparent that our country is approaching a grave emergency. In view of this, it seems astonishing that the leaders of two great political parties should spend their energy and the time of the House in trifling discussion of unworthy personalities. Canada is not concerned about Mr Bennett's opinion of Mr King or Mr King's opinion of Mr Bennett. She is gravely concerned about the existing emergency and her future destiny.

I remain, Sir, Yours, etc.,

April 4, 1936

HOLIDAY IN THE SOUTH

Sir,

Today I returned from a six weeks' holiday of which all, except one week, was spent at The Cloister Hotel, Sea Island, Georgia, a most delightful resort. The lawns, herbaceous borders, flowers, birds and the sunshine made our visit most enjoyable.

On my way south, I was entertained by Hugh Bullock in New York at a luncheon. Besides myself, the guests numbered fifteen of whom all were prominent, either in business, finance or economics ... Hugh Bullock took a straw vote as to who would be the next President. Sixteen ballots were handed in with the following result:

Dickinson	1
Hoover	2
Landon	3
Roosevelt	10

This was significant, as probably there was no supporter of Roosevelt at the table.

Hugh also took a vote on the quotation price of US Steel common at the end of twelve months. The quotations ranged from 63 to 159, the average being about 95. This seems to disclose a remarkable feeling of uncertainty as to the future.

Leaving Sea Island on March 29, we reached the Biltmore on the following day (Monday), and during our stay in New York we saw several excellent plays, including, *The First Lady*, with Jane Cowl; *Saint Joan* (Katharine Cornell and Brian Aherne); *Call It A Day* (Gladys Cooper and Philip Merivale and Jeanne Dante); *Victoria Regina* (Helen Hayes); and *Libel*, a play by Edward Wooll.

A notable incident, just before my return, was the government's refusal to provide for the service of Alberta's bonds, except upon conditions that, with respect to further borrowings, the province would submit to the rulings of the Federal Loan Commission. Premier Aberhart refused to accept the jurisdiction of the commission because, as he averred, it would prejudicially affect the fiscal autonomy of Alberta. Throughout the Dominion there is strong commendation of Mr Dunning's stand which will tend to strengthen confidence (somewhat severely shaken) in the fiscal policy of Canada.

I remain, Sir, Yours, etc.,

May 5, 1936

LEAGUE OF NATIONS

Sir,

Apparently the Italians have overrun Ethiopia. Emperor Haile Selassie has arrived at Djibouti and is said to be embarking on a British warship. All Italy is rapturously acclaiming victory; the Germans are delighted; the British government is disconcerted; and the British people are exasperated.

As first Japan, then Germany and now Italy have flouted and defied the League of Nations; it is apparent that its usefulness has reached the vanishing point.

In Great Britain there is a proposal that the League shall continue but under a Covenant that does not include punitive measures for disregard of its obligations.

Lewd fellows of the baser sort who have delighted to deride the League will now rejoice in its failure and will sharpen their dull wits for still more derisive contempt.

The ideal and the endeavour that established the League set forth what is noblest and best in human effort to repress and if possible to end the awful violence and destruction of war, to assure peaceful determination of international disputes and to maintain public right throughout the world. Perhaps there may have been too far-reaching an attempt to establish a perfect structure; but the ideal and the purpose were ennobling. And the failure is not of the League alone. In the tragic failure of humanity itself lies deadly peril, fraught with untold and unimaginable disaster.

And the League need not have failed. Assuredly it would not have failed if the rulers of United States had possessed wisdom at all comparable to that country's influence and power. It has been well said that in 1919, United States abdicated the moral leadership of the world. Endowed with a heritage of opportunity never before vouchsafed to any nation, it abandoned its birthright for a mess of pottage, for relatively insignificant party feuds, for the party lust of power. This is an eternal disgrace, not so much to the people of United States as to their leaders at that juncture.

The avoidance of European entanglements is unceasingly heralded in that country and apparently is hailed by its people as the highest expression of political wisdom. In the life of a nation half a century or even a century is but as a moment. It will be strange if within that period United States is not involved in entanglements that it never would have encountered had it upheld and joined the Covenant.

With United States leading and dominating the League, neither Japan, nor Germany, nor Italy would have dared pursue the course they have taken. In the absence of that leadership, these three nations have been enabled to uphold force as the vital consideration, its dominance as the highest political wisdom, its use as the ultimate resort. Thus they have led the world along the path of destruction. Again the devils enter into the swine so that they run violently down steep places into the sea and perish.

If President Wilson, in addition to his high ideals and splendid qualities, had possessed the saving grace of common sense and the spirit of compromise, sometimes essential for attaining a great purpose; if his opponents had not been inspired by so deadly a hatred and determination to secure his defeat; if the people of United States had realized that no nation can live to itself alone, the history of the world during the past fifteen years, and perhaps for all time to come, would have been vastly different and humanity could have cherished higher hope for the future.

In this turmoil of fear and hatred, of distrust, envy, jealousy and suspicion, of antagonistic nationalism, of supreme reliance on sheer force and violence, one may wonder whether what we call our civilization is destined or indeed has the right to survive.

This letter is written in great sadness; it expresses the feeling of pessimism which now possesses me, but which I hope may yet pass. So, my last word is *Sursum corda.*

I remain, Sir, Yours faithfully,

June 27, 1936

INVITATION TO UNVEILING OF VIMY MEMORIAL – 82nd BIRTHDAY AND OTHER MATTERS

Sir,

The accompanying letter from the Prime Minister and copies of my replies explain themselves. I had not the faintest idea of undertaking so great a journey and asked Dr Laidlaw to estimate my condition and to advise whether it would be prudent to accept. Subsequently,

Dr Laidlaw advised that I might safely undertake the journey upon condition that immediately after the Vimy Ceremonial I should spend three weeks at a spa in order to correct a condition or tendency which he described.

On June 6, I attended at the Experimental Farm the opening of the new Saunders' Administration Building. The speeches were altogether too long and the ceremony became rather tiresome. In the course of his address the Prime Minister ventured to quote *Si monumentum requiris, circumspice*. He forgot the third word of the quotation, and, much to the amusement of the audience, I prompted him with the necessary *requiris*, for which he thanked me. [See attached press reference to this incident]

In English public life a most unhappy event has transpired. Rt. Hon. J.H. Thomas [Chancellor of the Exchequer] has been found guilty of disclosing advance information concerning the budget. No one believes that he did this with intention or for his personal advantage; but, in this case, and in other similar instances, public opinion in Great Britain is on a much higher plane than in Canada or in the United States. Thomas has retired from office and from parliament. In our country it is generally believed that hints as to impending changes in the tariff have been given and that they could have come from no source except from some member of the cabinet. No action has ever been taken.

During this month, Sir John Caulcutt, Deputy-Chairman of Barclays Bank (Dominion, Colonial and Overseas) visited Canada. He arrived in Ottawa on the fourteenth; and for two hours after luncheon on that day we had an interesting and useful discussion respecting world and Empire conditions, and afterwards respecting the affairs of Barclays Bank (Canada). ...

My eighty-second birthday occurred on June 26; and a flood of cables, telegrams, letters and calls greeted me throughout the day. ...

Today, with Mr Justice Crockett, I listened to President Roosevelt's speech of acceptance which we considered not quite worthy of the occasion, as it seemed to embody an appeal to the mob and lacked any high quality of statesmanship.

During this month I have been much distressed by the unfortunate illness of my friend, Edgar Rhodes,[35] who suffered a stroke while engaged in salmon fishing at Cascapedia. Fortunately, his daughter, Sybil and her husband were with him at the time. After consultation with Dr Hugh Laidlaw, I arranged with the Prime

35 Hon. Edgar N. Rhodes, formerly Speaker of the House of Commons; Premier of Nova Scotia and later Minister of Finance in Mr Bennett's administration.

Minister that a private car would be sent to Matapedia as soon as the physicians considered that Rhodes could safely be moved to Ottawa.

World conditions, especially in Europe, are becoming more involved and threatening. No human intelligence is capable of forecasting the issue.

I remain, Sir, Yours etc,

June 5, 1936

To the Right Honourable
Sir Robert L. Borden, GCMG, KC, DCL, LL D,
201 Wurtemburg Street
Ottawa

My dear Sir Robert:

My colleagues and I desire to join in extending to you an invitation to attend, as a guest of the Government of Canada, the unveiling of the Vimy War Memorial in France on Sunday, July the 26th.

We feel that, as Prime Minister of Canada during the period of the war, you will welcome the opportunity, if at all possible, of being present at the dedication of the Vimy Memorial. We feel, equally, that the honour of your presence at the ceremony would be deeply appreciated by the members of the Canadian Legion of the British Empire Service League, under whose auspices the ceremony is being held, and would be welcomed by all the citizens of Canada.

Yours very sincerely,
(Sgd) W.L. Mackenzie King

PS It is expected, of course, that should you be able to accept this invitation, you would wish to be accompanied by Lady Borden, whom we desire to include in this invitation. W.L.M.K.

June 5, 1936

To the Right Honourable W.L. Mackenzie King, CMG, PC, MP, &c
Prime Minister of Canada
Ottawa

Private

My dear Prime Minister,

Before giving a formal answer to your most kind note of today, I hasten to express our grateful appreciation and our thanks.

As you know, it is necessary at my age to husband most carefully one's strength; and before definite decision as to whether I could undertake the journey, I must consult my physician who, at the moment, is absent from the city but with whom I hope to get into touch early next week.

But in any case, I shall always hold in happy memory your most courteous and thoughtful invitation and especially the very kind and generous terms in which it is couched.

With kind regards, I remain, my dear Prime Minister,

Yours faithfully,

June 11, 1936

My dear Prime Minister,

I have already expressed to you our appreciation and our thanks for your most kind invitation to attend as guests of the government of Canada the unveiling of the Vimy War Memorial in France on Sunday, July twenty-sixth.

My reply has been delayed until I could consult my physician who now has assured me that I may safely undertake the journey. I therefore accept with very great pleasure your most courteous and thoughtful invitation; and I very deeply appreciate the most kind and generous terms in which it is expressed. It will indeed be a privilege and an honour to be present at this solemn and impressive ceremonial.

I deeply regret, however, that my wife's engagements in Ottawa will prevent her from accompanying me.

With renewed thanks and very kind regards, I remain, my dear Prime Minister,

Yours faithfully,

June 8, 1936

Ottawa Journal

BORDEN PROMPTS PRIME MINISTER

Supplies Latin Phrase During Speech at Experimental Farm

When a word of a Latin phrase eluded him at the dedication of the William Saunders Building on the Experimental Farm grounds on

Saturday afternoon, Prime Minister King was prompted in the quotation by Sir Robert Borden, Canada's war-time Prime Minister.

Speaking of the great contribution made by the late Dr Saunders to the national welfare of Canada and the Experimental Farm system in particular, Mr King said: 'The lines carved on the tomb of Sir Christopher Wren may most appropriately be applied to Dr Saunders, namely *Si monumentum* ...'

'*Si monumentum* ...,' he repeated as the following word of the epitaph escaped him momentarily.

Sitting directly below the platform, Sir Robert Borden suggested, '*Si monumentum requiris, circumspice.*'

'Thank you, Sir Robert,' acknowledged the Prime Minister. 'Really, Mr. Chairman, I shouldn't have started on Latin without having the exact wording in mind.'

The following three Limbo letters deal with Sir Robert's journey to the unveiling of the Canadian War Memorial at Vimy Ridge, his visit to the Canadian war graves and his sojourn of three weeks in England before returning to Canada in the *Empress of Britain.*

The original of each of these letters records social events in England and in France with a certain amount of detail as to the host or hostess and fellow guests. Most of this has been eliminated by me – suffice it to say that Sir Robert was lavishly entertained, met many old friends and obviously had a most enjoyable trip.

I have endeavoured to identify for the reader certain of those individuals to whom Sir Robert refers in these letters by a footnote following each letter.

France
July 29, 1936

JOURNEY TO VIMY MEMORIAL

Sir,

On July 9, I learned from Ned Rhodes that his father (my old friend and former colleague, Hon. E.N. Rhodes) desired to see me before I left for England. So, on that day, I called upon him and of course found him greatly changed. His speech was in part unintelligible, although I understood a good deal of what he attempted to say. At times when he was at a loss for a word or could not utter it, a shrug of impatience and a quizzical smile were in evidence. However, I left him in strong hope that he would yet recover. [Mr Rhodes died in March 1942.]

On July 10, I had several business meetings in Montreal. Accompanied by General Mewburn, Col H.C. Osborne and Dr Ross Millar, I left that evening on the S.S. *Quebec* for Quebec where we arrived early next morning. Commodious suites were furnished to us by the courtesy of the company. Colonel Osborne was appointed general manager of the party, a position which he cheerfully accepted. We arrived at the *Empress of Britain* shortly before noon; and I was requested to broadcast a few words in company with Hon. Ian Mackenzie, and Hon. C.G. Power. On board the boat, John and Alistair Buchan, Mr Redfern and Captain Adeane gave us greetings on behalf of the Governor-General. ...

During the voyage ... I had an interesting conversation with Sir Percival Phillips, who was war correspondent in Ethiopia and who had just returned from attending the presidential conventions in United States. In his opinion, Mussolini is a greater peril than Hitler, but not greater than the men behind Hitler. He considers the English people undisciplined compared with those of the continent. ...

Just outside the Strait of Belle Isle, enveloped in fog and surrounded by icebergs and other steamers, our ship remained motionless for nearly six hours.

At Cherbourg, Mr Roy, with the Préfet of Cherbourg came aboard. As we were approaching Southampton (just twenty-four hours late) I was surprised at dinner by Mr W.M. Goodenough who had come out on the tender and who, with Captain Forster of the Canadian Pacific, did everything for me. We arrived at London at 11 pm.

Numerous telegrams and letters awaited me in my room at the Ritz. On the following day, I called at Buckingham Palace and wrote in the King's and in Queen Mary's book; called on the Duke of Connaught at Clarence House and had a long talk with Bessborough who is gravely concerned about the European situation. ...

On the twenty-third I attended the luncheon of the Canadian Women's Club, presided over by Lady Bessborough. The principal speaker was Mrs Baldwin, who spoke acceptably, and then I was called upon. I met scores of friends and acquaintances. That day we left for Paris. The sea was very rough and I had a most uncomfortable crossing. Hon. Philippe and Madame Roy and Jean Désy met us at Paris and drove us to the Ritz where I had a delightful apartment. ...

At 10.30 am on July 26, we left for Vimy in a crowded but well-arranged train. A long line of buses awaited us and conveyed the crowd from Vimy to the Ridge. The site of the memorial is most impressive and the Memorial itself dominates the landscape. The King arrived at 2.15 and the President of France at 2.50. We were presented to both. The chaplains were inaudible; but Mr Power read the Prime Minister's message very distinctly. Lapointe and Mackenzie spoke; and the latter called upon the King to unveil the memorial. The King spoke first in French (it was said that his accent was not of the best). His speech in English was appropriate; at times eloquent. Following the King, the President of the Republic, an accomplished and eloquent speaker, delivered an excellent address. It was a most solemn and impressive scene. ...

Estimates of the immense throng varied from seventy-five to one hundred and eighty thousand; probably even the first estimate is somewhat exaggerated.

There was a certain irony in the situation, as Mr Lapointe, who spoke for Canada, had fought desperately to prevent the passage of the Military Service Bill which alone could have provided reinforcements for the Canadian Army Corps. Without those reinforcements, the morale of the Corps would have suffered terribly; and its splendid record throughout the weary months of 1918 would have been impossible. In 1919, a Canadian officer said to me, 'We had gone forth on the pledge of Canada's honour that we would be supported to the end. If reinforcements had failed, we might have failed. After the election of 1917, everyone of us felt that he could lick a ton of Germans.'

Mr Ian Mackenzie's speech had evidently been committed to memory. It was full of eloquent periods, theatrical rather than moving.

When I left Canada I was under the impression that I would be privileged to speak at the unveiling; and since my return I have been told, many times, of the intense disappointment that my voice was not heard. Having been invited to attend, and being the only Prime Minister who had served as such throughout the war, it might have seemed appropriate that I should be asked to speak. But the volume of eloquence seeking outlet from the lips of ministers was altogether too great to permit the five minutes originally allotted to me, as I understand.

Before leaving Canada, I had prepared a short message which would not have occupied more than three minutes. En route I learned definitely that at the ceremony of unveiling my lips were to be silent. It seemed that, under the circumstances, the people whom I had served during the War with my very heart's blood, might expect some words from me. So on July 23, I gave them my message (copy appended).

On July 27, Colonel Osborne and I dined with the Granville-Barkers. On the following day Jean Désy told us of the very warm welcome and of the wonderful hospitality offered, not only by the government but by the cities and municipalities of France, to the Canadian pilgrims whose visit seems to have stirred very deep emotion in the French nation. The city of Blois sent its mayor to Paris to arrange for a luncheon to five thousand Canadians in that city. Paris abounded in hospitality, providing lodging for many thousand Canadians and tendering them an official luncheon.

On July 29, I began my visits to the war cemeteries. Colonel Osborne and I left for Arras where we were met by Colonel Frank Higginson with whom we lunched. After inspecting his office, we visited the Faubourg-d'Amiens Cemetery. ...

A fuller description of my visit to the cemeteries will be given in a further letter to your journal.

Faithfully yours,

MESSAGE TO THE CANADIAN PEOPLE

London: July 25

Before leaving for the Vimy celebrations in France on Sunday, Sir Robert Borden, war-time premier of Canada, gave the Canadian Press the following message:

> Around the stately memorial at Vimy we shall be gathered in solemn but proud tribute to the sacrifice and achievement it commemorates. It will long endure, but not longer we trust than the memory enshrined in our hearts. We the living shall not stand there alone but in the midst of a vast concourse, a mighty congregation of the dead who will be with us and of us and those voices inaudible to the dull sense of flesh, speak ceaselessly to those whose spirit is attuned to these memories.
>
> But in vain are those voices and fruitless sacrifice unless we,

the living, consecrate ourselves anew to the purpose and endeavor that liberty shall prevail, that peace and good-will among men and between nations shall be abiding upon earth.

So may God direct us.

NOTE

Major-General the Hon. S.C. Mewburn was a prominent lawyer and businessman in Hamilton, Ontario, and was Minister of Militia and Defence in Sir Robert's Union government from 1917–1920.

Colonel H.C. Osborne was Secretary-General, Canadian Agency, Imperial War Graves Commission.

Hon. Ian A. Mackenzie was then Minister of National Defence in Mr Mackenzie King's government and Hon. C.G. Power was then Minister of Pensions and National Health in the same government.

John and Alistair Buchan are sons of the then Governor-General, Lord Tweedsmuir and Mr A.S. Redfern was at that time Secretary to the Governor-General.

Hon. Philippe Roy was at that time Envoy Extraordinary and Minister Plenipotentiary of Canada to France.

Mr W.M. Goodenough was then Chairman of Barclays Bank.

Jean Désy was then Counsellor to the Canadian Legation in Paris.

Lapointe – the Hon. Ernest – was then Minister of Justice in Mr Mackenzie King's government.

London, England
August 3, 1936

VISIT TO WAR GRAVES

Sir,

To me, the visit to the war graves was much more solemn and impressive and moved me more deeply than the unveiling ceremony at Vimy.

The Faubourg-d'Amiens cemetery at Arras brought back to me very vividly all the long-drawn agony of the war years. During 1915, in fifty-three hospitals throughout England and France I had visited wounded Canadians. One's spirit was thrilled by their cheerfulness and heroism, but bruised by the realization of their suffering. As I passed through the long lines of hospital beds, every Canadian would raise himself as he saw me approaching and on his lips would be a smile, even if he were enduring intense pain. In this cemetery, a flood of these recollections overcame me and for a time I could not speak.

Later, I was soothed by the brooding peace that seems to hover over each cemetery. One could feel that peace, although one knew that every armament and munition factory in Europe was working at high pressure to provide means for the self-destruction of civilization.

No words can adequately describe the wonderful simplicity and beauty of these homes of the dead. Nowhere did I see the words 'Unknown Soldier'; where identification had failed, the inscription read: 'A soldier of the Great War,' and then, at the bottom of the stone were the words, 'Known to God.'

I have vivid recollections of the Neuve Chapelle Indian Memorial, the Ploegsteert Memorial, the Canadian Memorial at St Julien, Tyne Cot Cemetery at Passchendaele and the Canadian Memorial, Hill 62, Mount Sorrel.

We [Sir Robert was accompanied by Col Henry Osborne] visited Skindles Hotel, Poperinghe; then proceeded to Ypres where we dined and spent the night at a hotel of the same name. The name 'Skindles' was bestowed by a British officer during the War who knew of an inn bearing that name in England. It was adopted by the Belgian proprietors who are doing a thriving business and who received us most cordially.

Perhaps the most vivid of all my memories of this tour is that of the last post, sounded at the Menin Gate on the evening of July 29. The gate is a most impressive structure upon which are recorded the names of fifty-six thousand officers and men whose graves have not been identified. The memorial consists of a 'Hall of Memory', one hundred and twenty feet long and sixty-feet wide, covered in by a coffered half-elliptical arch in a single span. At each end is an archway thirty feet wide and forty-eight feet high. The names are incised in Portland stone panels fixed to the inner walls of the hall, up the sides of the staircases and inside the loggias. Among them is the name of my kinsman, Robert Clarence Borden, who, with his brother, Douglas Borden [both from Wolfville, Nova Scotia] enlisted as a private in the 85th Nova Scotia Regiment. Robert Clarence was corporal of his platoon during the Canadian attack on Passchendaele; his sergeant was killed; and Robert, taking command of the platoon, who reached their objective, was killed. (October 30, 1917.)

On the morning of July 30, we were received by the Burgomaster of Ypres, Monsieur Van der Ghote, and signed the golden book of distinguished visitors.

After visiting several cemeteries during the forenoon, we arrived at Cassel in time for lunch and then proceeded to Calais where we boarded S.S. *Canterbury* for Folkestone and London where we arrived at seven o'clock that evening.

The ceremonial at Vimy, and especially the visit to the war graves, are indelibly impressed upon my memory and will remain with me as long as life lasts. ...

I remain, Sir, Yours, etc.,

August 28, 1936

SOJOURN IN ENGLAND

Sir,

Upon my return to London, I attended a number of theatrical performances, many of which were excellent. I recall especially, *Pride and Prejudice,* at St James's Theatre, *Anthony and Anna,* at the Whitehall, *Whiteoaks* at the Playhouse, *Lilac Time,* at the Coliseum, *Spring Tide* at the Duchess, The Russian Ballet at Covent Garden, *Miss Smith* at the Duke of York's Theatre, *As You Like It,* at the Open Air Theatre, Regent's Park, *The Two Bouquets,* at the Ambassador's and *Heroes Don't Care,* at St Martin's.

Returning to my rooms at the Ritz, I was informed that the management had received instructions that I was to be the guest of the Bank [Barclays] during the remainder of my sojourn in England and 'every comfort, consideration and attention' was to be accorded to me.

Several times I had the privilege of attending luncheon at the bank and of meeting many of the directors. The chief butler, Day, informed Miss Cummins that he had waited on me in Canada thirty-two years ago when he was in the employ of the Earl of Dundonald; so I sent for him and congratulated him.

On Sunday, August 2, the Perleys and I drove to Cliveden where we were warmly welcomed by Bill Astor and later by Waldorf and Nancy [Lady Astor]. At luncheon ... Nancy put me on her right; and we had a most interesting conversation. An amusing incident occurred when I thought I had lost my hat and went about making a 'devil' of a fuss. I was looking for a brown hat which I had been wearing every day during the previous week and had completely forgotten that on this occasion I had worn a gray hat which was before my eyes at the time. Later, we visited the beautiful cemetery at Cliveden[36] which bears the inscription:

> They are at peace. God proved
> them and found them worthy for Himself.

In the afternoon we called upon Sir John Hanbury-Williams,[37] to whom has been allotted for his lifetime residence in the Henry III Tower [at Windsor Castle] which dates from 1210. He told us that records of its construction are available and that the price for a load of stone, brought from Oxford, was (if I remember correctly) one shilling, which, of course, might mean ten or fifteen dollars in our money.

On August 4 we left for Chatsworth to spend the week-end with the Devonshires. The Duchess was gracious and charming as ever; the Duke, who suffered a stroke some years ago, seemed intellectually bright but can walk only very slowly.

During my visit, I read Violet Markham's life of her grandfather, Sir Joseph Paxton who had laid out the grounds at Chatsworth. We heard many tales of Bess of Hardwicke who had four husbands, inheriting fortunes from each. Her second husband was Sir William Cavendish; and she endowed the Cavendish family with her great wealth. Hardwicke Castle contains a wealth of portraits. It is an enormous structure and in the days of Bess it outshone any residence in the neighborhood. The Duke who accompanied us on our visit to Hardwicke Castle did not attempt to ascend any of the stairways. In returning from the castle, he pointed out to me a hill where he and the late King had been shooting grouse in December, 1913. At the end of the day, the Duke said to the King: 'I hope, Sir, that you will be with us at Bolton Abbey next August 12.' 'Victor,' said the King, 'before the next twelfth, we will be thinking of things much more serious than grouse-shooting.' When the Duke inquired the meaning of the King's statement he was told that conditions in Europe were so confused and threatening that war was practically inevitable.

36 Cliveden was the estate of Lord and Lady (Nancy) Astor on which a hospital was maintained by the Astors for Canadian soldiers during the 1914–18 war. Sir Robert visited there many times during that war.

37 The late Major-General Sir John Hanbury-Williams – at that time an Extra Equerry to the King.

On the afternoon of August 5, the Duchess took us over the state apartments at Chatsworth which are splendid beyond description. We made our adieux at four o'clock and reached London at eight that evening.

On August 7, Mr Goodenough lunched with me; afterwards we discussed the affairs and future development of Barclays Bank (Canada). On the same day I arranged to return to Canada by the *Empress of Britain* on August 22. In making this arrangement, I was not in the least aware that my wife was ill, as she had forbidden any intimation to me.

On August 9, the Perleys and I visited Stansted Park as guests of the Bessboroughs. George [Canadian born son of Lord and Lady Bessborough] was in splendid form and not in the least shy. I photographed him in various attitudes; but, unfortunately, the camera had been damaged and none of the snapshots came out. Tomlin, the head gardener, accompanied me on a tour of the beautiful gardens; and I found him quite learned with respect both to wild and cultivated flowers. There are wonderful trees and the garden was a wealth of bloom. Before leaving for London the next morning, I had an amusing conversation with George to whom I confided, and upon which he agreed, my conviction that it is really quite impossible for a small boy to avoid being mischievous.

On August 10, Miss Cummins informed me that arrangements were completed for my visit to Scotland; and she firmly resisted any attempt on my part to pay for my passage. Private compartment, both going and returning, had been arranged; reservations had been made at the North British Hotel; and, as in London, a motor car was placed at my disposal during my visit to Edinburgh. Any attempt on my part to raise objection was quietly brushed aside.

Miss Cummins entered the service of Barclays Bank Limited about twenty years ago at a salary of one pound per week. Under the late F.C. Goodenough, for whom she eventually became Secretary, she received a wonderful training. She has the commanding intelligence of a man of the highest ability, but, at the same time, she possesses the instinctive intuition of a woman. Mr W.M. Goodenough told me that not only does she perform the various duties of Chairman's secretary, but she supervises all detail of business management and, in addition, she has a remarkable grasp of financial and business affairs.

In Edinburgh, I had my niece, Mabel Ashmere [Borden] and her husband, Aubrey Gordon Nicholls, with their boy Peter Borden Nicholls as my guests at the North British Hotel. Peter is a very beautiful child of less than nineteen months. He has his mother's lovely hair and complexion and his father's brilliant eyes. I have never seen a child of that age so endowed with poise and self-possession.

We visited the great War Memorial but, on account of the crowd, we failed to get a real conception of its variety and beauty. We also visited the Scottish-American War Memorial (by Dr Tait McKenzie) which bears the inscription: 'If it be life that waits, I shall live forever unconquered. If death, I shall die at last strong in my pride and free.'

We attended several theatres and visited Roslyn Castle before my departure for London on August 19.

On the twenty-second, I left for Southampton. ... Many friends greeted me on board the *Empress*. ... The voyage was uneventful. One found it necessary to shun cocktail parties to which there were numerous invitations. ...

During the journey I read Colonel H.F. Trew's *Botha Treks*. Barney Baruch and Mrs Mendez spoke to me of George Dangerfield's book, *The Strange Death of Liberal England*.

We docked at Quebec about noon on August 27; and there was much confusion as to luggage. ...

Having left Southampton on Saturday, August 22, at one pm, I reached my home at 10.45 on the following Thursday (August 27). It would have been a most joyous homecoming, except for my sadness on discovering that my wife had been ill for about four weeks. I found her in great distress, as she was physically unable to meet me at the station.

However, during my absence, she had carried out great improvements in the renovation of my office and on the grounds.

I am most happy to be once more in my own home; and I remain, Sir,

Yours, etc.,

September 24, 1936

ON READING DANGERFIELD'S *STRANGE DEATH OF LIBERAL ENGLAND*

Sir,

On September 21, I attended the Canadian Club luncheon at which

Lord Thankerton[38] was guest of honour. His address was not particularly impressive. I was interested to learn that he is a son of the famous Lord Watson before whom I had appeared before the Judicial Committee on two or three occasions.

It is just twenty-five years ago since we overwhelmed the Laurier government and came into power. I had been leader of the Opposition since 1901, a longer period, I believe, than any previous occupant of that position had served. There had been many vicissitudes during the ten years of my service; and I had faced many reversals without and many intrigues within.

My wife's health has improved somewhat since my return from England; but by no means has she regained her usual health and strength. On September 23, she became quite discouraged. Dr Laidlaw thinks she is suffering from 'undulant fever', so named because of alternate progress and recession throughout the period of illness.

On the evening of September 23, I learned that my friend and former colleague Honourable Newton W. Rowell had been appointed Chief Justice of Ontario; and immediately I got into touch with him at the Chateau to say how greatly rejoiced I was by these tidings.

Since my return I have read with much interest George Dangerfield's *Strange Death of Liberal England*. It is brilliantly written, the author being something of a stylist, but occasionally marred by a tone of condescending superiority. There is the suggestion that, in the author's opinion, the difficulties and perplexities of each situation could have been solved by a person endowed with the vision and prescience of George Dangerfield. In other words, if the author had stood in the place of each statesman whom he estimates, all would have been well, or at least much better. I knew intimately several of the men whose supposed weakness and futility come under Mr Dangerfield's animadversion; and I venture to think that in some instances his judgment is superficial. Then the book tails off into a rather weak ending which seems to have little connection with the preceding chapters. No one could fail to admire the genius and revere the memory of Rupert Brooke; but his brilliance was quite insular; and it seemed to me that on occasion he lacked imagination. In this connection, I venture to enclose an extract from my introduction to *Canada in the Commonwealth* ...

I remain, Sir, Yours, etc.,

38 English law lord who was in Canada attending the annual meeting of the Canadian Bar Association.

Extract from Sir Robert's introduction to *Canada in the Commonwealth*[39] being the Rhodes Memorial lectures, the first series of which was given by him at Oxford University in May and June of 1927. ED.

Thus, it is perhaps small wonder that a brilliant young Englishman of wide culture, vivid imagination, and splendid diction, who visited our country fourteen years ago, and who published his rather hasty impressions, should have manifested regrettable unacquaintance with its history. He found our countryside lonely, our mountains and forests, our great rivers and lakes, unimpressive, appealing in no way to the imagination. There were no memories, no voices, no dead.

> It is an empty land. To love the country here – mountains are worshipped, not loved – is like embracing a wraith. A European can find nothing to satisfy the hunger of his heart. The air is too thin to breathe. He requires haunted woods and the friendly presence of ghosts ... How far away seem those grassy moonlit places in England that have been Roman camps or roads, where there is always serenity ... It is possible at a pinch to do without gods. But one misses the dead.[40]

If Rupert Brooke had just listened, voices of the past were calling to him in all his journeying. They whispered to him on either side of the St Lawrence, from the Long Sault of the Ottawa, in the thunder of the Chaudière, on each battle-field by which he passed, from many a wilderness on which he looked. Can there be no ghosts save where the Roman once made his pathway? Between the surges of Cape North and the western ocean there is many a grave of explorer and adventurer on which the flower of remembrance will never fade, many a God's acre where sleep pioneer wardens of the wilderness and around which linger memories more appealing to Canadians than any associations that a Roman encampment could awaken.

For, in truth, from Louisburg to Esquimalt the land teems with memories of adventure and romance, of courage and endurance, of devotion and heroism. The vales of the ocean provinces, the broad countrysides of Quebec and Ontario, the mighty waterways, the vast western plains, the northern wilderness, the majestic summits

39 *Canada in the Commonwealth* was published by the Oxford University Press in 1929.

40 *Letters from America*, by Rupert Brooke, pp. 153–6.

of the Rockies and the shores of the Pacific are not dumb, but eloquent to one who will listen and can understand.

Following his return to Canada at the end of August, 1936, Sir Robert continued to be active in attending public functions, in meeting with distinguished persons and in reading. He became increasingly concerned with world conditions as is evident from parts of the following three Limbo letters.

He and Lord Lothian – the former Philip Kerr, whom he had met as Mr Lloyd George's secretary during the war and who, for a time during the second world war, was to be Britain's ambassador to the United States – were very good friends. Indeed, Philip Kerr in 1927 was Secretary to the Rhodes Trust and he and Sir Robert had seen much of each other when, in the spring of that year, Sir Robert resided in All Soul's College in Oxford at the time of delivering the first series of the Rhodes Memorial lectures.

October 8, 1936

VISIT OF EARL OF LOTHIAN

Sir,

On October 3, Philip Kerr (Earl of Lothian) came at 5.30 and for an hour and a half we talked over world affairs.

He is certain that there will be an explosion in Europe and he earnestly hopes that it will be toward the East rather than towards the West.

In his opinion, the only hope for world peace lies with the two great democracies, British Empire and the United States. If they could be united in an alliance, or even in understanding, he feels that peace could be maintained during the remainder of this century, as it was maintained by the dominance of Great Britain's naval power during the last century.

During his approaching visit to Washington, he purposes to get into touch with important permanent officials upon whom he will endeavour to impress his view as to the peril within which the United States will lie if Great Britain and her Empire should be overthrown. In that case, United States would be obliged to face, unaided, the combination of military powers that had destroyed the British Commonwealth.

He believes that Germany and probably Italy must embark upon war in the early future. Hitler would prefer to attack Russia, but his military advisers believe that Great Britain would afford an easier victory. Kerr is convinced that as soon as Great Britain is involved in any struggle, Italy will take possession of Egypt and the Sudan; and the disintegration of the British Empire will then have become assured.

On October 7, I attended a luncheon given by Honourable Norman Armour [United States Minister to Ottawa] in honour of the International Joint Commission. I acted as deputy head, sitting opposite to Norman; on my right Senator A.O. Stanley and on my left Senator William Hearst. At Mr Armour's request I spoke briefly.

Senator Stanley gave me a most interesting account of Kentucky and her people. *Inter alia,* he declared that in her wonderful blue grass, in her magnificent race-horses and last, but not least, in her beautiful women Kentucky surpassed the world. Against this last claim, I entered a caveat.

During this and the previous month, the European situation, arising out of the civil war in Spain has become very acute. Russia has put a verbal ultimatum to countries assisting insurgents.

No one can fail to realize that the present menace could only have arisen in an insensate world.

I remain, Sir, Yours, etc.,

October 19, 1936

ON WORLD AFFAIRS

Sir,

Recently with very deep interest I have read *The Far Eastern Crisis,* by Henry L. Stimson. The book covers a period of about eight months. The author is restrained and courteous in his references to Great Britain. He states the facts fairly as they occurred. There may have been conditions which he, perhaps, could not realize and which deterred Great Britain from taking a firmer stand. But, the record does not inspire respect for British statesmanship. It seems apparent that Sir John Simon is much more competent as lawyer and advocate than as statesman and Foreign Secretary.

On October 12, J.W. Dafoe called. He was pessimistic as to the outcome of world conditions which he regards as both dangerous and puzzling. He is rather scornful of Lothian's outlook, as he still has hope that the League of Nations may play a great part in maintaining world peace.

On the same afternoon, Mrs C.C. Robinson of Geneva gave us a vivid account of present methods in Germany in the education of the youth. Another war will be attended with every horror that human ingenuity can devise.

On October 17, Owen Lattimore who lives in China, and who has made a keen study of Eastern conditions, gave me a penetrating and instructive account of existing relations between China and Japan. He regards it as possible that Japan may, for an extended period, dominate, control and exploit China; but he agrees that in the ultimate issue, China is too strong to be absorbed. I told him of Sir John Jordan's firm opinion that China was much more likely to absorb than to be absorbed.

On Sunday, October 18, I went into hospital for four days, returning the following Thursday. I underwent every conceivable test to ascertain my condition; and the results were pronounced highly satisfactory. Some of these tests were quite disagreeable, but for the most part I was not inconvenienced.

I remain, my dear Sir, Yours, etc.,

November 30, 1936

NOVEMBER ACTIVITIES, 1936

Sir,

During this month I attended many functions and spoke oftener than I anticipated or desired.

On the ninth instant I presided at the annual dinner of the League of Nations Society in Canada. The Prime Minister, [Mr King] as guest-speaker, reviewed at some length the transactions and incidents at the recent meeting of the Assembly of the League; and he set forth a useful as well as an interesting estimate of conditions through which Europe is passing.

In introducing the Prime Minister I thought it desirable and useful to express my personal view with respect to the past service and probable future of the League, and with respect to world conditions. A copy of my address is appended, together with letters from Nicholas Murray Butler, Sir Austen Chamberlain and John W. Dafoe.

On Armistice Day (November 11), we did not attend the service on Parliament Hill, as the weather was quite uncongenial; but we listened to the broadcast. In the evening my wife and I were guests of the Canadian Legion at the Armistice Dinner at the Chateau. I sat on the left of G.D. Rochester, President of the Legion. Air Marshal Bishop made a stirring speech in which he emphasized, with great force, Canada's responsibility for the unity and preservation of the Empire. He was loudly applauded. There were many calls for me; finally I spoke briefly and was given a very cordial reception.

On the sixteenth I attended the Canadian Club luncheon at which Dr Wallace (newly appointed Principal of Queen's University) delivered an excellent address. I was called upon to express the thanks of the audience and received a remarkable ovation when I arose to do so.

On November 17, in Montreal at the annual meeting of Barclays Bank (Canada) I delivered the appended address which had an excellent reception and was published widely, not only in Canada but in Great Britain.

On the twenty-fourth instant I received an enthusiastic reception in delivering an address of welcome to the delegates at the opening of the First National Safety conference. The Secretary of State (Honourable Fernand Rinfret) was extremely generous and complimentary in introducing me and I expressed appreciation and thanks.

During the month I spent a good deal of time preparing for transmission to friends in England a memorandum of my impressions respecting business and political conditions in Canada during 1936. This memorandum I sent to the Duke of Connaught, the Duke of Devonshire, Lord Willingdon, Lord Bessborough, Sir William Clark, Honourable Philippe Roy and General Smuts. (Copy appended.)

On the twenty-fifth I lunched with our neighbour, Mrs Palmer, and a few other ladies to meet Ruth Draper; and afterwards I attended her wonderful recital at the Little Theatre. Miss Draper was surprised and impressed by my vivid recollection of her recitals at the Hotel Majestic in Paris (1919) and on several other occasions.

Copy of my letter (November 27) to General Smuts, respecting the future of the League is appended.

During the month my wife's health has gradually been improving, although she has not yet fully emerged from the long and tiresome illnesses which have afflicted her since the middle of July last.

I remain, Sir, Yours, etc.,

NOTE

In the foregoing Limbo letter Sir Robert refers to his address at the League of Nations Society banquet as being appended. It was not. But the *Ottawa Citizen* of November 10, 1936, carries a rather full report of the address as follows:

FUTURE PEACE OF WORLD TO REST IN REALM OF SPIRIT

But for the dissociation from the League of Nations covenant of that nation 'from which in large measure had come the inspiration out of which the covenant arose,' perils that confront and confound the world today would never have arisen, Sir Robert Borden, Canada's wartime Prime Minister, declared last night.

Presiding over the League of Nations Society banquet, a part of peace action week ceremonies arranged by the society, the veteran Canadian statesman delivered a brief address prior to the speech of Prime Minister Mackenzie King.

Disappointment in the failure of the League of Nations to meet early expectations, but thankfulness for the service it had achieved and belief in it as a future force for peace were all expressed by Sir Robert. He foresaw a final all-powerful force for peace in a public opinion expressed in the collective and compelling voice of the nations united in a more intimate relationship than at present.

'We must confess,' said Sir Robert, 'to a feeling of disappointment and sadness that the League has not fully realized the expectations awakened at its inception. That there has been such failure it is impossible to deny, but let us remember that in the absolute sense there has been no failure.

'If the League should dissolve tomorrow the world would have abundant reason to be grateful for its past service. And it can still render worthy service, although its future seems clouded and uncertain.

'If the most powerful nation on earth, then endowed with the moral leadership of the world, the nation from which in a large measure had come the inspiration out of which the covenant arose; if that nation had not seen fit to dissociate itself from the covenant, perils that confront and confound the world today would never have arisen.

'This I say not by way of criticism but with an emotion of very deep regret that the world thus lost leadership which should have led the nations along the way of international right and wholesome co-operation.

'But this was not to be and there is no more striking illustration of the limitation of human intelligence than in the results that have followed the Great War which, as we hoped and believed, was to end all war.

'It was impossible to foresee or to estimate the reaction of surging forces, tendencies and influences, powerful, complex, conflicting, that drove the nations along a perilous path until today every armament factory is working at tremendous pressure while violence, naked and unashamed, strives to dominate the earth.

'Treaties, covenants, pacts – these are all to the good unless so openly and shamelessly violated and disregarded that they become a by-word and a mockery. I am of those who believe that the future peace of the world will rest in the realm of the spirit. In the final issue it may depend upon elusive and indefinable but powerful influence which we call public opinion; the public opinion of the world expressed in the collective and compelling voice of the nations united; perhaps, in a more intimate relationship than at present.'

November 16, 1936

My dear Sir Robert

It was kind of you to send me a marked copy of the *Ottawa Citizen* of November 10, with its admirable report of your address at the League of Nations Society banquet. It is a gratification to be able to say to you that I agree with every word of your speech as reported and congratulate you on making it.

What you say, in all kindness about the failure of the Government of the United States to cooperate with the rest of the world after the Treaty of Versailles had been negotiated in 1919, is as true as gospel. Some day I shall be able to tell the story of what happened within the range of my own personal knowledge and observation. It is too soon yet and passion still runs too high to make it worth while to publish that part of the happenings of the summer of 1919 which is familiar to me. May I say, however, that it justifies to the full what you said at the League of Nations Society banquet?

It may be that the clouds will lift one of these days and that despite unhappy and threatening appearances, the world will get back where it was when the war ended.

With warm regards and all good wishes, I am

Sincerely yours,
(Sgd) Nicholas Murray Butler

24 Egerton Terrace,
SW 3.

16th December, 1936

Dear Sir Robert,

My wife and I thank you cordially for your Christmas greetings and heartily reciprocate your good wishes.

Thank you for sending me the text of your address at the annual dinner of the League of Nations Society in Canada. We must all share your hope that this great effort for peace and understanding among nations may not fail. You will, I am sure, have noticed and approved the language of our Foreign Secretary on the subject. It is not easy at this moment to see what the future of the League is to be, but it would be a calamity indeed if it were to perish like so many earlier attempts to find an alternative to war.

Yrs. sincerely
Austen Chamberlain

December 21
Winnipeg

My dear Sir Robert,

Your kind Christmas greeting is very acceptable.

My friendship with you, now growing into the decades has been one of the satisfactions of my life – the more so as it began before we were as agreed upon fundamentals as we are now and have been for many years. I admired the felicity and awareness of your remarks at the League dinner last month. I find it difficult myself to find justification for the course towards the League taken either by the British or Canadian government. I am afraid that Canada will have to take the responsibility of having dealt two heavy blows to the League within a single year.

I shall be in the east the latter part of January – partly on CIIA business which calls for some decisions of moment. (What with the CIIA & the IPR I find myself carrying considerable responsibility.) If you have not by that time departed for the south I shall expect to have the pleasure of seeing you.

My best regards to yourself and Lady Borden in which Mrs Dafoe joins.

Yours Faithfully
(Sgd) J.W. Dafoe

ADDRESS AT ANNUAL MEETING OF BARCLAYS BANK (CANADA) ON NOVEMBER 17, 1936

During the past year a gradual advance toward ultimate recovery has been unmistakable; and in no country has this indication been more marked than in Canada. Unfortunately, this steady progress is over-shadowed by the menace of international controversies and antagonisms which seem to become increasingly dangerous as, more and more, the resources of the world are devoted to the increase of armaments. Great Britain, who led the way in disarmament, has been compelled to adopt measures for self-defence.

Unless, however, we are to lose faith in humanity, we must believe that present tendencies represent only a passing phase, that mankind will recover its balance, and that a truer and saner spirit will arise and prevail.

I have spoken of our country's progress. The abundance of its varied resources cannot be denied. But we must not forget the eternal verity that 'A man's life consisteth not in the abundance of the things which he possesseth.' What is true of the individual is equally true of the nation.

Thus, above all considerations of material progress we must take into account the spirit of our nation, the stability of our institutions, the ideals of our people, our ethical standards both in public and in private life. In these qualities, as well as in courage, resourcefulness and determination in the face of difficulty, danger and hardship, Canada has not failed. But never should her people forget that their faith is pledged in the covenant of their government and must be kept inviolate.

On the other hand, we cannot disregard the material welfare of our people; and it is important to note the development and achievement made manifest during the past year.

Taking into consideration all contributing factors, it is abundantly clear that the economic condition of Canada has advanced into a more favourable position during the past twelve months. The statistical information upon which this statement is based has been derived, in large measure, from the Dominion Bureau of Statistics, a very efficient organization under the highly capable direction of Dr R.H. Coats.

Except where otherwise indicated, the following comparisons of production and other factors relate to the nine-month period, ending September 30, 1936, as contrasted with the like period of 1935.

FOOD AND FIELD CROPS

The physical volume of production was low in 1936. It is anticipated that the output will reach approximately 80 per cent of the average output for the period 1926 to 1930. The severe drought in the south of the prairie provinces and in some western sections of Ontario is responsible for this result. However, the Maritimes had an exceedingly good year; the yield in Quebec was slightly above average; and in British Columbia conditions were normal.

The production of wheat, oats, barley and rye was smaller than in 1935; while there was a slight increase in flax-seed.

But it is estimated that owing to higher quality of wheat and increased prices for all grains and for potatoes, as well as increased production of butter, cheese and hogs, the total value will be greater than in 1935.

MANUFACTURING

A wholesome expansion, with a gain of nearly 10 p.c. (based on 29 factors) is indicated. In food, pulp and paper, rubber, textiles, iron and steel, non-ferrous metal and non-metallic mineral industries, the gains are especially large; and in most of them the situation is more satisfactory than in any years since 1930. ...

Copper exports were more than maintained. The output of motor-cars declined by more than 8 p.c.

Construction was at an even lower level than in 1935, while building-permits in 58 cities showed a decline of nearly 20 p.c.

EXTERNAL TRADE

There has been a remarkable and most satisfactory development in external trade.

Total trade exceeded the billion dollar mark for the first time in any corresponding period since 1930. ...

FEDERAL REVENUES

Federal revenues show satisfactory advance. An unrevised statement of receipts, up to the end of October, 1936, indicates an increase in revenue of approximately $40,000,000 over the corresponding period of 1935.

For the last three months, the gain over the corresponding months of 1935 has been in excess of $5,000,000 per month. The largest increases are in excise taxes (chiefly sales tax) $18,500,000; and in income taxes, $17,000,000. However, customs revenues show an advance of more than $3,000,000.

RAILWAY FREIGHT MOVEMENT

A gain of 5 p.c. in car-loadings is indicated during the first forty-three weeks of the present year. Pronounced gains are indicated in the shipment of coal, as well as in the movement of grain, livestock and ore, especially in the western division.

The gross operating revenues of the Canadian National Railways were 6 p.c. greater while the corresponding revenues of the Canadian Pacific advanced 9 p.c. during the period.

BANKING AND INSURANCE

The Bureau reports that on the 1926 basis, index of bank debits was 132.9 in September, 1936, against 102.9 in September, 1935. The percentage of bank-debits to deposits was 147.2, as against 122.0 in September, 1935.

The increase in current loans during September, was much greater than normal for the season, the new movement possibly presaging a reversal of the downward trend prevailing since the autumn of 1929.

New business written by Life Insurance companies having, in force 90 per cent of the total business in Canada, but not including industrial and group business, increased by over $5,000,000, or about 2 p.c. over the amount for 1935. A corresponding comparison of the business written in United States shows a 5 per cent decrease in 1936.

SECURITY PRICES

The prices of stocks traded in on Canadian exchanges advanced by more than 27 p.c. during the period; and there was also pronounced advance in high-grade bond prices.

CANADA'S TOURIST TRADE

'Tourism', essentially a post-war development, has become one of Canada's major industries, affording a lucrative source of revenue for many of our citizens and stimulating many and varied lines of business. The 'invisible' export represented by the tourist trade has, in recent years, ranked ahead of any of our commodity exports, not excepting wheat and newsprint, and is the largest single item in maintaining a healthy condition in our international balance sheet.

Tourist travel, which must be classed as a luxury, inevitably falls off in times of depression. From $117,000,000 in 1933, the lowest point in a decade, tourist expenditures in Canada rose to approximately $202,000,000 in 1935. For 1936, the amount will probably reach $250,000,000.

The expenditures of Canadian tourists abroad, which were approximately $51,000,000 in 1933, are also on the up-grade and will amount to somewhat over $80,000,000 in 1936, still leaving a very satisfactory balance in Canada's favour.

The Bureau reports substantial recovery in industrial employment. The 1926 index (100) of employment has risen from 76.0 at April 1, 1933, to 110.1 at October 1, 1936, when it was higher than in any month since the late autumn of 1930. This is based upon data from over 10,000 firms whose staffs include some 1,044,200 persons. As, during the last two years, there has been considerable diminution in the number engaged on unemployment relief projects, the gains recently recorded in monthly employment surveys are apparently due to revival in business rather than to work undertaken primarily for relief.

Increases in employment have been registered throughout Canada, except in the drought-stricken districts. The situation appears more favourable than in any similar period during the past five years; and in the prairie provinces employment, in the last few months, has been brisker than in the same months of any year since 1931.

... The closely related problems of unemployment and relief confront every civilized country. Measures for relief hitherto prevailing in Canada have been disjointed and unsystematic. The sooner our various governmental authorities deal resolutely, fully and systematically with the question the better it will be for the welfare of our country. In a certain element among persons on relief there is, unquestionably, a marked tendency to regard themselves as permanent pensioners of the state, to decline work on any convenient pretext and to consider idleness on relief as their absolute right. Every available means should be applied to correct this tendency which is highly undesirable for the state and most detrimental to the individual.

Care of the sick, the destitute, the helpless, the unemployable, and provision for the unemployed must find a permanent place in our social order. Every reasonable consideration must be given to those bravely struggling against misfortune and vainly, although eagerly, seeking employment.

In the construction industry even the meagre results of 1935 have not been equalled in 1936, while in United States there has been an increase of no less than 76 per cent. The significance of this industry as a factor in economic revival is everywhere acknowledged. Thus, it is not only opportune but highly important to consider the work and the proposals of the National Employment Commission under the chairmanship of Mr Arthur B. Purvis.

Early in September last the Federal government, on the recommendation of the Purvis Commission, announced a national housing policy embracing the following proposals:

1 A Home Improvement Plan having for its object the improvement of existing dwellings.
2 A low cost housing plan to provide dwellings for those who cannot afford to pay an economic rent, with its corollary the abolition of existing slum areas in the main cities.
3 An improved Dominion Housing Act to provide medium priced housing facilities for those who can afford to purchase their homes provided payments are spread over a long period and interest on outstandings is calculated at a reasonably low rate.

Utilizing the experience of other countries, the Commission decided to model the first plan upon the United States effort, which had stood the test of two years' experience. This plan is based upon a limited guarantee by the Federal government to lending institutions making advances to home owners.

It is understood that the Commission is presently engaged in developing the second feature, a plan for low cost housing. This plan may perhaps be based on the experience of the United Kingdom, which in this field has shown itself in advance of other countries.

The third feature of the Commission's proposals will probably embrace the revision of the Dominion Housing Act of 1935 or the preparation of a broader Act.

It is hoped that these proposals will result in a strong revival of the construction industry. Thus contractors and builders should spare no effort to equip themselves with skilled labour, for which there has been little training in recent years.

The banks of the country can be relied upon to give every reasonable encouragement and assistance to bona fide borrowers desirous of taking advantage of the Home Improvement Plan.

... In Great Britain, conditions of employment now closely approach, if they have not already reached, the normal. ...

General business conditions seem equally favourable in that country. Thus, Great Britain, leading the nations in the endeavour for peace, maintains firmly her place in the van of recovery.

Marked economic progress in United States during the period is indicated by the Federal Reserve Board report of 16 p.c. advance in industrial production. The situation at present is more satisfactory than at any time during the depression. Improvement in general business and industry has been so marked and consistent that it was retarded but little by the intense activities of the election campaign just concluded.

As compared with September, 1935, there was an increase of more than 1,000,000 workers in the industries surveyed. But it is estimated that 11,000,000 wage-earners are still unemployed.

The result of the recent election makes it probable that the convention of last year, providing for reduction of tariffs and for wider trade between Canada and United States, will be continued. This new freedom of trade between these neighbouring countries, intimately related to each other in many aspects, should be of marked advantage to each.

Apart from international antagonisms, the tendency toward aggression and the lack of wholesome co-operation, conditions abroad are quite encouraging. Indeed, from the record of the past twelve months, it would appear that the world is on the point of emerging from the morass of depression.

Tariff barriers continue, however, to impede international trade and co-operation, and economic nationalism still holds the stage. On the other hand, the importance of measures enacted recently in France and other gold bloc countries merits comment.

The long-anticipated devaluation of the French franc sanctioned on October 2nd was followed by action on somewhat similar lines with respect to their currencies by the governments of Holland

and Switzerland. In addition, the Greek, Turkish, and Latvian currencies were adjusted approximately to a Sterling basis.

By their three-power monetary agreement, the governments of Great Britain, United States and France propose to use the appropriate resources of their respective Exchange Equalization Funds, for the purpose of minimizing any disturbance of the basis of international exchanges resulting from the proposed currency adjustments. This agreement has enhanced the prospect of successfully closing the abnormal gaps which now separate price levels in different countries.

The parties to the agreement have invited other governments to co-operate towards the realization of the policy laid down, and Belgium has indicated its adhesion to the principles involved, which include the need for development of international trade and progressive relaxation of the present system of quotas and exchange control.

It is fully realized that there are many difficulties to be surmounted and that problems beside trade barriers and exchange restrictions require attention, but these recent developments should be hopefully accepted as a starting point from which a fresh international and stable monetary system may eventually be evolved, leading to the solution of those political problems which have been created in so many countries by economic troubles.

Further recovery will closely follow stabilization of exchange and monetary values, resumption of international trade and co-operation, return of confidence and assurance of peace. All these *desiderata* are within the grasp of the nations. Although in some aspects world conditions are still unsatisfactory, there is reason to hope that the most difficult incidents of the existing crisis are behind us. Of this there is firm assurance if the peace of the world can be maintained.

November, 1936

MEMORANDUM

Private and Confidential

1 Business Conditions

The main features are set forth in Sir Robert Borden's Address at the annual meeting of Barclays Bank (Canada), on November 17, 1936.

The trade arrangement between Canada and United States, which had its inception last year, is apparently operating to the advantage of both countries. There is considerable satisfaction in Canada that the result of the recent Presidential election seems to assure the continuance of this advance toward freer trade relations.

2 Political Conditions

In various communities from Atlantic to Pacific there is not a little unrest as to the attitude of our government on Empire defence. In some quarters, the policy of isolation has gained strength; but, on the other hand, the attitude of the government is seriously questioned by those who believe that our nationhood is a vain thing unless it is accompanied by acceptance and fulfilment of responsibility. The recent action of the government in acquiring from Great Britain two destroyers has, perhaps, been hastened or even induced by this view. An important element of our population are those who believe that a powerful, well-armed British Empire is the securest safeguard for world-peace, and the strongest protection against further development of a reign of violence.

Otherwise, in the Federal arena, the policies and proposals of the present Liberal government have almost wholly commended themselves to the great majority of Canadians. The Administration includes several men of distinctive ability; and every community of our varied population and territory seems to be adequately represented.

Mr Dunning, Minister of Finance, has fully justified the general satisfaction at his accession to that office. It is understood that during his recent visit to London he made a favourable impression not only upon members of the British government with whom he came into contact, but upon leaders in business and finance. His burdens have not been lightened by the vagaries of several provincial governments. Whenever occasion arose, he has dealt with them wisely and firmly.

Mr Norman McLeod Rogers, Minister of Labour, is a young man of distinctive ability and high idealism. His training in the Labour department is probably useful in broadening his outlook. At first he gave evidence of a rather impulsive temperament in precipitously abolishing unemployment camps before establishing any substitute therefor. This action is already creating an unfortunate condition in some of our cities to which unemployed are thronging for food and shelter in lack of opportunity formerly afforded by the camps.

Among other Ministers well worthy of mention is Mr J.L. Ilsley, who holds the portfolio of Inland Revenue and whose ability and strength of character seem to be outstanding.

3 Inter-Provincial Political Affairs

Ontario

Legislation repudiating solemn contracts of the province is being vigorously attacked in the courts; and recently the court of appeal of Ontario has over-ruled the objection that no such action can be maintained without consent of the Attorney-General which, of course, has not been and will not be given. The deliberate repudiation of solemn contracts disgraced Ontario, but it did much more; it inflicted a most serious injury upon the credit of Canada, and it led the way to the absurdities that have subsequently developed in the political life of Alberta.

Mr Earl Rowe has recently acceded to the leadership of the local Conservative party; and he is carrying on a vigorous campaign against the Hepburn government.

Quebec

The Liberal party sustained an overwhelming defeat in this Province at the hands of Union-Nationale, under the leadership of Maurice Duplessis who has shown distinctive ability and extraordinary vigour in the leadership of the new administration. In the Committee of Public Accounts, both during the session of last year and that recently concluded, there have been unfortunate revelations which are not yet concluded.

In several quarters it was apprehended that the policy of the new administration might verge toward a radicalism that would be detrimental to the business interests of the province; but no such result has ensued. Mr Duplessis has shown great firmness under fierce pressure; and his prestige has been distinctly enhanced by his direction of public affairs.

Maritime Provinces

The conditions of business and of employment are apparently more satisfactory in these provinces than elsewhere in Canada. There seems to be a minimum of unemployment and a steady development of business activity.

Manitoba and Saskatchewan

These provinces appear to be under the direction of sane, progressive administrations. Except for the drought-stricken areas (which, unfortunately, are very extensive) conditions are quite satisfactory. But, very large sums will be required to make provision of food, shelter and other necessaries for those who, with heavy hearts but with grim determination, have faced a long succession of crop failures.

There is some apprehension that the policy of debt repudiation, initiated by Ontario and carried to an extraordinary degree in Alberta, may infect the other prairie provinces. But of this there is, at present, little evidence.

Alberta

Conditions in Alberta seem quite chaotic. From the very first, Premier Aberhart was far beyond his depth; and presently he is sinking deeper and deeper into the morass to which he was led by Mr Menard (Minister without Portfolio) who is thoroughly inexperienced in public life and wholly lacking in a sane business outlook. A few months ago it was said that Aberhart, upon an appeal to the people, would be overwhelmingly sustained. It is now said that this view is gradually changing as a result of his absurd policies. Withdrawal from Alberta of immense assets by banks and other corporations is beginning to awaken some portion of the population to a realization of the disaster toward which the province is heading. Some time ago there was initiated by the local Conservatives an effort to unite against the government all the forces opposed to its policies.

British Columbia

Conditions in British Columbia have been normal during the present year. Premier Pattullo was not, at first, credited with well-balanced outlook or wise policy in his economic proposals. There is a disposition to believe that in this respect he has gained a useful lesson from experience.

November 27, 1936

To General the Right Honourable J.C. Smuts, CH, MP, KC,
Doornloof, Irene (near Pretoria)
South Africa

Private and Personal

My dear General Smuts,

For more than sixteen years you and I have been most earnest advocates and supporters of the League of Nations, in the inception of which you had so great a part.

In May last, I set down in my journal some reflections which expressed the discouragement I then felt. ...

Since then I have gained more hope for the future of the League.

Its usefulness for great humanitarian purposes and for a concourse of the nations would justify a hundred times its continued existence, even if its Articles were so reduced as to put into the background, for the time being, the prevention of aggressive war by economic or military sanctions.

On November 9, in introducing the Prime Minister at the annual dinner of the League of Nations Society in Canada (at which I presided), I spoke briefly; and I venture to send you my little address. ...

So much for my lucubrations with regard to the League. From time to time we learn in the press that great prosperity prevails in the Union of South Africa. However, it is notable, but perhaps not remarkable, that in Canada progress toward recovery has been, on the whole, more consistent and even more rapid than in United States, notwithstanding the intensive policies and astonishing public expenditures in that country. This comparison has been noted and emphasized by various economic authorities in United States.

Possibly you may be interested in the enclosed memorandum which sets forth my estimate of present business and political conditions in Canada. If it were not for our unfortunate railway situation and the apprehension of widespread war in Europe, we should be beginning very soon to approach the normal. As it is, there has been distinctive progress during the present year; and there is every indication that it will continue.

We have had an exceptionally open autumn; and the weather has not yet become very cold. Unfortunately, we still lack that excellent canopy of snow which at this season usually covers eastern Canada and which is of marked advantage to farm lands as well as to city parks and lawns.

During the past six months I have read some interesting books:

Inside Europe, by John Gunther: interesting but not always reliable; compounded of first-hand and second-hand information, gossip and imagination.

The Strange Death of Liberal England, by George Dangerfield: brilliantly written but impaired by its tone of conscious superiority. If the author had stood in the place of each statesman whom he estimates, all would have been well, or at least much better.

These Hurrying Years, by Gerald Heard: a remarkable book, setting forth the dynamic transformations that have attended the present century.

The Faith of an Englishman, by Sir Edward Grigg: a comprehensive review of conditions supervening the World War; the future purpose and usefulness of the League is discussed.

I apologize for all the litter I am enclosing.

My wife and I hope to leave, early in February, for the congenial climate of Georgia, a winter climate far superior, in my experience, to that of Italy.

We join in Christmas greetings to you and yours; and in all good wishes for the New Year soon to dawn.

With kindest regards, I remain, my dear General Smuts,

Yours faithfully,

Sir Robert, as he says in the following Limbo letter, had known King Edward VIII for over twenty years and had 'warm affection' for him. In the latter part of 1936 the abdication crisis arose and this deeply upset him. There was no television then but Sir Robert listened carefully to his radio and followed the events with sadness.

The following two letters recorded his views on this unhappy incident. Dr H.L. Stewart, to whom he refers, was Professor of Philosophy at Dalhousie University and a regular and highly respected broadcaster on national and international affairs.

December 5, 1936

KING EDWARD VIII AND MRS SIMPSON

Sir,

The nations of the British Commonwealth and its dependencies have passed through deep waters during the past two weeks; they are still passing; the end is not yet.

For more than twenty years I have known King Edward. On the occasions of his visits to Canada during my premiership I came into intimate association with him, and I conceived for him not only sincere admiration but warm affection. Now I am disillusioned, shocked, amazed; and I cannot free myself from the abhorrent thought that, early in the year, when he requested parliament to make provision for his marriage, he had in mind a woman whose husband was then living and undivorced. I hope and pray that in this I may be mistaken.

During the past month, the King's insensate folly in determining to marry a woman twice divorced created a scandal which has been exploited to the fullest extent by lewd newspapers of the baser sort in United States; and that scandal has now developed into a constitutional crisis. Apparently, the King places before all obligation of duty, and above all concern for the welfare of the Empire his silly infatuation for this woman, and his desire to make her his queen. Endowed with two living husbands, other than the King, imagine her coronation! Would it not be appropriate that her former husbands, original and secondary, should have foremost places at the coronation?

It would be difficult to exaggerate the intense concern that disturbs our people. Last week, during a temporary indisposition which confined me to my room, I spent two sleepless nights in grieving over this deplorable incident and in endeavouring to forecast the future. For I was fully conscious that the issue of the present crisis might be so grave as eventually to disturb the Empire's unity. And all this because of the absurd infatuation of a middle-aged man for a twice-divorced woman. Physicians of this city are convinced that the King is suffering from a certain type of psychosis.

Since the growth of nationhood in the self-governing countries of the Empire, the Crown has been the perpetual symbol of the Empire's unity; and each Sovereign has been its living symbol. For the last hundred years there has been a reverence so deep and so abiding for the Crown, and indeed for each succeeding sovereign, that the unity of the Empire has withstood the severest shocks. This symbolic significance of the Crown has suffered grievously from the fantastic whim of a man who had vowed to follow in his father's footsteps. The lustre of the Crown has been tarnished; the King and the Throne discredited.

In his weekly broadcast, on Sunday last, Dr H.L. Stewart (Halifax) spoke with great power and dignity. ... During the course of his remarks he administered a well-deserved rebuke to Boake Carter (without naming him) [well known American radio broadcaster] who has utilized this incident for a contemptible purpose. Carter endeavours to persuade his listeners in United States that the British objection to a Queen with two living husbands other than the King is based upon antagonism to the American people. Nothing could be farther from the truth, as there are hundreds of girls in the

United States, any one of whom would have been hailed as queen with real enthusiasm, not only in Great Britain but throughout every Dominion.

I remain, Sir, Yours in tribulation,

December 30, 1936

KING EDWARD VIII – ABDICATION

Sir,

The crisis has finally passed in the abdication of King Edward VIII and in the accession of his brother, formerly Duke of York, as King George VI. This solution of what might have developed into a grave constitutional crisis has relieved the Canadian people, although it has greatly distressed them to realize that a young man who has served the Empire so finely and with such marked advantage should place above his solemn duty and the glory of his opportunity the vagary of his fantastic infatuation for a twice-divorced woman, a woman whose better feeling should have led her to withdraw from a situation so disgraceful and humiliating to the man she is supposed to love. But it is said that the better feeling to which I allude has not been one of her characteristics in the past.

On December 11, King Edward VIII gave a farewell broadcast to the Empire. In part, it was manly and moving, but it was marred by his declaration that he could not continue to carry on the burden of kingship without the support and comfort of the woman he loved. In this, he revealed a fatal weakness which caused men to rejoice at his abdication.

To Baldwin, who took upon himself without resort to his colleagues the burden of a tremendous responsibility (greater perhaps than any Prime Minister has faced for at least two centuries), the grateful homage of all the Empire's nations goes forth. On December 12, I expressed to him my personal feelings in a letter, copy of which I append.

Our new Sovereign, King George VI, will assuredly follow in his father's footsteps, placing his duty to the State above all other considerations. He will enjoy the counsel and support of his wife who may be expected to strengthen him as our revered and beloved Queen Mary undoubtedly did strengthen her husband throughout his reign.

307 DECEMBER 30, 1936

Edward VIII has been created Duke of Windsor and he has repaired to Enzsefeld where he will probably remain as a guest of Baron Rothschild until the dissolution of Mrs Simpson's marriage shall have been confirmed in due course. It is expected that as soon as the decree of dissolution shall have been made absolute he will marry this woman. Let us hope that he will find in this marriage some compensation for his tragic failure to place above a foolish obsession the duty and the service that he owed to his race and its traditions, and especially to the Empire's nations.

From the Duke of Connaught I have a letter in which he alludes to the tragic character of the episode through which we have passed. His letter and a copy of my reply are appended.

Yours, etc.,

PS Since writing the above I have received from Mr Baldwin the appended letter.

December 12, 1936

Private

My dear Mr Baldwin,

No Prime Minister was ever confronted with a task of higher responsibility or of more surpassing difficulty than that which it was your duty to sustain during the recent tragic episode. No one could have discharged that duty with greater sympathy or finer tact. The simplicity and dignity of your speech in the Commons yesterday were most moving, especially as you breathed throughout the fullest sympathy for the young man who has just renounced the throne. In 1919, during his first visit to Canada, I was brought into very close and intimate touch with the then Prince of Wales; and I very soon entertained for him not only a sincere admiration but a warm affection. I was wholly dismayed and shocked by his proposal to marry the lady in question. More than once my grief and concern cost me a night's sleep.

All our people were greatly saddened but it is abundantly clear that in this country public opinion regards the result as inevitable, seeing that King Edward's determination was fixed. But I fear that the episode has had harmful results which I trust time will efface. King Edward's usefulness had gone before his abdication. It is my earnest hope and prayer that he may find happiness during his remaining years.

Canada never can and never will forget this your most wonderful service to the Empire. You have the unstinted homage of our people.

With deep and heartfelt appreciation, I remain, my dear Mr Baldwin,

Yours faithfully,

2nd January 1937

10 Downing Street
Whitehall

My dear Sir Robert,

I thank you most warmly for your kind and generous letter.

It has been a strange time but what has happened was inevitable and I feel more confidence in the future for our own country and for the Empire.

You will find the new King his father over again.

I agree with all you say about King Edward.

He had and has many great gifts, but –

Accept our warmest greetings to Lady Borden and yourself, and Believe me to remain

Very sincerely yours
(Sgd) Stanley Baldwin

December 18th, 1936

Bath

My dear Sir Robert

I write to thank you many times for your kind letter, and good wishes for Xmas and New Year, which you have sent to me and to my daughter in both your and Lady Borden's name. These must have crossed my Christmas card to you both. I was very sorry to hear how poorly your wife had been during your short absence from Canada; I rejoice however to know that you found [her] much better on your return, and I hope that your projected visit to Georgia may restore

her to her usual health. I must now thank you so very much for sending me your memorandum on the business and political conditions of Canada. I have read it with the deepest interest, and it is so clearly worded that I have been able to take in the whole of the past troubles that the Dominion has so successfully surmounted. Most earnestly do I hope that the New Year of 1937 may bring renewed prosperity to the whole of Canada. My one great wish is that the Dominion may continue to show its loyalty to King and his Throne. We have just ended a most sad and anxious climax with credit and dignity to our Empire and the Throne; but the Royal Family has had to pass through very sad and trying days. Thank God that we have successfully surmounted what appeared at one moment to be insoluble. Our constitution has received a great shock, but I believe that we may look forward to King George VI proving a wise and constitutional Sovereign, who has the welfare and the traditions of his people deeply at heart and who will always put *duty before anything else*. He is lucky in having a most charming wife who is beloved, I believe, as much as Queen Mary.
With my best wishes to you both.

Believe me, Yours very sincerely,
(Sgd) Arthur

December 30, 1936

Sir,

I am most grateful for the letter which has just arrived from Your Royal Highness. The incidents to which you allude gave very grave concern to our people and at one time occasioned widespread dismay. Personally, I was very deeply grieved and my earnest solicitude as to what might ensue, cost me two sleepless nights. I can imagine the distress through which the Royal Family has passed.

We are happy in our confidence that King George VI, will ever by guided by the strong and unfailing sense of duty which distinguished his beloved father and of which Your Royal Highness has been so constant and conspicuous an exemplar. And we rejoice in the assurance that in our Queen he will have the invaluable support and comfort which our revered and beloved Queen Mary gave to his father throughout his reign.

The Crown is the permanent symbol and each Sovereign the living symbol of the Empire's unity and majesty. Your Royal Highness may be assured that the loyalty and devotion of our people were never firmer and surer than at present.

I have the honour to remain, Sir, Your most humble obedient servant.

NOTE

Sir Robert and Lady Borden went to Georgia in February of 1937. While there he suffered a heart attack. They returned to Ottawa in April. He dictated two more Limbo letters – one dealing with the Dominion Drama Festival, which was held in Ottawa at the end of April, and which I have included, immediately following the April 29, 1935, Limbo letter dealing with the Festival of that year, and the other with the despoiling of parts of his wildflower garden by young boys. This latter incident distressed him greatly.

These letters were never corrected and were in draft form only. The second draft letter is not included in this volume.

In the middle of May, Sir Robert suffered a severe heart attack and passed away on June 10, 1937. Lady Borden, for whose health he had had such great concern in his later years, survived him until September, 1940. ED.

This book

was designed by

ANTJE LINGNER

under the direction of

ALLAN FLEMING

and was printed by

University of

Toronto

Press

www.ingramcontent.com/pod-product-compliance
Lightning Source LLC
Chambersburg PA
CBHW082106090726
47910CB00009B/2605

* 9 7 8 1 4 4 2 6 5 2 1 1 8 *